50 HIKES

IN THE LOWER
HUDSON VALLEY

50 HIKES
IN THE LOWER
HUDSON VALLEY

FOURTH EDITION

Daniel Chazin

NEW YORK–NEW JERSEY
TRAIL CONFERENCE

THE COUNTRYMAN PRESS

A division of W. W. Norton & Company

Independent Publishers Since 1923

AN INVITATION TO THE READER

Over time trails can be rerouted and signs and landmarks altered. If you find that changes have occurred on the routes described in this book, please let us know so that corrections may be made in future editions. The author and publisher also welcome other comments and suggestions. Address all correspondence to:

Editor, 50 Hikes Series
The Countryman Press
500 Fifth Avenue
New York, NY 10110

For information about permission to reproduce selections from this book, write to Permissions, The Countryman Press, 500 Fifth Avenue, New York, NY 10110

For information about special discounts for bulk purchases, please contact W. W. Norton Special Sales at specialsales@wwnorton.com or 800-233-4830

The Countryman Press
www.countrymanpress.com

A division of W. W. Norton & Company, Inc.
500 Fifth Avenue, New York, NY 10110
www.wwnorton.com

978-1-68268-301-9 (pbk.)

10 9 8 7 6 5 4 3 2 1

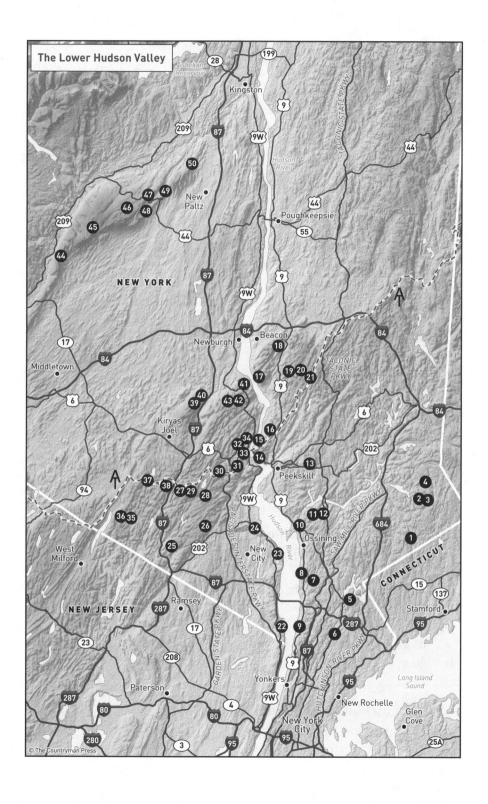

The Lower Hudson Valley

Contents

Hikes at a Glance

Hike	County	Distance (miles)	Difficulty	Elevation Gain (feet)
1. Mianus River Gorge	Westchester	4.3	E/M	933
2. Ward Pound Ridge—Leatherman's Cave Loop	Westchester	4	E/M	823
3. Ward Pound Ridge—Rocks Trail	Westchester	7.5	M/S	1,624
4. Ward Pound Ridge—Northern Loop	Westchester	5	E/M	820
5. Cranberry Lake Preserve	Westchester	3	E	466
6. Bronx River Pathway	Westchester	9.8	E	581
7. Rockefeller State Park Preserve Loop	Westchester	10.4/ 3.8	E/M	1,348
8. Rockwood Hall	Westchester	2.1	E	294
9. Old Croton Aqueduct State Historic Park—Tarrytown to Yonkers	Westchester	9	E	357
10. Old Croton Aqueduct State Historic Park—New Croton Dam to Ossining	Westchester	5.5	E/M	466
11. Teatown Lake Loop	Westchester	2.4	E	378
12. Vernay Lake/Hidden Valley Loop	Westchester	2	E	340
13. Sylvan Glen Park Preserve	Westchester	3.6	E/M	662
14. Anthony's Nose/Camp Smith Trail	Westchester/ Putnam	4.2	S	1,781
15. Manitou Point Preserve	Putnam	3.1	E	522
16. Osborn Loop/Sugarloaf Hill	Putnam	7	M	1,589
17. Breakneck Ridge/Undercliff Loop	Putnam	7.5	S	2,273
18. Fishkill Ridge	Dutchess	7	S	2,122
19. East Mountain/Round Hill Loop	Putnam	7.3	M	1,578
20. Jordan Pond/Perkins Trail Loop	Putnam	7.2	E/M	1,209
21. Heart of Fahnestock	Putnam	6.4/ 3.5	E/M	876
22. Tallman Mountain State Park	Rockland	4.3	E/M	452
23. Hook Mountain	Rockland	12/ 6	M/S	2,681
24. The Tors, High and Low	Rockland	6	M/S	1,722
25. Ramapo Torne	Rockland	4.8	M/S	1,422
26. Breakneck Mountain Loop	Rockland	6.9	M	1,495
27. Nurian/Appalachian Trail Loop	Orange	7	M/S	1,890

Time (hours)	Views	Kids	Camp	X-C Ski	Falls	Shuttle	Notes
3		Y			Y		Scenic gorge, closed in winter
3	Y	Y	P	Y			Historic cave, scenic view
5	Y		P				Six "rocks" attractions, scenic view
3		Y	P	Y			Cascading river, woods roads
2.5	Y	Y					Scenic ponds, historic quarry
6	Y	Y		Y	Y		Historic pathway, bikes allowed, public transportation
6/2		Y		Y			Carriage roads, lake, exhibits
1.5	Y	Y		Y			Ruins of mansion, views of Hudson River
5	Y	Y		Y			Nearly level, bikes allowed, historic stone-arch bridge
3	Y	Y		Y		Y	Nearly level, bikes allowed, historic stone-arch bridge
2	Y	Y		Y			Boardwalk over scenic lake, nature center
1.5	Y	Y		Y			Scenic lake and valley, nature center
2	Y	Y		Y			Historic stone quarry
4	Y					O	Spectacular views, some steep sections
2	Y	Y					Scenic views of Hudson River
4.5	Y	Y					Steep at start, carriage roads
6	Y						Craggy trails, views, dairy farm ruins
5	Y						Steep climbs, views, less-used area
4.5	Y						Less-used area, views
4							Farm fields, streamside walk, lakes
3.5/2		Y		Y			History, mining, old railbed, lakes
2.5	Y	Y					Scenic views of Hudson River
6.5/3.5	Y						Scenic views of Hudson River, historic ruins
4	Y	Y					Scenic views of Hudson River
4	Y						Scenic views, some steep climbs and descents
4							Deep woods, interesting boulders
4.5	Y						Massive boulders, scenic lakes, historic mine

Hike	County	Distance (miles)	Difficulty	Elevation Gain (feet)
28. Rockhouse Mountain Loop	Rockland/ Orange	7.5/ 6"	M	1,415
29. Iron Mines Loop	Orange	8	M/S	1,803
30. Menomine Trail/Black Mountain	Orange	4.5	M/S	1,031
31. Anthony Wayne Loop	Rockland/ Orange	5.5	M/S	1,850
32. Popolopen Torne	Orange	4.5	M/S	1,608
33. Bear Mountain Loop	Rockland/ Orange	4.2	S	1,388
34. Brooks Lake	Orange	1	E	192
35. Sterling Lake Loop	Orange	4.2	E	640
36. Sterling Ridge to the Fire Tower	Orange	7.4/ 5.5	M	807
37. Mount Peter to Arden on the Appalachian Trail	Orange	12.3/ 8.7	S	2,956
38. Indian Hill Loop	Orange	4.3	M	1,010
39. Schunemunk via High Knob	Orange	8	S	1,913
40. Schunemunk Mountain Loop	Orange	7.8	S	1,864
41. Storm King Mountain	Orange	2.5	M	852
42. Black Rock Forest—Southern Ledges	Orange	9	S	2,277
43. Black Rock Forest—Northern Loop	Orange	5.5	M	1,182
44. Shawangunk Ridge	Ulster	6.2	M	1,799
45. Verkeerder Kill Falls Loop	Ulster	9.6	S	1,332
46. Minnewaska State Park Preserve Loop	Ulster	9.2	S	1,654
47. Peters Kill Loop	Ulster	2	E	545
48. The Trapps to Gertrude's Nose	Ulster	10.1	S	1,836
49. Old Minnewaska Trail Loop	Ulster	7.5	S	1,552
50. Bonticou Crag	Ulster	4	S	992

Difficulty Key

E: Easy
M: Moderate
S: Strenuous

P: Possible, i.e.,
     lean-to available
Y: Yes

Min.: Minimal
O: Optional

Time (hours)	Views	Kids	Camp	X-C Ski	Falls	Shuttle	Notes
4/ 3"	Y	Y					Historic mine, old cemetery
5	Y						Historic mines, Lemon Squeezer rock formation
3	Y		P				Scenic lake, views from summit
4	Y		P				Steep climb, scenic ridge walk
3.5	Y						Spectacular views from summit, scenic gorge
3	Y						Steep climb, stone steps on descent, views from summit
1	Y	Y					Easy walk around scenic lake
2.5	Y	Y					Walk around scenic lake; historic furnace
4.5/ 3	Y	Y				O	Scenic ridge walk; views from fire tower
9/ 6.5	Y		P		Y	Y	Strenuous hike on the Appalachian Trail
3	Y	Y					Historic furnace, wide stone walls
6	Y					Y	Puddingstone conglomerate rock, scenic views
5.5	Y				Y		Puddingstone conglomerate rock, megaliths
2.5	Y						Open summit, spectacular views
6.5	Y						Expansive views, scenic ponds, historic building
3.5	Y	Y					Expansive views, scenic ponds, swimming
4.5	Y				Y	Y	Scenic ridge walk, views, pitch pines
6.5	Y				Y		Panoramic views, spectacular waterfall, pitch pines
6	Y				Y		Cascading stream, ptich pines, panoramic views
1.5	Y	Y			Y		Cascading stream, views of Catskills
6	Y						Panoramic views from congolmerate rock slabs, cliffs
5	Y						Panoramic views, carriage roads, Trapps cliffs
3	Y						Challenging rock scramble, panoramic views

Preface

Although this book has always been titled *50 Hikes in the Lower Hudson Valley*, previous editions have included hikes all the way up the Hudson as far as Albany County. In early 2018, the Countryman Press published a new book titled *50 Hikes in the Upper Hudson Valley*. To minimize conflict between the two books, it was agreed that the 12 hikes in "The North Country and the Catskills" section of the third edition of *50 Hikes in the Lower Hudson Valley* (as well as two other hikes) would be omitted from this edition. These 14 hikes have been replaced with new hikes, the majority of which are in Westchester County, where the number of hikes has been expanded from 6 to 14. New hikes have also been added to each of the other four sections of the book.

For this edition, most of the remaining hikes have been field-checked, and many updates and changes have been made. In some cases, the trail system in a particular park has been significantly revised, and the hike has been essentially rewritten.

I want to thank Jacques Van Engel, who revised Hike #7 (Rockefeller State Park Preserve), and Jane and Walt Daniels, who revised the introductions to the Westchester County and East Hudson Highlands sections. Finally, I wish to thank my friends Ryan Chombok, Devin McDermitt, Benzion Sanders, Ezra Sanders, James Sanders, Aaron Schwartz, Ariel Schwartz, and Eitan Schwartz, who accompanied me on trips to check out some of the hikes in this book.

Although the maps for each hike were prepared by the Countryman Press, the GPS tracks for each map were supplied by Jeremy Apgar, the NY–NJTC's talented cartographer.

Daniel Chazin

NY–NJTC

Introduction

The Hudson River is a 350-mile-long corridor of history and a monument to our natural heritage. For part of its length, the Hudson is an estuary—a place where seawater blends with fresh water, creating one of the most productive ecosystems on earth. This territory is the spawning ground and nursery for many species of fish, and it supports thousands of acres of tidal wetlands.

Southeastern New York State is dominated by the Hudson River, which flows past the wonders of its cities and industries. At the same time, the river touches some of the state's wilder lands, where the hiker can quickly escape the centers of civilization that dot the Hudson's banks. The wilderness at the Hudson's Adirondack headwaters needs no introduction. Some of the wildlands near the Hudson's southern cities are well known, whereas others are almost undiscovered. This guide includes a variety of day hikes that will introduce you to the best of southeastern New York's wildlands not far removed from the Hudson.

Settled by Europeans more than 350 years ago—and much earlier by Native peoples—the Hudson Valley has provided generations of Americans with rich farmland and has been a vital source of strength and inspiration for artistic expression in painting, poetry, and literature. The first visitors to the Hudson were mightily impressed by the fortress-like rocks of the Palisades, the rugged Hudson Highlands, and the mysteries of the distant blue Catskills. It is in these rocky hills and mountains bordering the Hudson that most of the hikes described in this guide take place.

The book leads you to the northern Palisades, the Ramapos, the Highlands, the isolated lump of Schunemunk, and the white cliffs of the Shawangunks. It takes you to the tops of this series of ranges, which stand as if designed to offer the best possible views of the Hudson and Mohawk Valleys.

THE HISTORY OF THE ROCKS AND MOUNTAINS

The drama of the southeastern New York landscape reveals a secondary story in the very rocks themselves. From the crystalline Hudson Highlands to the younger folded rocks of the Appalachians, you can see the parts of the puzzle that make up the region's geological history.

The Shawangunks were formed during the Silurian period, about 450 million years ago, when extensive sands and quartz-rich gravels were deposited in a shallow sea. Much later, the resulting sandstones and conglomerates were uplifted and differentially eroded.

The Hudson Highlands to the south are a series of granitic and metamorphic rocks. They were intruded and metamorphosed at great depth more than a billion years ago. Later, during the Taconic orogeny, the rocks were folded, faulted, and uplifted to their present form.

HIKING IN SOUTHEASTERN NEW YORK

This guide offers the hiker an excellent range of opportunities. For residents of southern New York State, the special appeal of most of these trails is their proximity to the New York City metropolitan area. All of the trailheads lie within two hours of the city. The area offers many more walks than are described in this book, and references to other hiking guides are given in the bibliography. Social hikers can find many walking groups that offer regularly scheduled trips to help them discover other hikes and prepare for outdoor adventures. The New York–New Jersey Trail Conference can put you in touch with many of these groups. Organizations such as the Catskill 3500 Club, the Appalachian Mountain Club, the Sierra Club, and chapters of the Adirondack Mountain Club all offer outing schedules that provide a variety of hikes. Each of these organizations—and most particularly the Trail Conference—also provides mechanisms for the hiker to return something to the land. With programs of trail maintenance, conservation, planning to prevent overuse, and education to promote wise use, these organizations help protect our wildlands.

Some of the hikes described in this book are not heavily trafficked. Others are, but even here, an early spring, winter, and late-fall trip will provide both solitude and expanded vistas in ways sure to please any wilderness seeker. Many trails crowded on weekends are much less frequented on weekdays.

Almost all the lands traversed by today's trails were once settled and used by farmers, miners, and loggers. Their presence inevitably is reflected in the lore that surrounds the trails, and we explore that history as well as the natural scene. Although this guide serves as an invitation to the mountain ranges and valleys of the southern part of the state, it cannot even begin to probe the vast history that enlivens each route. For further information, consult the bibliography at the end of this book.

BEFORE YOU START

There is an enormous range of hikes in this guide, from easy strolls to strenuous climbs. The information given about distance, time, and elevation change should help you gauge the difficulty of each hike and your preparedness. Almost all hikes follow clearly marked trails.

Preparedness is key to your enjoyment, and you should be suitably equipped before you start. Knowledge should include understanding the use of a map and compass to complement the information in this guide. If you are new to hiking, it may be a good idea to join a hiking group and learn from those with experience. The more background you have in the woods, the greater your safety as well as your enjoyment. Even if you're an experienced hiker, it is always safer to hike with others. A group of four people is often considered ideal, especially if you are hiking under adverse conditions, since if someone is injured, two of the hikers can go for help while one stays with the injured person.

Carrying a cell phone for use in an emergency is another sensible precaution. However, it is often not possible to get adequate reception in backcountry areas, and nonemergency use is often annoying to others on the trail who appreciate the natural outdoor experience.

THE WEATHER

Whenever possible, wait for a sunny day, as the hiking pleasures are much greater. However, even on sunny days you should be prepared for changes and extremes. It can be colder in the Hudson Valley than in the city, and storms can and do appear with little warning.

The weather can often be too hot in summer for strenuous hikes. Some people prefer walking in southern New York in late fall and early spring, but these times coincide with the most unpredictable conditions. Extremes from heat waves to snowstorms can occur—but the rewards of fewer people and expanded distant vistas in the leafless seasons make the experience worthwhile.

Walking in the winter months (and colder weather at any time of the year) is wonderful and brings its own rewards. Vistas are more easily seen when leaves are down from the trees, annoying black-flies and mosquitoes are gone, and fewer walkers are in the woods. However, the winter hiker needs to take additional precautions. Always remember to file a hike plan with a stay-at-home friend, be prepared to shorten your planned hike if necessary, and carry additional clothing and emergency supplies. In extreme cold or in windy conditions, watch your companions for signs of hypothermia and/or frostbite. Hypothermia can creep up unawares, as the temperature does not need to be very low for a person to be affected. You can become hypothermic in 50-degree weather if you become wet and are poorly prepared. Watch your companions for signs of poor reflex actions: excessive stumbling, the need for frequent rest stops, or a careless attitude toward clothing and equipment. Once uncontrollable shivering has started, it may be only a matter of minutes before the body temperature has cooled beyond the point of recovery. Immediate warmth for the affected person is the only solution.

If there is more than eight inches of snow on the ground, you may need snowshoes; if the trail is icy, crampons or other traction devices. Even if there is little or no snow in the city, the parks in the Hudson Valley could have a foot or more of the white stuff on the ground.

PREPARATIONS

Even with the best of forecasts, you should plan for the unexpected. You should bring along extra clothing in case of possible temperature changes, and rain gear should always be carried. Experiment with layers of light, waterproof gear. Places to swim are noted on these hikes, so you may wish to take along a bathing suit.

Some of the trails are quite smooth, while others are very rocky. For most of these hikes, a sturdy pair of well-broken-in, over-the-ankle boots is recommended. Lightweight boots with Vibram soles give wonderful traction; if they are lined with Gore-Tex, they will also be waterproof. Wearing two pairs of socks—an inner lightweight pair and a heavy outer pair—helps to prevent blisters by allowing the socks to rub against one another instead of skin. Avoid cotton socks; wool or synthetic socks are much better for your feet and will stay much drier.

Carry a sturdy day pack large enough to hold your lunch, plenty of water, and a few necessities. You may wish to bring along a whistle, a waterproof case with dry matches, a knife, lip balm, and/or a space blanket (to be used in case of emergency).

Carry a map of the trail and a compass,

a flashlight in case you are delayed beyond dusk, and a watch. It is also advisable to carry a small first-aid kit containing a few bandages, first-aid cream, and moleskin for the unexpected blister.

You may wish to take along a small bottle of insect repellent. Some hikers prefer one that contains DEET (N-diethylmetatoluamide), while others prefer a natural repellent. Blackflies often bite in early spring, and mosquitoes later in the season.

Fill a plastic bag with toilet paper, and throw in a few moist towelettes or a liquid sanitizer to use before lunch on those dry mountaintops.

Even if you do not require prescription eyeglasses, you may wish to wear sunglasses, as it's all too easy to run into an overhanging branch or twig. If you're helpless without your glasses, carry an extra pair.

You'll enjoy the hikes more if you carry binoculars and watch for birds. A small magnifying glass can add to your discoveries of nature. You may wish to carry a small, lightweight altimeter which provides a good clue to progress on a mountain. Of course, if you have a smartphone, such a device is often included as part of an app.

When you hike, you should always carry more water than you think you will need. Dehydration on summer days is a real possibility, and it can even happen on a sunny, leafless early spring or winter day. These mountains are dry much of the year, and there are few springs. It's becoming increasingly dangerous to trust open water sources because of the spread of *Giardia lamblia*, so don't drink from a stream, no matter how lovely it looks, without first purifying the water.

Remember, hiking should be fun. If you are tired or uncomfortable with the weather, turn back and complete the hike another day. Do not create a situation in which you risk your safety or that of your companions. Be sure someone knows your intended route and expected return time. Always sign in at trailhead registers where available. The unexpected can occur. Weather can change, trail markings can be obscured, you can fall, and you can get lost. Nevertheless, you won't be in real danger if you have anticipated the unexpected.

Timber rattlesnakes are a threatened species. Be cautious when hiking, and on no account interfere with individual snakes or their dens.

Mountain bikers and/or equestrians may be encountered in some areas. User conflicts continue to occur. Hikers often resent the silent approach from behind, the encroachment and possible trail destruction from knobby wheels. Equestrians dislike the speed at which some bikers travel the trails, which often scares horses. Cyclists must always yield the trail, but it is still a good idea for hikers to remain alert. If you wish to avoid bicycles and horses, choose a hike in an area where they are not allowed.

Rifle hunting is allowed in Storm King, most of Sterling Forest, and some other areas described in this guide. Bow hunting is allowed in other areas, such as Fahnestock State Park and Westchester County. No-hunting zones include Harriman-Bear Mountain and most of Minnewaska State Park Preserve. Deer season usually runs from late November into mid-December; specific dates are available from the New York State Department of Environmental Conservation. If you choose to hike in hunting areas during deer or bear season, be sure to wear a blaze-orange hat and/or vest.

LYME DISEASE

Lyme disease is caused by a tick-borne spirochete that may produce a rash, flu-like symptoms, and joint pain. If left untreated, it may cause chronic arthritis and nervous-system disorders. The disease is difficult to diagnose but treatable if diagnosed early.

The deer ticks that transmit Lyme disease are found in the areas covered in this guidebook, and hikers should take preventive measures. There is no fool-proof way to protect yourself from these very small ticks, so make sure to check yourself frequently; tuck pants into socks and boots; put insect repellent containing DEET on your pants, shoes, and socks (note that DEET may weaken elastics), and wear tightly woven and light-colored clothing (making it easier to see the ticks). Staying on the trail and avoiding tall grass is also a good preventive measure. Above all else, we strongly recommend that you shower and change clothes at the end of your hike, as this is the best time to perform a complete body check. Change out of your hiking clothes to prevent any ticks that are present from attaching themselves to you. If you suspect that you may have contracted Lyme disease, contact your physician right away.

BEHAVIOR IN THE WOODS

So, now you are safe in the woods, but what about the woods themselves? The environment that may threaten you can be just as fragile as you are, and you are responsible for protecting it.

Trail erosion is becoming a serious problem in many areas. Please stay on the trail at all times to minimize damage to soils, tree roots, and vegetation. Never cut across switchbacks, and use stepping-stones whenever possible to cross wet areas of the trail. Do not pick wildflowers or dig up woodland plants.

Leave no sign of your presence. Use privies if available. If not, bury your personal waste at least 200 feet from water or from a trail. When you camp, do not bathe with soap in lakes or streams; when picnicking or camping, carry wash water and dishwater back from the shore. If you're camping, carry a stove for cooking, and do not build fires. In most parks, fires are prohibited except in designated receptacles. Respect the rights of others, and help preserve natural areas for future hikers.

The woolly adelgid has been active in the Hudson Valley for the last few years. Many hemlock trees are dying as a result of its depredations, and large stands of once-magnificent hemlocks have already succumbed in our hiking areas. The loss of hemlock groves with their deep shade changes the character of our woodlands. When deciduous hardwoods replace hemlocks, more light filters through. The forest floor dries out, and the vernal pools used by frogs and salamanders for breeding shrivel. This aphidlike insect was introduced inadvertently to the United States from Asia in 1924. Originally discovered in Oregon, the infestation has now spread to the eastern states. The insect feeds on new twig growth and can be seen at maturity between late winter and early spring at the base of individual hemlock needles when the insects cover themselves with easily seen white, cottony wax that remains attached to the branches even after the insect has left. Individual trees can sometimes be saved by spraying. A natural predator of the insect does exist, and some encouraging results are being seen in areas where the imported ladybird beetle has been introduced.

GEOCACHING

Geocaching is a high-tech treasure hunt using the Global Positioning System (GPS) to find "caches" hidden in the woods. This activity has added a new dimension to the adventure of being outdoors, and it can add an exciting dimension for the children hiking with you.

Geocaching began in the Seattle area in 2002, and it is estimated that caches now exist in every state of the United States and in more than 200 countries, with more than 15,000 active participants and many variations on the main theme. The player chooses a code name, logs on to www.geocaching .com, and enters a zip code to find a list of names and coordinates for close-by caches. Then it's up to the skill of the player to use a portable GPS unit to find the treasure. Most of the pleasure is in the hunt, but once the cache has been found, the cacher signs the log using his nom de plume and, if he wishes, takes something from the cache—replacing it with an equal or better quality item. The "find" is subsequently registered on the cache page, which keeps track of the number of "finds." New York State requires that caches be registered and a permit number assigned.

Letterboxing (www.letterboxing.com) is a similar pastime, but instead of using a GPS unit to obtain coordinates, this game uses instructions and puzzles to locate the treasure, and a rubber stamp and pad is needed to validate the find.

Other sites such as navicache.com are also available.

NOTES FOR USING THIS GUIDE

The hike description tells you how to reach the trailhead itself, but getting to the nearby highway or town is up to you.

Summaries at the beginning of each hike list hiking distance, elevation gain, time on the trail, and United States Geological Survey (USGS) topographic map (or maps) and/or the NY–NJTC trail map for the area the hike traverses. In some cases, other maps are also listed. Unless otherwise noted, distances are for the round-trip or circuit.

Elevation gain refers to the total change in cumulative elevation for the hike. Where the terrain is relatively level, no numerical figure has been used. Hiking times are estimated. The times provided are designed to allow a reasonably experienced hiker to follow the route at a moderate pace, with a moderate amount of time allowed for breaks. Faster hikers may be able to cover the route in less time, while those who are not in the best of shape or who wish to take more frequent or longer breaks will require more time to complete the hike.

All of the hikes in this book are accompanied by a map showing the route of the hike. If you don't know how to read a map, you should learn to do so before hiking. Spend time, if you can, walking with someone who does know how to read a map. The same instructions are appropriate for the use of a compass. You may not need either on the easiest of this guide's trails, but walking these routes with map and compass will allow you to become comfortable with their use so that you can extend your hikes beyond the ones described or to more difficult hikes.

Many trails are blazed with paint according to the designated trail color, either on trees adjacent to the trail or on rock underfoot, but in some locations, plastic or metal disks are nailed to trees. Two blazes, one above the other, indicate a turn in the trail, the direction of the turn being indicated by the off-set of the upper blaze. Standing at one blaze, the hiker can normally expect to see the next one ahead, though where the footway is clear—such as on a woods road—blazes may be less frequent. Three blazes indicate the beginning or the end of a trail. Some trails border on or cross private property, so please honor any NO TRESPASSING or KEEP OUT signs, leave any gates you may find along the route of your hike in the same condition as you found them, and generally be respectful of the landowner.

Keep in mind those two familiar mottos: Take only photographs, leave only footprints and "carry in, carry out." It's a good idea to bring along a small plastic bag to enable you to take out litter left by others.

LONG-DISTANCE TRAILS

Three long-distance trails traverse the Hudson Valley.

The Appalachian Trail (AT) is a National Scenic Trail that passes through on its 2,190-mile journey from Georgia to Maine. Through-hikers are those completing the AT's entire length in one trip, most taking about six months on the trail and adopting trail names for the journey. Other hikers tackle the project by hiking separate sections, one or more at a time, and still others walk the trail as day hikers. The first section of the AT from the Bear Mountain Bridge to the Ramapo River south of Arden in Harriman-Bear Mountain State Parks was built by volunteers of the NY–NJTC in 1922–23. Marked with white rectangles, the AT is administered by the Appalachian Trail Conservancy, headquartered in Harpers Ferry, West Virginia. For more information, go to www.appalachiantrail.org.

The Long Path, marked with aqua blazes, begins its northward journey at the George Washington Bridge. For many years, the trail's northern terminus was at Windham in the Catskills, but the trail has now been extended as far north as the Mohawk Valley, and there are plans to extend the trail into the Adirondacks. Administered by the NY–NJTC, the Long Path is currently over 350 miles long. The Shawangunk Ridge Trail, which extends from High Point State Park in New Jersey to the northern Shawangunks, is part of the Long Path system. Joining the other two traditional long-distance trails is the Highlands Trail, blazed with diamond-shaped teal-colored markers. This trail, about 150 miles long, links the Delaware and Hudson Rivers. An extension east of the Hudson River to Connecticut has been proposed. The not-yet-complete route uses established trails, with some new construction where necessary and connections made by short sections of paved road. The system links over 26 county, state, and federal parks, forests, and open spaces, and is the result of cooperation among the NY–NJTC, conservation organizations, state and local governments, and local businesses.

These three trails are maintained by volunteers, as are most other trails described in this book.

OTHER HELPFUL INFORMATION

New York–New Jersey Trail Conference (NY–NJTC)
600 Ramapo Valley Road
Mahwah, NJ 07430
201-512-9348
www.nynjtc.org
e-mail: info@nynjtc.org

The NY–NJTC coordinates the construction and maintenance of over 2,150 miles of hiking trails, including the Appalachian Trail in New York and New Jersey, and the Long Path, which connects the metropolitan area with the Catskills and beyond. The organization publishes hiking guidebooks and maps, which may be purchased directly from the conference or from outdoor stores, with significant discounts for members on purchases made directly from the conference (see the bibliography).

Approximately 100 hiking clubs and conservation organizations belong to the conference, along with nearly 10,000 individual members. All interested hikers are invited to join, and annual dues include, among other things, a subscription to the *Trail Walker*. This quarterly publication includes informative articles and trail updates. For a list of local hiking clubs, a complete list of publications, and to order books and maps, call the NY–NJTC or visit their website, www.nynjtc.org. The website also includes descriptions of over 400 hikes, many of which are in the lower Hudson Valley.

For the Shawangunks:

Mohonk Preserve Visitor Center
3197 US 44/NY 55
Gardiner, NY 12525
845-255-0919
www.mohonkpreserve.org (A contact e-mail form is available at this site.)
The Mohonk Preserve manages this unique natural resource and supervises access to preserve lands. An admission fee is required from non-members.

Mohonk Mountain House
1000 Mountain Rest Road
New Paltz, NY 12561
855-883-3798

www.mohonk.com
Admission fee required except for overnight guests and Mohonk Preserve members.

Other:

Scenic Hudson, Inc.
One Civic Center Plaza, #200
Poughkeepsie, NY 12601
845-473-4440
e-mail: info@scenichudson.org
www.scenichudson.org
Founded in 1963, Scenic Hudson is a nonprofit environmental organization and separately incorporated land trust. They are "dedicated to protecting and enhancing the scenic, natural, historic, agricultural, and recreational treasures of the majestic 315-mile-long Hudson River and its valley."

Open Space Institute
1350 Broadway, #201
New York, NY 10018
212-290-8200
www.osiny.org
Responsible for preserving many thousands of acres in the Hudson Valley.

The Nature Conservancy
195 New Karner Road, #200
Albany, NY 12205
518-690-7850
www.nature.org/ourinitiatives/regions/northamerica/unitedstates/newyork/index.htm
Founded in 1951, The Nature Conservancy is the world's largest private, international conservation group. The organization manages and protects natural areas, and some hikes in this guide are in conservancy preserves. As threats to remaining wild places escalate, The Nature Conservancy is working in New York to counter and preempt them.

New York State Office of Parks, Recreation, and Historic Preservation
625 Broadway
Albany, NY 12207
518-474-0456
www.nysparks.com/parks
The New York State OPRHP welcomes 65 million visitors a year to its parks, historic sites, and recreation areas from Jones Beach to Niagara Falls. Regional offices, or commissions, administer the specific sites.

Taconic State Park Commission
9 Old Post Road
Staatsburg, NY 12580
845-889-4100
The Taconic State Park Commission manages the lands of the OPRHP on the east side of the Hudson. It is responsible for state parks and historic sites there, including Hudson Highlands State Park Preserve and Fahnestock State Park.

Palisades Interstate Park Commission
3006 Seven Lakes Drive
Bear Mountain, NY 10911-0427
845-786-2701
The Palisades Interstate Park Commission manages the lands of the OPRHP on the west side of the Hudson. It is responsible for state parks and historic sites there, including Nyack Beach, Hook Mountain, Rockland Lake, High Tor, Harriman-Bear Mountain, Sterling Forest, Schunemunk Mountain, Storm King, and Minnewaska State Parks.

Free USGS topo maps are available online: store.usgs.gov.

MAP LEGEND

——— Described trail	═══ Interstate highway
- - - - Important trail	═══ Secondary highway
◄——— Hike direction arrow	——— Minor highway, road, street
——— Perennial stream	- - - - Unpaved road, trail
- - - - Intermittent stream	+—+—+ Railroad
——— Major contour line	—··— International border
——— Minor contour line	- -·- -· State border
National/state park, wilderness	🅿 Parking area
National/state forest, wildlife refuge	🚶 Trailhead
Perennial body of water	• City, town
Intermittent body of water	🔆 Overlook, scenic view
Swamp, marsh	Λ Campground, campsite
Wooded area	⊓ Shelter
	✕ Mountain peak
	▪ Place of interest
	⏶ Appalachian Trail

I.

WESTCHESTER COUNTY

Introduction to Westchester

Extending some 35 miles from the New York City boundary north to the Hudson Highlands, Westchester is a mix of suburbs, horse farms, light industry, malls, commuting routes, corporate headquarters, and cities. Although developed, the region offers plenty of hiking opportunities through natural and historic areas. Hikes are available throughout the county, ranging from short walks in small parks to longer hikes in larger parks—some of which even offer the opportunity to camp overnight. The county's park system is extensive, and there are many private preserves, municipal parks, and a few state parks to round out the offerings.

In 1609, explorer Henry Hudson, sailing under the English flag, thought he had found a route to China. As he sailed up the river that would bear his name, he passed Native American villages. A hundred years later, the Native American peoples had all but disappeared, but their influence is still reflected in the names of towns, villages, rivers, and roads: Katonah was "principal hill"; Ossining, "place of stone"; Chappaqua, "rustling land"; and Kisco, "muddy place."

The railroads arrived in the 1840s, and land began to be developed—some areas as estates and country retreats, and others as towns and farms. At the same time, New York City began purchasing land to construct a reservoir system to provide drinking water for its residents. Later, in the early twentieth century, Westchester County began acquiring land for parks. The support of land preservation persists in the twenty-first century with public-private partnerships expanding public access to open space.

Hiking opportunities in Westchester County are plentiful, especially considering the area's proximity to New York City, and the trails are generally less strenuous than those located farther north in the Hudson Highlands. The rolling hills feature streams, ponds, wetlands, stone walls, and rock outcrops; many woods roads built to provide access to private lands are now delightful hiking routes. Westchester County also offers a number of linear trails, some of which follow abandoned railroad rights-of-way. Others use the route of a historic aqueduct or follow parkways built for automobiles. For more information about county parks in Westchester County, go to www.parks.westchestergov.com. Those wishing to explore additional hiking opportunities in Westchester should consult *Walkable Westchester*, a comprehensive guide to over 200 parks and 600 miles of trails, published by the New York–New Jersey Trail Conference.

Mianus River Gorge

TOTAL DISTANCE: 4.3 miles

WALKING TIME: 3 hours

ELEVATION GAIN: 933 feet

MAPS: USGS 7.5' Pound Ridge; Mianus River Gorge Preserve trail map

TRAILHEAD GPS COORDINATES: N 41° 11' 11" W 73° 37' 18"

Protection of this stretch of the Mianus River was The Nature Conservancy's first project when, in 1953, the infant organization became involved with a group of local citizens to preserve this unique area. In 1964, the Mianus River Gorge was registered as a National Natural Landmark and became the first area to be granted this designation. The preserve is now managed by an independent nonprofit organization, the Mianus River Gorge Preserve, Inc.

The Mianus River begins in Greenwich, Connecticut, and flows north through New York before reversing its direction and turning south through the gorge toward Long Island Sound. The river is named for Chief (or Sachem) Mayano of the Wappinger tribe, whose name in the Wappinger language means "he who gathers together," and who was killed near the gorge in 1664. In 1600, the seven Wappinger tribes probably numbered about 8,000 people in thirty villages, but epidemics of smallpox and malaria and the Wappinger War of 1643–45 seriously depleted their numbers. Only a few hundred remained in the lower Hudson valley after 1700, and almost all were gone by 1758.

Three trails traverse the Mianus River Gorge: the Old Growth Forest Trail (red), the Old Farmland Trail (blue), and the River Trail (green). This hike is a "lollipop-loop," with the "stick" of the lollipop at the far end. The hike begins by following the green trail, continues south on the red trail, and returns on the blue trail. Although these trails are identified by color on the preserve map, they are not blazed on the ground, and are marked only by colored arrows on signposts at junctions. However, the trails are clearly defined and easy to follow. Side trails lead to an old mica mine, an overlook, a waterfall, and the shore

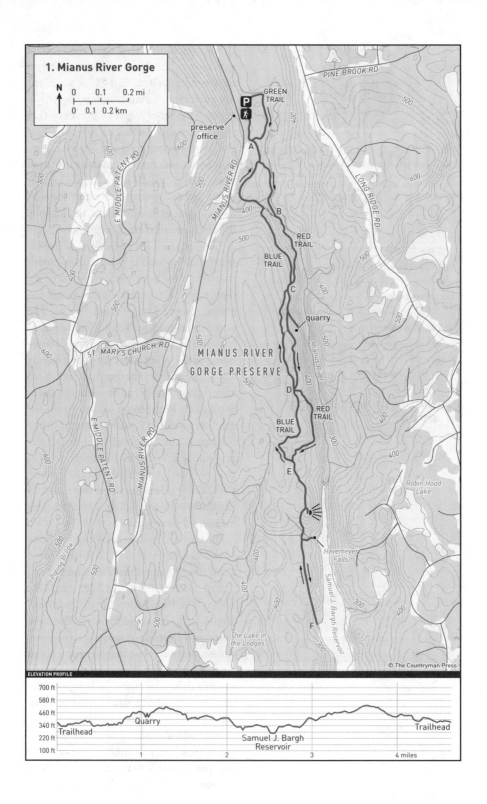

1. Mianus River Gorge

N

| 0 | 0.1 | 0.2 mi |
| 0 | 0.1 | 0.2 km |

GREEN TRAIL

P

preserve office

A

B

RED TRAIL

BLUE TRAIL

C

quarry

MIANUS RIVER GORGE PRESERVE

Mianus River

D

RED TRAIL

BLUE TRAIL

E

Robin Hood Lake

Havemeyer Falls

F

Samuel J. Bargh Reservoir

The Lake in the Ledges

PINE BROOK RD

E MIDDLE PATENT RD

MIANUS RIVER RD

ST. MARY'S CHURCH RD

E MIDDLE PATENT RD

MIANUS RIVER RD

Poring Brook

LONG RIDGE RD

© The Countryman Press

ELEVATION PROFILE

| 700 ft |
| 580 ft |
| 460 ft |
| 340 ft |
| 220 ft |
| 100 ft |

Trailhead   Quarry   Samuel J. Bargh Reservoir   Trailhead

1   2   3   4 miles

of a reservoir. Important junctions are marked by letters (A to F) on signposts, and features of interest are identified by numbers (1 to 10).

The Mianus River Gorge is a private preserve, not a public park. It is managed primarily to protect the natural resource, not for recreational purposes. Thus, neither bicycles nor dogs are allowed in the preserve, and picnicking is permitted only in the Map Shelter area. Although there is no entry fee, the preserve relies on donations to continue its work, so you are encouraged to make a donation. The preserve is open daily between April 1 and November 30 from 8:30 a.m. to 5:00 p.m. For more information, go to www.mianus.org.

GETTING THERE

From Exit 4 on I-684, proceed east on NY 172 for 1.6 miles, then turn left onto NY 22 north. NY 172 and NY 22 run together for 1 mile into Bedford, where the triangular village green is reached and NY 22 departs to the left. Bear right to stay on NY 172 (Pound Ridge Road) toward Pound Ridge and Stamford. In 0.9 mile, you'll come to a traffic light (and gas station), where you turn right (south) onto Long Ridge Road. In another 0.6 mile, turn very sharply right onto Millers Mill Road (a gravel road). Continue for 0.1 mile, and immediately after crossing a bridge, turn left onto Mianus Road. The entrance to the preserve is on the left, 0.6 mile farther on. The preserve office is on the right side of the road, just beyond the preserve entrance (the address of the preserve office is 167 Mianus River Road, Bedford, NY 10506).

Alternatively, from Connecticut's Merritt Parkway, Exit 34, take Long Ridge Road (CT 104) north for 7.7 miles, entering New York State along the way.

Turn left onto Millers Mill Road, then left again onto Mianus Road, and continue for 0.6 mile to the preserve entrance on the left.

THE HIKE

When you arrive, proceed to the Map Shelter, where there are informative exhibits on the history and ecology of the preserve. Trail guide booklets, which include a map, are available here. Begin the hike by heading north (left when facing the kiosk) on a level section of the green trail. You'll soon reach a bench, overlooking the river, which honors Lucy Adams, a local educator and preservationist.

The trail now descends to the Mianus River and follows it for a short distance, then turns right, away from the river. Soon the path again parallels the river. Next you'll cross a tributary stream on a footbridge of huge rocks. The trail now turns right and climbs to point A. Here, you should turn left, now following all three trails—green, red, and blue. The trail proceeds through a hemlock forest high above the river, which may be seen through the trees down to the left.

At the next junction (marked by a signpost), turn left and follow the green trail, which descends to the river. On the right, the high fence is a deer exclosure. After crossing a tributary stream on huge rocks, you'll reach a particularly beautiful section, where the river cascades through large boulders.

The trail now climbs out of the gorge and reaches point B. Here, the green trail ends, and you should turn left onto the red trail. Once again, the trail descends into the gorge, then climbs to reach sign 4, which marks the Rockwall Breach—the narrowest point across the gorge. Just beyond, you'll pass sign 5,

MIANUS RIVER GORGE

the site of the first land acquisition for the preserve. This location has been named "Monte Gloria" in honor of Gloria Anable, a founder of the preserve.

Proceed ahead on the red trail, which continues to parallel the river in the gorge (the stream can be heard, but not seen, below to the left). After running alongside a moss-covered stone wall, the trail curves to the right and reaches point C, where the blue trail joins briefly. Turn left here and climb to the next junction (marked by a signpost), where you'll turn left again to continue on the red trail. A short distance ahead, you'll pass a rock on the left with interesting striations.

Soon, you'll reach a sign for the "Quarry." Turn left and follow a side trail that descends to the Hobby Hill Quarry (marked by sign 6). Here, mica, quartz, and feldspar were mined in the nineteenth century by local farmers. Please honor the preserve's request not to take away any samples. Follow a short loop trail around the quarry, then return to

the red trail and turn left. At the next junction, where a branch of the blue trail leaves to the right, turn left to continue on the red trail. The red trail continues to parallel the gorge, now far below on the left.

When you reach point D, bear left and continue along a trail constructed in 2018–19 by the Jolly Rovers Trail Crew. This section of the red trail, which runs along the side of the gorge, features rock steps and stone cribbing to support sidehilling.

After climbing out of the gorge, the trail reaches point E, where the blue trail begins on the right. Turn left to continue on the red trail. Soon, the trail passes sign 7, which marks the site of a vernal pool, and reaches a sign for an OVERLOOK. Turn left and follow a short side trail to sign 8, which marks the site of an east-facing overlook. You can see a mountain beyond the gorge, but the view of the Mianus River and the reservoir is obscured by trees during leaf-on season.

Return to the red trail and turn left.

HAVEMEYER FALLS

Soon, you'll cross a stream on flat rocks and reach a sign for the FALLS. Turn left and follow a side trail, past sign 9, to Havemeyer Falls—a seasonal waterfall. After heavy rains, this waterfall can be truly spectacular, and you will want to spend some time at this beautiful spot. When you're ready to continue, return to the red trail and turn left again.

The trail now descends gradually to its terminus at a kiosk adjacent to the Samuel J. Bargh Reservoir, which supplies water to several localities, including Greenwich. Bargh was the president of the Connecticut American Water Company when the reservoir and dam were constructed. This location, point F, marks the end of the trail.

After taking in the view of the reservoir, retrace your steps along the red trail to point E. Here, you should bear left and begin to follow the blue trail, which you'll be taking all the way back to the start of the hike. Unlike the green and red trails, which run along the gorge, the blue trail follows an inland route that passes through former farmland. Along the way, you'll cross a number of stone walls built by farmers to mark property boundaries.

At point D, the red trail comes in from the right and immediately leaves to the right. You should bear left to continue along the blue trail. Just after passing a deer exclosure on the left, you'll notice a wide path that heads left. Continue straight ahead on the blue trail. At the next fork (with blue-blazed trails heading in both directions), bear left. After passing through a grassy area, and then an area covered with ferns, you'll descend to point C. Here, you should bear left, now following both the blue trail and the red trail. Just ahead, at another junction marked by a signpost, you should again bear left to continue on the blue trail.

After bearing right and descending a little, you'll reach another junction with the red trail at a T-intersection. Turn left and again follow the joint blue and red trails. Soon, you'll cross a stream on rocks and begin to climb. A short distance ahead, you'll pass a deer exclosure on the right, then another on the left.

At the next T-intersection, turn left, now following the blue, red, and green trails. You hiked this trail section on the way in, and you can once again see the Mianus River below on the right. When you reach point A, the green trail departs to the right, but you should continue ahead, following blue and red arrows. After passing a deer exclosure gate on the right, you'll reach the parking area of the preserve, where the hike began.

Ward Pound Ridge— Leatherman's Cave Loop

TOTAL DISTANCE: 4 miles

WALKING TIME: 3 hours

ELEVATION GAIN: 823 feet

MAPS: USGS 7.5' Pound Ridge; Ward Pound Ridge Reservation trail map (available online at parks.westchestergov.com); NY–NJTC Westchester Trails map

TRAILHEAD GPS COORDINATES: N 41° 14' 52" W 73° 35' 40"

Covering over 4,300 acres (about 6 square miles), Ward Pound Ridge Reservation is the largest park in Westchester County. The basic tract was assembled and acquired in 1925–26 and was named for the nearby town of Pound Ridge. Originally, the Native Americans had a "pound" in the area where they kept live game until needed for food. The "Ward" was added later to honor William Lukens Ward, Westchester's Republican county leader from 1896 to 1933, who was instrumental in establishing the county's park system. In addition to the trails, picnic areas, and camping areas, the park is home to the Trailside Nature Museum (914-864-7322). The park office can be reached at 914-864-7317.

There are over 45 miles of trails in Ward Pound Ridge Reservation, which makes possible a wide variety of hikes. Most of the trails follow old woods roads which date back to the days when the area was farmland. This hike climbs to a west-facing overlook (one of only two panoramic viewpoints in the park) and explores the fascinating Leatherman's Cave.

GETTING THERE

To get to the park, take Exit 6 off I-684 (at the merge between I-684 and the northern end of the Saw Mill River Parkway). Proceed east on NY 35 for 3.6 miles to NY 121, and turn right onto NY 121. The park entrance is almost immediately on your left. After passing the tollbooth (a per-car fee is charged on weekends, daily in the summer), turn right onto the first paved road, Michigan Road. Pass the side road to a camping area, and park at the end of the road near a circular turnaround.

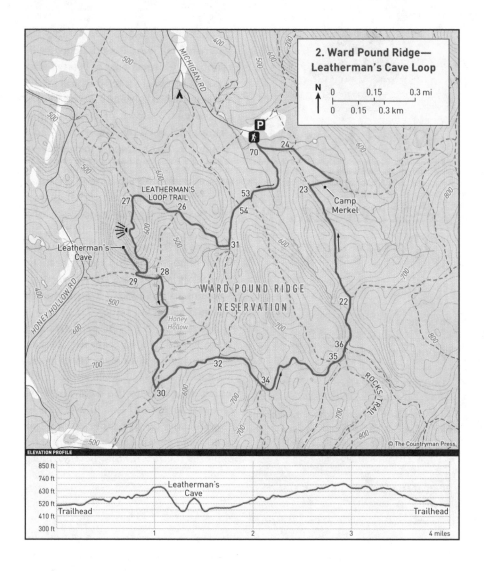

2. Ward Pound Ridge—
Leatherman's Cave Loop

N

| 0 | 0.15 | 0.3 mi |
| 0 | 0.15 | 0.3 km |

MICHIGAN RD

LEATHERMAN'S
LOOP TRAIL
26

27

Leatherman's
Cave

28

29

HONEY HOLLOW RD

Honey
Hollow

70

24

53

54

31

23

Camp
Merkel

22

36

35

WARD POUND RIDGE
RESERVATION

32

34

30

ROCKS TRAIL

© The Countryman Press

ELEVATION PROFILE

850 ft				
740 ft				
630 ft	Leatherman's			
520 ft	Cave			
410 ft	Trailhead			Trailhead
300 ft				
	1	2	3	4 miles

THE HIKE

From the circle at the end of the road, bear right and follow a road blocked by a wooden gate. Just beyond the gate, pass a kiosk on the right (trail maps are usually available there). Directly thereafter, you'll reach a fork in the trail, marked with a brown number as junction #70. (Most junctions in the park are marked with brown numbers; these numbers are referenced in this description and on the park map.) Bear right, following the metal trail markers with red and green arrows. This first section of trail is higher than the surrounding ground. Constructed by the Civilian Conservation Corps (CCC) in the 1930s, the path traverses a wetland. Most of the park had been heavily farmed, and evidence of that bygone era abounds in the many stone walls and foundations you'll see along the hike.

In a third of a mile, you'll reach

junction #53, with a branch of the green-blazed trail continuing straight ahead. Bear right, staying on the trail marked by both red and green metal blazes. Continue ahead past junction #54, and you'll soon come to junction #31. Here you should turn right onto the white-blazed Leatherman's Loop Trail. In a quarter mile, you'll reach junction #26. Continue straight ahead, but turn left at the following T-junction (#27) and continue to follow the LL blazes, which proceed along a narrow, winding footpath to the top of a hill, passing some interesting rock outcrops along the way. At the top, you'll come to a fine viewpoint from rock ledges just to the right of the trail. At an elevation of 665 feet, the viewpoint offers an expansive western vista across to the Cross River Reservoir, built in the early 1900s. On a clear day, you can see the Hudson Highlands.

After your "view break," continue following the LL blazes as the trail descends, turns right near a stone wall, and passes a massive rock outcrop and overhang. Ward Pound Ridge has many truly magnificent rock outcrops, and this one is among the best.

In a quarter mile, you'll reach junction #29. Turn around, go back a few feet the way you came, and you'll see a tree with arrows pointing in two directions and a sign TO JUNCTION MARKER 27. Bear left at this tree and follow a white-blazed trail uphill to the Leatherman's Cave. The cave itself is not very large—it's more of a rock shelter than a true cave—but its story makes it interesting.

Leatherman's Cave is named after a mysterious homeless man who wandered through the area from 1883 to 1889. He traveled a 365-mile circuit, stopping at the same 34 campsites on a regular schedule. His loop went from Danbury (Connecticut) to Waterbury, then to Saybrook and along the Connecticut River. Then he headed toward

LEATHERMAN'S CAVE

ALONG A TRAIL IN WARD POUND RIDGE

Long Island Sound, New Canaan, Wilton, White Plains, and back to here. He was clad in 60-pound clothes made of old leather, and mostly communicated using crude signs. People often left food for this gentle soul or invited him in for a meal. Another one of his camps is preserved on the Mattatuck Trail near County Route 6 in Connecticut.

According to one account, the Leatherman was born in Lyon, France, the son of a wealthy wool merchant, but because of economic ruin or an unhappy love affair, he left for America and soon began his treks. His photograph, a printed handout, and other information about him are available at the Trailside Nature Museum.

After your visit to the cave, return to junction #29 and turn left, following the LL blazes for two minutes to junction #28. Here, the Leatherman's Loop

Trail turns left, but you should bear right and continue on a white-blazed woods road through Honey Hollow (so named because a farmer kept bees here in the 1800s).

Soon the trail crosses a bridge over a stream and begins a gentle climb. At the top of the rise, the white-blazed trail turns left at a fork and almost immediately reaches junction #30, where it ends at a junction with the Red and Green Trails. Bear right at the fork, now following red and green blazes. After continuing past junction #32, you'll parallel a stream on the left and climb gradually on a winding woods road.

When you reach junction #34, bear left, leaving the green-and-red-blazed trail, and continue on a white-blazed trail. After descending to cross a stream, the white-blazed trail follows a winding road for 0.4 mile until it reaches junction #35. Here, you should make a broad left turn onto a red-blazed trail (do not turn sharply left onto a green-blazed trail). Just ahead, you'll reach a junction where the Rocks Trail joins from the right. Continue ahead, and you'll immediately come to junction #36, where you proceed straight ahead on the Rocks Trail (do not turn right). After crossing a stream, you'll climb to junction #22. Here, the Rocks Trail turns right, but you should turn left and continue on a yellow-blazed trail, which heads downhill.

In half a mile, you'll reach junction #23, the former site of the park's main CCC camp. Known as Camp Merkel, it was in operation from 1933 to 1941, when America's entry into World War II ended the CCC program. Turn right at this junction onto an unmarked trail, passing the steps and foundations that are all that remains of "CO210 Camp SP Katona." The CCC camp may be gone, but the work of the CCC boys remains for us to enjoy: trails, bridges, shelters, and even the Trailside Nature Museum.

Just past the CCC camp, you'll reach a T-junction. Turn left onto the Red and Yellow Trails, soon passing through an open field and curving to the left. After bearing right at junction #70, you'll pass a kiosk and gate and reach the parking area where the hike began.

Ward Pound Ridge—Rocks Trail

TOTAL DISTANCE: 7.5 miles

WALKING TIME: 5 hours

ELEVATION GAIN: 1,624 feet

MAPS: USGS 7.5' Pound Ridge; Ward Pound Ridge Reservation trail map (available online at parks.westchestergov.com); NY–NJTC Westchester Trails map

TRAILHEAD GPS COORDINATES: N 41° 14' 52" W 73° 35' 40"

For most of the way, this hike follows the Rocks Trail, built by volunteers of the New York–New Jersey Trail Conference in 2010. The most challenging in the reservation, the trail leads to six features of interest, each of whose names includes the word "rock": Dancing Rock, Bear Rock Petroglyph, Spy Rock, Castle Rock, Raven Rocks, and Indian Rock Shelter. Unlike most of the other trails in Ward Pound Ridge, the Rocks Trail follows footpaths, rather than woods roads, for most of its length. The trail has several relatively steep elevation gains and losses, but by following it in the counter-clockwise direction (as this hike does), you'll be going down, rather than up, the steepest portion.

GETTING THERE

To get to the park, take Exit 6 off I-684 (at the merge between I-684 and the northern end of the Saw Mill River Parkway). Proceed east on NY 35 for 3.6 miles to NY 121, then turn right onto NY 121. The park entrance is immediately on your left. After passing the tollbooth (a per-car fee is charged on weekends, daily in the summer), turn right onto the first paved road, Michigan Road. Pass the side road to a camping area, and park at the end of the road near a circular turnaround.

THE HIKE

From the circle at the end of the road, bear right and follow a road blocked by a wooden gate. Just beyond the gate, pass a kiosk on the right (trail maps are usually available at the kiosk). Shortly thereafter, you'll reach a fork in the trail, marked with a brown number as junction #70. (Most junctions in the park are marked with brown numbers; these

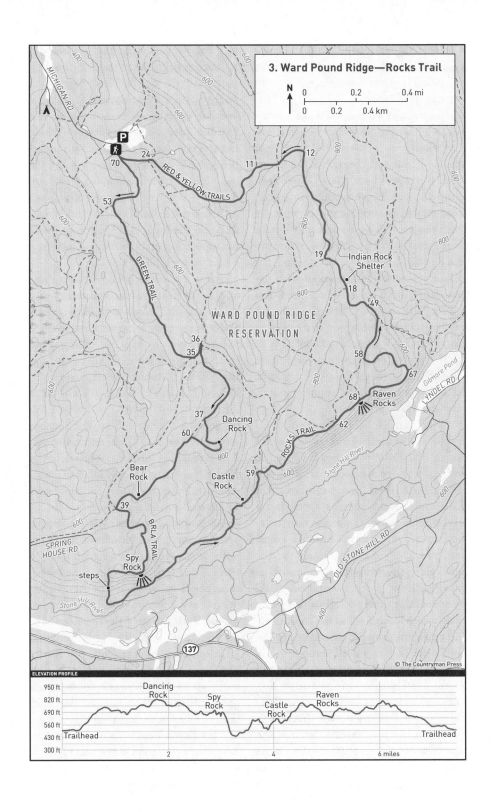

3. Ward Pound Ridge—Rocks Trail

N

| 0 | 0.2 | 0.4 mi |
| 0 | 0.2 | 0.4 km |

MICHIGAN RD

P

24

70

53

11

12

RED & YELLOW TRAILS

GREEN TRAIL

19

Indian Rock Shelter

18

49

WARD POUND RIDGE

RESERVATION

36

35

58

67

Gilmore Pond

LYNDEL RD

68

Raven Rocks

37

60

Dancing Rock

62

ROCKS TRAIL

Stone Hill River

Bear Rock

Castle Rock

59

39

B RLA TRAIL

Spy Rock

steps

OLD STONE HILL RD

SPRING HOUSE RD

Stone Hill River

137

© The Countryman Press

ELEVATION PROFILE

950 ft		Dancing					
820 ft		Rock	Spy	Castle	Raven		
690 ft			Rock	Rock	Rocks		
560 ft							
430 ft	Trailhead						Trailhead
300 ft		2		4		6 miles	

numbers are referenced in this description and on the park map.) Bear right, following the metal trail markers with red and green arrows.

In a third of a mile, you'll reach junction #53, where you should bear left, continuing to follow the Green Trail (the Red Trail and a branch of the Green Trail turn right here). The Green Trail climbs steadily on a woods road, then descends to junction #35 (the number is on the back of a tree and may not be immediately visible). Turn left here onto the Red Trail, but just ahead, turn right onto the Rocks Trail, marked with the letters "RT" on a white background. You will be following the Rocks Trail for the next 4.5 miles (with a side trip to Dancing Rock on a white-blazed trail).

The Rocks Trail proceeds uphill on a woods road through laurel thickets. After about half a mile, at junction #37, a white-blazed trail begins on the left. Turn left and follow this white trail uphill to Dancing Rock—a large flat rock surface that was used for dancing by local farmers to celebrate the conclusion of the harvest. Imagine it devoid of trees and crowded with rejoicing farmers. Note some of the stone constructions nearby: platforms and fire rings, well over 100 years old. Notice too the moss along the access trail—some of the most brilliant green vegetation you'll ever see. Continue to follow the white trail, which loops behind the rock, passing stone ruins, and descends to rejoin the Rocks Trail at junction #60.

Turn left and continue along the Rocks Trail, which climbs a little and crosses under power lines. The path briefly parallels the power lines, then bears left. As it descends through the woods, the trail passes Bear Rock on the right. Bear Rock is named for a potentially ancient carving of what appears to

be a bear's head, etched onto a boulder of leucogranite. According to the July 1972 Bulletin of the New York State Archeological Association, 12 designs are distinguishable, measuring up to a half-inch deep. The investigator made out the contour of a bear, a twin deer-bear profile, and a wild turkey—with the rest of the images unclear. However, Jim Swager, who wrote the book *Petroglyphs in America*, called the carving "questionable" and was not willing to stake his reputation on positively identifying it as a petroglyph.

After paralleling the power lines again, the trail reaches junction #39 and turns left. Soon it crosses two stone walls and reaches a junction with a yellow-blazed horse trail, maintained by the Bedford Riding Lanes Association (BRLA), which goes off to the right. Follow the Rocks Trail, which turns left and descends. At the base of the descent, turn right and cross a seasonally wet area on puncheon and rocks. After crossing two more stone walls, the Rocks Trail turns sharply left and parallels a stone wall, while a yellow-blazed BRLA trail continues ahead.

At the end of the stone wall, the Rocks Trail bears right and climbs to Spy Rock, with south-facing views through the trees. During the Revolutionary War, this rock ledge was used by Americans to observe the movements of British troops. Unfortunately, the recent growth of vegetation limits the views from this location. Now descending, the Rocks Trail passes a ledge on the left, offering more views. It continues down into a gully with impressive cliffs on the right, then climbs out and crosses a level area. The trail soon begins a steady descent, first gradually, then more steeply on a series of 84 rock steps, constructed by a local resident approximately 50 years ago and rehabilitated when the Rocks Trail was opened in 2010.

At the base of the descent, the Rocks Trail bears left and heads northeast, following a level woods road through a pretty valley. Just past a deer exclosure on the right, the Rocks Trail turns sharply right, leaving the woods road, and continues on a footpath. It briefly parallels the road, then begins to climb. After crossing an underground intermittent stream and an old stone wall with some cut stones, the trail climbs more steeply. It levels off, then continues on an undulating route along the side of the hill, with several rather steep ups and downs.

After briefly joining an old woods road, the Rocks Trail crosses an intermittent stream and climbs to pass beneath the power lines. Just beyond the power lines, the path passes a huge boulder on the left, known as Castle Rock (visible behind the trees). The trail now follows a woods road to junction #59, where it turns right. Ahead, the woods road is a white-blazed trail.

The Rocks Trail crosses a wet area on puncheon, descends a little to cross an intermittent stream on rocks, then climbs steadily to reach a high point, where the trail crosses exposed rocks. It then descends a little and continues along the edge of the escarpment, with views to the right through the trees across the Stone Hill River valley. After passing junction #62, the Rocks Trail reaches Raven Rocks (junction #68)—a spectacular south-facing unobstructed overlook from a cliff (use caution, as there is a sharp drop here!). The view is the best on this hike, and a bench has been placed here, so you may wish to take a break and enjoy the panorama.

BEAR ROCK PETROGLYPH

VIEW FROM RAVEN ROCKS

From Raven Rocks, the Rocks Trail continues ahead along the escarpment. It soon begins to descend, crossing an intermittent stream on puncheon. After briefly leveling off, the Rocks Trail turns left at junction #67 and begins to climb. It passes through dense mountain laurel thickets and reaches junction #58, where it turns right. After crossing another intermittent stream, it reaches junction #49, where a white-blazed trail begins on the right. Continue ahead on the Rocks Trail, which climbs gradually and then levels off.

Immediately after passing junction #18 (where another white-blazed trail begins on the left), you'll come to the Indian Rock Shelter (on the right). It is the last of the six "rock" features along the hike. Native Americans frequented this spot because the overhanging rocks offered protection from the rain. Continue ahead on the Rocks Trail, which crosses two streams on wooden bridges.

After crossing the second bridge, bear left, uphill, to reach junction #19, at an intersection with the Red and Yellow Trails. Here, the Rocks Trail turns left, but you should turn right onto the joint route of the Red and Yellow Trails, soon passing dramatic cliffs on the left. Continue to follow the Red and Yellow Trails along a wide woods road for about a mile, returning to the parking area where the hike began.

Ward Pound Ridge— Northern Loop

TOTAL DISTANCE: 5 miles

WALKING TIME: 3 hours

ELEVATION GAIN: 820 feet

MAPS: USGS 7.5' Pound Ridge; Ward Pound Ridge Reservation trail map (available online at parks.westchestergov.com); NY–NJTC Westchester Trails map

TRAILHEAD GPS COORDINATES: N 41°15' 34.7" W 73°35'4 4.3"W

The northern section of Ward Pound Ridge Reservation (north of Reservation Road) features woods roads with relatively gentle grades. This hike loops around the northern section of the park, and the last mile of the hike parallels the cascading Cross River.

GETTING THERE

To get to the park, take Exit 6 off I-684 (at the merge between I-684 and the northern end of the Saw Mill River Parkway). Proceed east on NY 35 for 3.6 miles to NY 121, and turn right onto NY 121. You will shortly arrive at the park entrance on your left. After passing the tollbooth (a per-car fee is charged on weekends, daily in the summer), proceed ahead for 0.3 mile and turn left into the Meadow Picnic Area.

THE HIKE

From the kiosk at the northwest corner of the parking area, proceed north on a wide path, following the Fox Hill Trail, marked with "FH" blazes. After crossing a wet area on a boardwalk and a stream on a bridge, the trail continues between stone walls. When the "FH" blazes turn right, continue ahead and cross a bridge over the Cross River. Just beyond, you'll reach junction #1, where you'll turn left onto the Brown Trail.

At junction #46, turn right and follow the Brown Trail uphill on a wide woods road. The trail levels off, then resumes its climb. When you reach the top of the climb at junction #45, bear right to continue along the Brown Trail, which now descends. After traversing a relatively level section, the trail climbs steadily.

Continue ahead at junction #44, where another road joins from the left. Just ahead, at junction #5 (marked by

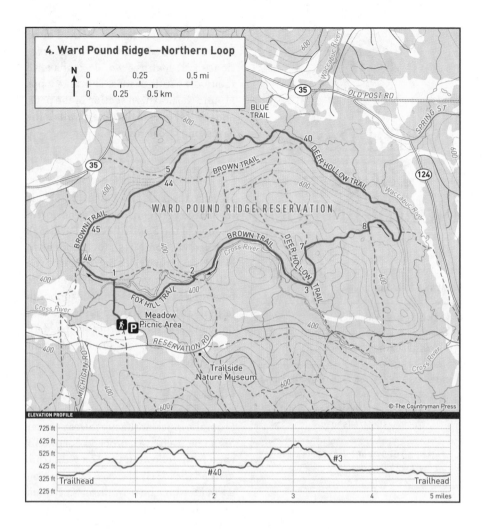

© The Countryman Press

a cairn on a stump), turn left, leaving the Brown Trail, and follow the Deer Hollow Trail, marked with "DH" blazes. This trail follows along the hillside, with Deer Hollow below on the right.

In a quarter mile, the Deer Hollow Trail begins to descend, passing a trail register on the right (please sign) and a blue trail on the left that leads into the Lewisboro Town Park. At the base of the descent, the path crosses an intermittent stream, then climbs again, passing a yellow trail on the left. From the crest of the rise, the trail descends steeply, then more gradually. It soon begins to parallel a stream on the right and passes the start of another blue trail on the left.

After passing a fenced-off horse farm, with Route 35 visible in the distance, the trail crosses the stream, passes through a gap in a stone wall, and continues past a wetland on the left. At junction #40, a white-blazed trail enters from the right, but you should proceed ahead on the Deer Hollow Trail.

The trail now follows a relatively level route, with some minor ups and downs. It passes rock outcrops to the right, continues to parallel the wetland on the left, and goes through an area with thick barberry bushes. After paralleling a stone wall for some distance, the trail climbs a little, then makes a short, steep descent. You are now about a quarter mile from Route 124, which may be heard and seen through the trees.

Soon, the trail begins to climb, passing more rock outcrops on the right. When it reaches a point where the road ahead is badly eroded, the trail bears right and continues on a footpath. It turns sharply right, rejoins the road, and soon bends left to reach junction #8. Here, you should turn right onto a white-blazed trail and follow it for a third of a mile to junction #7.

Turn left at junction #7 onto the Brown Trail, which soon descends—first steeply, then more gradually. At junction #3, turn right, briefly rejoining the Deer Hollow Trail, but when the two trails diverge (at a sign for JUNCTION MARKER 42), bear left to stay on the Brown Trail, which descends to cross a wet area on a wide boardwalk.

For the next three-quarters of a mile, the Brown Trail follows a woods road along the Cross River, below on the left (to avoid several wet sections, it detours slightly to the right). This is a particularly scenic section of the hike, with the trail paralleling the cascading stream.

WETLAND ALONG THE DEER HOLLOW TRAIL

THE CASCADING CROSS RIVER

Most of the way, the trail is elevated above the stream, but it dips down occasionally to approach the stream.

When you reach junction #2, turn left, cross the bridge over the river, then immediately turn right to proceed west on the Fox Hill Trail, which continues to parallel the stream. After passing high above the stream, below on the right, the trail passes by a playground and picnic area on the left. A short distance beyond, the Fox Hill Trail reaches another bridge over the river. Turn left (do not cross the bridge), and retrace your steps on the Fox Hill Trail back to the parking area where the hike began.

Cranberry Lake Preserve

TOTAL DISTANCE: 3 miles

WALKING TIME: 2.5 hours

ELEVATION GAIN: 466 feet

MAPS: USGS 7.5' Ossining; Cranberry Lake Preserve map

TRAILHEAD GPS COORDINATES: N 41°04' 54.9" W 73°45' 21.2"

When you enter the tranquil Cranberry Lake Preserve, you might think that you're entering the forest primeval. You're surrounded by trees and walk along pleasant, quiet ponds and bogs that seem to have been there forever.

But it wasn't always this way. Just over a century ago, the area encompassed by the preserve was bustling with activity. New York City's increasing need for water had led to the construction of the nearby Kensico Dam, and a large supply of stone was need to face the dam. A quarry was established just a mile away from it, with heavy machinery installed to lift the huge blocks of rock and crush pieces that were too small for the dam project. To move the enormous blocks, railroad tracks were installed.

The quarry was abandoned when the dam was completed in 1917, but its scars on the landscape remain. On this hike, you'll have the opportunity to explore not only the shaded trails and peaceful waters of the western part of the preserve, but also the remains of the quarry in its eastern section. Trail junctions in the preserve are marked by numbers on trees, which are referenced in the description below.

GETTING THERE

From I-287 (the Cross Westchester Expressway), take Exit 6 (Route 22, North White Plains/White Plains) and continue on N.Y. Route 22 North (North Broadway) for 2.9 miles. After passing the Kensico Reservoir on the left, turn right at a traffic light onto Old Orchard Road. In about 100 feet, turn right into the Cranberry Lake Preserve and continue ahead for 0.3 mile to the Nature Center, where parking is available. (If the entrance gate is closed, or if you intend to stay until after 4:00 p.m., park

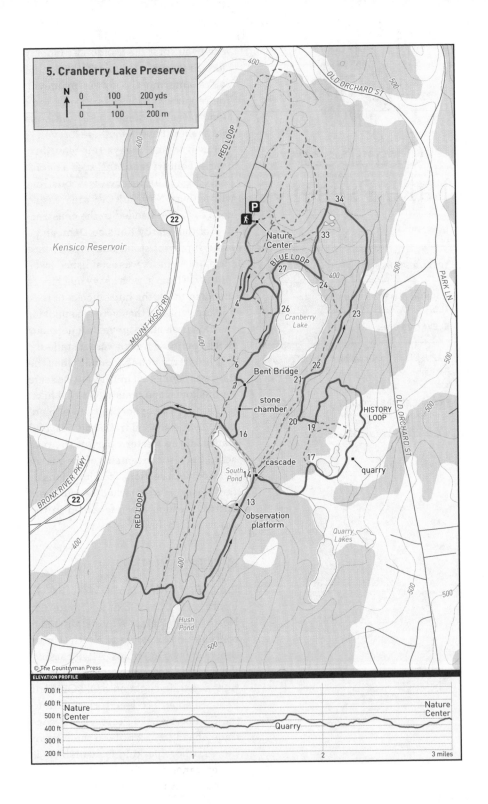

5. Cranberry Lake Preserve

N

| 0 | 100 | 200 yds |
| 0 | 100 | 200 m |

OLD ORCHARD ST

400

500

RED LOOP

P

Nature
Center

34

33

BLUE LOOP

27

24

Kensico Reservoir

22

400

4

26

Cranberry
Lake

23

MOUNT KISCO RD

400

6

Bent Bridge

7

stone
chamber

22

21

PARK LN

500

HISTORY
LOOP

16

20

19

OLD ORCHARD ST

BRONX RIVER PKWY

22

RED LOOP

South
Pond

cascade

14

17

quarry

13

observation
platform

Quarry
Lakes

400

Hush
Pond

500

500

500

© The Countryman Press

ELEVATION PROFILE

	700 ft				
	600 ft	Nature			Nature
	500 ft	Center			Center
	400 ft			Quarry	
	300 ft				
	200 ft		1	2	3 miles

outside the gate and walk along the road to the Nature Center.)

THE HIKE

From the Nature Center, proceed south on a wide yellow-blazed path. At a blue sign to the lake (junction #4), turn left and follow an orange-blazed trail downhill to the shore of Cranberry Lake, then turn right (at junction #26) onto a trail with blue and yellow blazes. After briefly following the shore of the lake, the trail climbs to ledges overlooking it, continuing to run parallel to the lake. At the end of the lake, the trail descends. After crossing a boardwalk, you'll reach junction #6.

Turn left onto a wide path, briefly following blue, red, and purple blazes, then turn left at the next junction (#7) onto an orange-blazed trail, immediately crossing the Bent Bridge over a bog. The trail continues along old stone walls and passes the "stone chamber"—probably an old root cellar. At the end of the orange trail (junction #16), turn right onto a wide path (an old railroad bed) and follow it to a Y-intersection, with a sign for the New York City Watershed grown into a tree (junction #18).

Bear left here, now following the Red Loop Trail. This trail, which circles the park, will be your route for most of the remainder of the hike. On the right, marking the boundary between the park and New York City Watershed lands, is an expertly laid dry stone wall, built over a century ago and still in nearly perfect condition today (except where damaged by fallen trees). Soon, the trail bears left and heads south, continuing to follow the wall.

At the southern end of the park, with private homes visible ahead through the trees, the red trail turns left and begins to head east. Be alert for a sharp right turn (marked by an arrow on a tree to

CRANBERRY LAKE

POND AT THE SITE OF THE ABANDONED QUARRY

the left) and head downhill toward Hush Pond, continuing to follow the red trail. Cross the outlet of the pond on puncheons, bear left (north), and soon begin to parallel a wetland on the left. In a short distance, the trail continues along a level dirt road, with cliffs on the right.

Soon, the cliffs are supplanted by a concrete wall. This wall is a remnant of a facility built around 1912 to crush stone too small for use in the construction of the Kensico Reservoir. Just beyond a crumbling section of the wall, you'll reach junction #13, where a blue-blazed trail leads left to a wooden observation platform. Unfortunately, the view over South Pond is largely obscured by vegetation.

Return to the main trail and turn left (north), now following both blue and red blazes. Soon, you'll reach a pleasant cascade with a bench (junction #14). Turn right, leaving the wide road, and proceed uphill on a footpath, now following the purple-on-white blazes of the History Trail, which parallels a stream on the left.

At the top of the rise, the trail bears left and crosses a wet area on puncheons, with a chain-link fence (marking the boundary of the preserve) on the right. After passing abandoned tennis courts on the left, the trail curves to the

The trail bears left and continues around the rim of the quarry, then reenters the woods and begins to descend. At the base of the descent, you'll reach a line of crumbling concrete supports. Bear left here, continuing to follow the purple-on-white blazes.

After passing some more concrete supports on the left, you come to a T-intersection, with both white and purple-on-white blazes visible. Turn right at this intersection, then immediately turn left at junction #19 and descend on a footpath. When you reach junction #20, turn right, joining the Red Loop Trail.

The trail now descends rather steeply. At the base of the descent (junction #21), the blue trail joins from the left, and the trails cross a boardwalk. Just beyond, at junction #22, the trails again split. Bear right, continuing to follow the red and purple-on-white trails, which cross another boardwalk and then proceed along stump slices. Bear right at junction #23, continuing to follow the red and purple-on-white blazes.

After curving to the left, the trail reaches a T-intersection (junction #34), with cliffs ahead. Here, the red and purple-on-white trails turn right, but you should turn left, now following yellow blazes. At the next junction (#33), bear left, continuing to follow the yellow blazes, and descend to the lake. At junction #24, turn right and follow yellow and blue blazes, with the trail paralleling Cranberry Lake. After passing junction #27, you'll reach a viewpoint over the lake (with the view partially obstructed by vegetation). Just beyond, you'll reach junction #26. Turn right onto the orange trail, follow it back up to the yellow trail at junction #4, and turn right on the yellow trail to return to the Nature Center where the hike began.

right and reaches junction #17. Here, you bear right and follow a dirt path around a pond. At the fork ahead, bear left to continue around the pond in the counter-clockwise direction.

After passing on the right a set of wheels from a railroad car, follow the History Trail as it bears left and climbs to the top of cliffs overlooking an abandoned quarry (the trail in this area is marked by purple paint blazes). From 1912 to 1917, stone used to construct the nearby Kensico Dam was quarried here, and you can see drill marks in some of the rocks around the quarry, as well as iron rods drilled into the rocks.

Bronx River Pathway

TOTAL DISTANCE: 9.8 miles

WALKING TIME: 6 hours

ELEVATION GAIN: 581 feet

MAPS: USGS 7.5' White Plains, Mount Vernon

TRAILHEAD GPS COORDINATES: N 41°04' 19.3" W 73°46' 07.1"

Some readers might find it surprising that this hike, which parallels a major highway, the Bronx River Parkway, has been included in this book. After all, the purpose of a hike is to get away from civilization and experience nature. Why would one choose to spend a day walking along a roadway, with automobiles constantly speeding by?

Despite what one might assume at first glance, this hike is actually a delightful one. The pathway parallels not only the parkway but also the scenic Bronx River, and for most of the way, the walking route is located some distance from the busy parkway. Moreover, the proximity of the route to the Metro-North Harlem Line not only makes this hike accessible by public transportation, but it also provides those who arrive by car with a convenient way to return to the start of the hike. Since the grades are gentle, and the path is paved for nearly the entire distance (only a 1.1-mile section north of Hartsdale has a dirt surface), this is a great hike for those who are looking for a less rugged experience. Finally, as will be explained, the route of the hike is a historic one.

The Bronx River Pathway, the route of this hike, is a component of the Bronx River Parkway Reservation, an 807-acre linear park that was created as an adjunct to the Bronx River Parkway. The creation of the parkway was part of a larger project to clean up the area along the Bronx River in southern Westchester County, which had become unsightly and unsanitary. The work extended over an 18-year period, from 1907 to 1925. As a plaque on the Valhalla Viaduct relates, the work included the removal of 370 buildings and "5 miles of billboards," as well as the planting of 30,000 trees and 140,000 shrubs. When opened in 1925, the Bronx River Parkway was the first

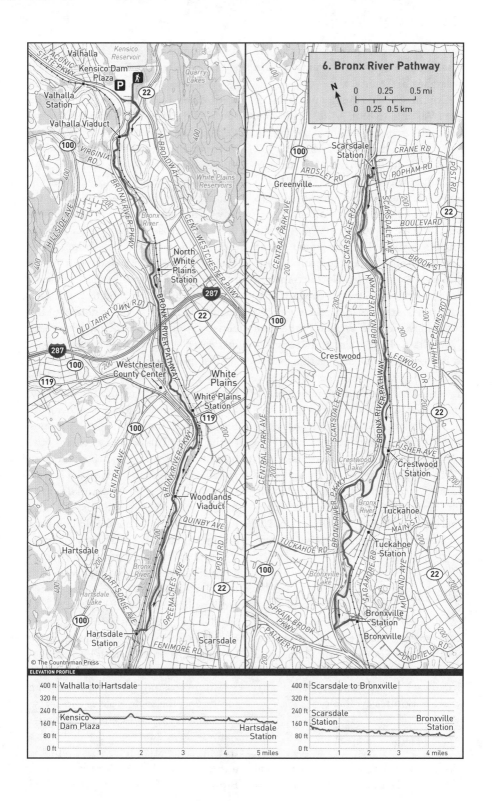

parkway in the United States, and the reservation was the first county park in Westchester County.

This hike covers the 12-mile distance from Valhalla to Bronxville. Originally, the pathway followed the parkway for this entire 12-mile stretch, but in 1967, a 1.6-mile section from Hartsdale to Scarsdale was eliminated as part of a project to improve the parkway. (There are plans to restore this 1.6-mile section, but as of 2018, this gap in the route remains.) The remainder of the pathway from Valhalla to Bronxville is still intact, and Metro-North trains are used to bridge the gap between Hartsdale and Scarsdale. Mileages are given separately for each section of the hike (Valhalla to Hartsdale, and Scarsdale to Bronxville), and each section can be hiked independently (although parking near the Scarsdale station may be difficult to find, except on Sundays).

Your hike may be enhanced by the audio commentary provided by the Westchester Parks Foundation, which offers information on the history of the pathway and on flora and fauna along it, with signs along the route indicating the appropriate number of each feature. The tour may be accessed at www.thewpf.org.

GETTING THERE

From I-287 (the Cross Westchester Expressway), take Exit 6 (Route 22, North White Plains/White Plains) and continue on N.Y. Route 22 North (North Broadway) to the Kensico Dam Plaza, where parking is available.

THE HIKE

The pathway begins on the east side of Kenisco Dam Plaza, near the steps to the top of the dam. The trail heads south, passing The Rising, a memorial to Westchester County residents who were killed in the terrorist attacks on the World Trade Center on September 11, 2001. At the entrance to the plaza, after passing a fitness station on the left, the path crosses the access road to Route 22 and turns left to parallel it. After continuing beneath an overpass, the pathway turns right and passes ballfields on the left. It crosses Washington Avenue North and goes over the Valhalla Viaduct, which spans the Metro-North railroad tracks. A plaque in the stonework of the viaduct—designed to look like a suspension bridge—gives details of the construction of the parkway, which was dedicated at this viaduct in 1925.

The pathway now turns left and follows an attractive, wooded section between the railroad and the parkway. Soon you'll cross a footbridge over the Bronx River—the first of many crossings of the river. The pathway crosses Virginia Road at 1 mile and then Parkway Homes Road, which leads to the Metro-North rail yards. After paralleling the Bronx River, the pathway crosses Fisher Lane at 1.6 miles. You should continue straight ahead on a paved path that gently climbs a hill, then descends to cross a footbridge high above the river (with the North White Plains Metro-North station visible on the left). At the base of the descent, the pathway turns right at a T-intersection, proceeds through park-like meadows, and turns left to parallel the parkway.

After crossing the Bronx River on a footbridge, the route crosses Old Tarrytown Road at 2.3 miles, and passes under I-287 bridges. Just beyond, you'll pass a transmission station for a gas pipeline and cross another footbridge over the Bronx River. After crossing an exit road from the parking lot of the Westchester County Center, the pathway proceeds through a wooded area. It briefly parallels the main access road to the parking lot, then turns left and crosses the road on a marked pedestrian path. The pathway now turns right and follows a paved path along the perimeter of the lot. After passing a fenced-in brick building on the left, the pathway turns right at 3.2 miles, with a 1913 pedestrian tunnel leading to the White Plains Metro-North station visible on the left.

The pathway now crosses a footbridge over a tributary of the Bronx River and closely parallels the river, passing under three bridges. After the third bridge, another path enters from the left. At 3.6 miles, you'll turn right and cross a footbridge over the river, continuing between the river on the left and the parkway on the right. At 4.1 miles, looming overhead, the massive arches of the Woodlands Viaduct carry the parkway across the valley, the pathway, the river, and the railroad.

About 150 feet beyond the viaduct, the pathway makes a sharp left to cross the river on a footbridge. It immediately continues under the railroad and turns right to wedge between the parkway and the river. Here, the pathway become dirt-surfaced, and it remains unpaved for most of the way to Greenacres Avenue (except for several inclined sections). At 4.6 miles, the pathway passes through a low arch of a bridge that carries the parkway over the pathway and the river, then heads uphill onto a bluff above the river, with a path connecting to Walworth Avenue on the left.

Soon, the pathway descends to the river level and traverses the most natural of all its sections, with homes on

ALONG THE BRONX RIVER SOUTH OF THE WHITE PLAINS STATION

the bluff to the left, and woods between the river and the parkway to the right. You'll pass a small dam at 5.1 miles, after which the river curves back under the highway, while the pathway bears left and follows a narrow trail along a fence behind the private County Tennis Club of Westchester.

After proceeding past a small pond constructed for the Haubold Gunpowder Mill in the 1840s, the pathway reaches Greenacres Avenue at 5.3 miles. This marks the end of the first section of the pathway. Turn right onto Greenacres Avenue and cross the bridge over the parkway to reach the Hartsdale Metro-North station (now a Starbucks coffee shop, where refreshments are available). Metro-North trains heading south to

Scarsdale (where the pathway resumes) and north to North White Plains run every half hour (connections at White Plains to Valhalla operate hourly).

At the Scarsdale station, the pathway resumes just west of the station building. It descends on a paved path to the Bronx River, turns left and passes Scarsdale Falls, then bears right and crosses the river on the picturesque three-span Tooley Bridge. The pathway continues between the river and the parkway, and then crosses beneath an overpass. The south side of the overpass contains an inscription commemorating the parkway's construction in 1925. The pathway now enters Garth Woods, named for David Garth, whose estate donated the land to the Parkway Commission in 1915.

THE TOOLEY BRIDGE SOUTH OF THE SCARSDALE STATION

A short distance ahead, the parkway splits, and the pathway briefly parallels the northbound parkway, then turns left to cross a branch of the river on a rustic bentwood bridge. After recrossing the river on another bridge, you'll pass through an attractive area with many large trees and benches along the path. At 0.5 mile (from the Scarsdale station), the pathway bears right and heads under the northbound parkway. The walkway is just inches from the water in the Bronx River, and it may be necessary to duck, as the girders are only about five-and-a-half feet above the path. The pathway crosses a long truss footbridge over the river and proceeds south through a wide, wooded corridor between the northbound and southbound lanes of the parkway.

After traversing an open area with more benches and an occasional wood duck house, the pathway reaches the intersection of Harney Road with the northbound lanes of the parkway at 0.9 mile. Here, the route turns left, crosses the northbound parkway, then immediately turns right and crosses Harney Road. You'll cross a tributary stream on a footbridge, then, a short distance beyond, recross the Bronx River on another truss footbridge, with the stone abutments of an old bridge visible on the left.

Now following a route between the river on the left and the parkway on the right, the pathway passes a small stone building, originally a gas station, at 1.2 miles. The pathway recrosses the river on another truss footbridge and, at 1.5 miles, crosses Leewood Drive. To the left, the road goes under the railroad tracks through a narrow, one-lane stone-arch underpass.

For the next half a mile, the pathway follows a wooded route, with the railroad on the left and the parkway, partially screened from view by the trees, on the right. Deciduous trees are interwoven with towering pines. After passing a maintenance yard for the Westchester County Parks, the pathway bears right at 2.1 miles and follows a service road to Thompson Avenue, with the Crestwood station on the left.

The pathway crosses Thompson Avenue. After bearing left, away from the river, the pathway reaches the north end of Crestwood Lake. As it follows the eastern shore of the lake, apartment buildings block the view of the railroad, and the parkway curves to the west. For a short distance, neither the railroad nor the parkway can be seen from the pathway. After passing ballfields on the left, the pathway reaches the south end of the lake at 2.7 miles. Here, it crosses a footbridge over its outlet, just below a stone dam, and heads north along the western shore of the lake. It soon comes out at the parkway, where it crosses an exit ramp leading to Read Avenue.

Now closely paralleling the parkway, the pathway passes a cul-de-sac and crosses Scarsdale Road at 3.1 miles. After passing beneath an overpass, the pathway bears left, parallels an entrance ramp to the parkway, then follows along its shoulder, crossing the Bronx River and passing the intersection of Elm Street with the entrance ramp. A short distance beyond, as the ramp curves sharply to the left, the pathway crosses the ramp and proceeds ahead through a landscaped area to the intersection of Yonkers Avenue and Garrett Street, with Tuckahoe Road just to the right. Crossing this busy intersection, the pathway enters a wide section of the Bronx River Reservation and reaches the northern end of Bronxville Lake at 3.7 miles. Paths lead around both sides of the lake,

DAM ALONG THE BRONX RIVER

but the path along the left (east) side is farther from the noise of the traffic on the parkway. Many benches line the pathway along the lake.

At the southern end of the lake, the easterly path crosses a bridge over the outlet (with the Bronxville Waterfall on the right) and reaches a T-intersection, where the westerly path rejoins. Turn left to continue south on the pathway. A short distance ahead, where the pathway splits again, follow the left fork, which soon passes the foundations of the former Swain's Mill (on the opposite bank of the river) and crosses Pondfield Road. After proceeding through another wide section of the reservation, the pathway ends at 4.5 miles at Palmer Avenue. To reach the Metro-North Harlem Line Bronxville Station, turn left (east) onto Palmer Avenue. Metro-North trains heading north to North White Plains run every half hour, but connections at White Plains to Valhalla operate hourly.

To return from the Valhalla station to your car at Kensico Dam Plaza, walk south to the old station, currently a restaurant. Cross over the Taconic State Parkway at the traffic light (Cleveland Street), turn right onto Broadway, the village's main street, and continue until you reach a church. Just beyond the church parking lot, take the faint path heading off to the left through the woods to the Kenisco Dam Plaza.

Rockefeller State Park Preserve Loop

TOTAL DISTANCE: 10.4 miles (3.8-mile alternate)

WALKING TIME: 6 hours (2-hour alternate)

ELEVATION GAIN: 1,348 feet

MAPS: USGS 7.5' White Plains; Rockefeller State Park Preserve brochure map; NY–NJTC Westchester Trails map

TRAILHEAD GPS COORDINATES: N 41° 06' 42" W 73° 50' 14"

Rockefeller State Park Preserve was created in 1983 when the Rockefeller family deeded 715 acres to New York along with an endowment fund for its upkeep. Subsequent donations have increased the preserve's size to over 1,400 acres. A beautiful visitor center, opened in 1994, contains exhibits on the historical and natural features of the park. A pleasant place for a walk or a stroll, the preserve is open for public use during daylight hours. The office phone is 914-762-0209.

Attracted by the commanding views of the Hudson Valley, oil magnate and philanthropist John D. Rockefeller, Sr. began buying land in the Pocantico Hills area in 1893. His estate would eventually reach 40,000 acres. A 40-room Georgian mansion, "Kykuit" (Dutch for "lookout"), was built as the family home. During the 1900s, the Rockefellers restored much of the land to a natural state. An earthen dam created Swan Lake in 1932, and to this day some family land is still used for growing corn and breeding cattle.

The Rockefellers built 55 miles of carriage roads during the 1920s and 1930s. Designed to highlight the beauty of the area, they have been traditionally (but informally) open for public use. These carriage roads are open to walkers, runners, and equestrians, though bicycles are not allowed. Much of the hike is in the park proper, but some portions of the hike use carriage roads on the adjacent property of the Greenrock Corporation. Trail junctions are marked with blue plastic wands, giving the names of the intersecting trails. As the carriage roads are smooth-surfaced and well maintained, any good walking shoe or sneaker will suffice.

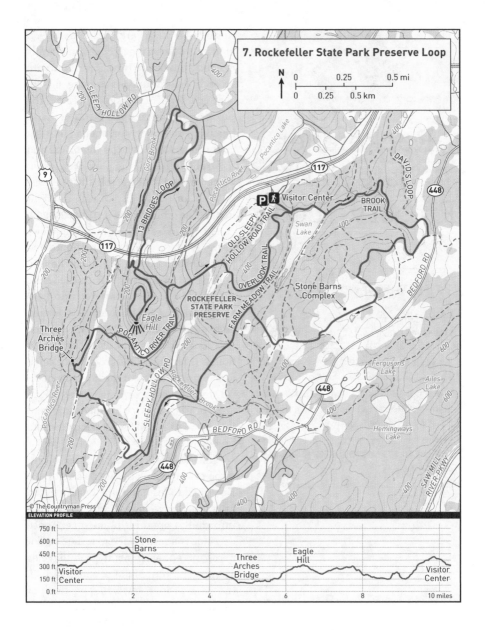

7. Rockefeller State Park Preserve Loop

ELEVATION PROFILE

GETTING THERE

Take the New York State Thruway (I-87) to Exit 9 (at the eastern end of the Tappan Zee Bridge). Proceed north on US 9 through Tarrytown and Sleepy Hollow for 3 miles to a junction with NY 117. Turn right onto NY 117 for 1.4 miles to the park entrance. In season, there is a parking fee.

THE HIKE

The hike begins at the tollbooth. From the parking lot, cross the road, pass the visitor center, and continue to Swan

Lake. Here, you should turn left onto the Brothers Path, which runs along the northern shore of Swan Lake. Keep bearing right until you cross the earthen dam and the outlet of the lake on stepping stones. Turn left here onto the Old Railroad Bed.

You are now walking on the right-of-way of the former Putnam Division of the New York Central Railroad, built in 1881. When John D. Rockefeller Jr. wanted to expand his estate around 1930, he financed the cost of relocating the line to bypass his estate. The former rail line is now a delightful hiking trail.

Continue ahead on the Old Railroad Bed for only 500 feet and turn right onto the Brook Trail. You'll follow this path uphill for the next 0.8 mile, paralleling a cascading brook and crossing it several times. After passing a junction with David's Loop on the left, you'll come to a breached dam. The Brook Trail briefly curves away from the brook but soon returns to it. Then, to the right, a side trail crosses two bridges and soon rejoins the main trail. After crossing another bridge, you'll see a drained cistern on the left, with a large solitary rock that was never removed. The Brook Trail now passes the other end of David's Loop on the left and heads slightly downhill to reach a T-junction with the Ridge Trail. You have now hiked for 1.4 miles.

Turn right onto the Ridge Trail. Bear right at the first intersection, then turn left at the second junction onto the Simental Trail and continue heading uphill. At the next intersection, the Simental Trail departs to the right, but you continue straight, now following the Rock Wall Loop, which parallels an old stone wall on the left. When you reach the next junction, with a red farmhouse on the right, turn left onto a gravel road

with stone walls on both sides. When the trail briefly levels off at the crest of the rise, you can catch a glimpse of the Hudson River on the right. This is one of the two spots on this hike from which the Hudson River can be seen.

The trail now heads downhill, curves to the right, and reaches a T-junction with a paved road. Here you turn right. The impressive stone building in front of you is known as the Stone Barns. It features the Blue Hill Grain Bar, where drinks and snacks are available.

As you approach the Stone Barns, bear left at the first intersection, pass to the left of the Stone Barns, then bear right at the next intersection and continue downhill along the paved road toward the greenhouses. When you reach the parking area for the greenhouses, bear left and continue on a gravel path, the route of the Stone Barns Path (with a vertical metal pole on each side of the trail and a caution sign on the right). In another 500 feet, turn right at a T-junction and soon begin to descend. Continue straight ahead when the Headwater Trail leaves to the right and the Greenrock Road crosses. Just beyond, the carriage road bends sharply to the left; immediately thereafter, bear right onto another carriage road, with an open concrete storage area on the left. Continue ahead as the Maple Loop joins from the left and proceed downhill to a junction at the bottom of the valley with the Farm Meadow Trail. You have now hiked for 3.1 miles.

If you've had enough hiking for the day, turn right onto the Farm Meadow Trail, continue to Swan Lake, and proceed ahead on the Brother's Path, with the lake on your right. At the end of the lake, turn left to return to the visitor center parking lot. If you choose this option,

CASCADE IN THE POCANTICO RIVER

your hike will have been about 3.8 miles long.

To continue along the route of the hike, turn left onto the Farm Meadow Trail, which soon leaves park property and continues through lands managed by the Greenrock Corporation. Several side trails leave to the left and to the right, but you should continue straight ahead to the crest of a hill, with a red barn on your right. The trail now descends, crosses a brook, and reaches a T-junction with the Hudson Pines Road (a wire fence is just beyond). Turn right and follow the carriage road downhill, and bear right at the next intersection.

Soon, you'll begin to parallel the paved Sleepy Hollow Road. At the next intersection, turn right and cross beneath the paved road on a stone-arch underpass. You've now walked 4.3 miles.

If you wish to cut the hike short at this point, turn right on the other side of the underpass and, in 350 feet, bear right at the fork onto the Canter Alley Trail. You are now walking parallel to a tiny but picturesque brook. Continue to parallel the brook, crossing it several times, until the brook ends at the Pocantico River. Cross the river and turn right onto the Pocantico River Trail. Continue to follow the Pocantico

River Trail, which parallels the river, until you reach a steel truss footbridge over the river. Turn right onto the Old Sleepy Hollow Road Trail, which soon crosses the paved Sleepy Hollow Road, and continue ahead to the parking area. The total length of your hike will have been 6 miles.

To continue along the route of the hike, turn left on the other side of the underpass and head uphill on the Douglas Hill Loop, which curves to the right. Keep right at the first fork and continue with an old wooden fence on your left and views of the countryside below on the right. Bear left at the next junction and continue downhill, then bear right at the following intersection and continue until you reach a T-junction. Turn right and head downhill, with the Old Croton Aqueduct running parallel to you on the left, until you reach a marked triangular intersection, where you turn right.

Before making this turn, however, continue straight ahead to the bridge right in front of you which crosses the Pocantico River. This bridge, known as the Three Arches Bridge, is generally considered to be the finest stone bridge built by the Rockefellers.

Return to the previous intersection and continue on the Pocantico River Trail, which parallels the river below you on the left. At the next bridge, where the Witch's Spring Trail begins on the left, turn right to continue on the Pocantico River Trail. After passing an abandoned concrete bridge on the left, turn left at the next intersection and cross the river.

On the other side of the bridge, you'll reach a concrete signpost marking the junction of the Pocantico River Trail with the Gory Brook Road Trail. Turn right to stay on the Pocantico River Trail. The river is now on your right, and the route will soon take you through open fields. At the next intersection, with a stone-arch bridge on the right, turn left to continue on the Pocantico River Trail, which now comes nearer to the river. After passing by a smooth-topped stone wall, with cascades in the river that are especially lovely if the water level is high, you reach a junction with the Eagle Hill Trail. You have now hiked for 6.2 miles.

If you've had enough hiking by now, bear right at the junction and cross a steel truss bridge over the Pocantico River. Continue ahead on the Old Sleepy Hollow Road Trail, which crosses paved Sleepy Hollow Road and continues ahead to the parking lot. This hike would cover, in total, just under 7 miles.

To continue along the route of the hike, turn left onto the Eagle Hill Trail. After a short climb, you'll reach a junction with the Eagle Hill Summit Trail. Turn left and head uphill. When you reach a fork (the start of a loop), bear left, and you'll soon reach a viewpoint, with the Kykuit mansion of the Rockefeller estate visible on the opposite hill. Just beyond, you'll come to a stone bench on your right, from which the Hudson River can be seen. Continue ahead to complete the loop, then bear left and descend to the Eagle Hill Trail. You've now hiked 7.6 miles.

To return to the parking lot from here, turn right onto the Eagle Hill Trail, retrace your steps to the Pocantico River Trail, then cross the steel truss bridge over the Pocantico River and continue ahead on the Old Sleepy Hollow Road Trail to the parking lot. You will have hiked a total of 8.5 miles.

But to continue along the route of the hike, proceed ahead, crossing a steel bridge over NY 117. One might wonder why such a substantial limited-access

THREE ARCHES BRIDGE

road was built here, as it is certainly out of character for the area. Interestingly, this section of highway was part of a major controversy in the mid-1960s. NY 117 was to be upgraded to connect with the planned Hudson River Expressway, I-487. A major interchange was to be built on landfill in the river. By the time the plans for I-487 were abandoned, this upgraded section of NY 117 had already been constructed.

On the other side of NY 117, proceed ahead along the 2-mile-long 13 Bridges Loop. There are a few junctions, but this trail is well signed and easy to follow. The 13 bridges, of standard design, are primarily on the last part of the loop as it crosses and recrosses meandering Gory Brook. This part of the preserve, somewhat distant from the parking area, is less traveled and usually quite peaceful.

But it was not always so. Gory Brook was named for a Revolutionary War skirmish that left the stream red with the blood of British troops.

After crossing under NY 117, the 13 Bridges Loop ends. Turn left and head uphill on the Eagle Hill Trail, follow it back to the Pocantico River Trail, and cross the bridge over the river. Continue on the Old Sleepy Hollow Road Trail and cross the paved Sleepy Hollow Road. In another 0.2 mile, you'll reach a junction with the Ash Tree Loop. Turn right, and at the next junction turn left onto the Overlook Trail, which meanders high above Swan Lake, offering beautiful views over the lake. When you reach a five-way junction with a signboard, a sharp left will take you back to the visitor center. The complete hike is 11.6 miles long.

Rockwood Hall

TOTAL DISTANCE: 2.1 miles

WALKING TIME: 1.5 hours

ELEVATION GAIN: 294 feet

MAPS: USGS 7.5' White Plains; NY–NJTC Westchester Trails map

TRAILHEAD GPS COORDINATES: N 41°06' 40.5" W 73°51' 42.8"

Rockwood Hall is the site of the former home of William Rockefeller (1841–1922), a younger brother of the more famous John D. Rockefeller. In 1886, William purchased Rockwood, a 200-acre estate, and built Rockwood Hall, a mansion with 204 rooms. Frederick Law Olmsted designed the landscape, which includes many ornamental trees. When built, Rockwood Hall was the second largest private home in the United States.

Following Rockefeller's death in 1922, the estate was converted into a country club, which soon went bankrupt. In 1938, the property was acquired by John D. Rockefeller, Jr., William's nephew, who arranged for the mansion to be razed in 1941–42.

The Rockefeller family donated Rockwood Hall to New York State in 1999, and it is now a part of Rockefeller State Park Preserve. Although the buildings are gone, the foundations remain. The carriage roads that were constructed by the Rockefeller family offer an opportunity for a delightful stroll through the property, with panoramic views over the Hudson River. Bicycles are not allowed, and while equestrians are permitted (with a permit), the carriage roads are rarely used by horses. Although not blazed, the roads that form the route of this hike are easily followed.

GETTING THERE

Take the New York State Thruway to Exit 9 (on the east side of the Tappan Zee Bridge). Turn right at the top of the ramp onto US 9 (South Broadway), and continue north on US 9 through the Village of Tarrytown. After 1.7 miles, you'll come to a complex intersection where you should bear left to continue on US 9. In another 1.8 miles (3.5 miles from the

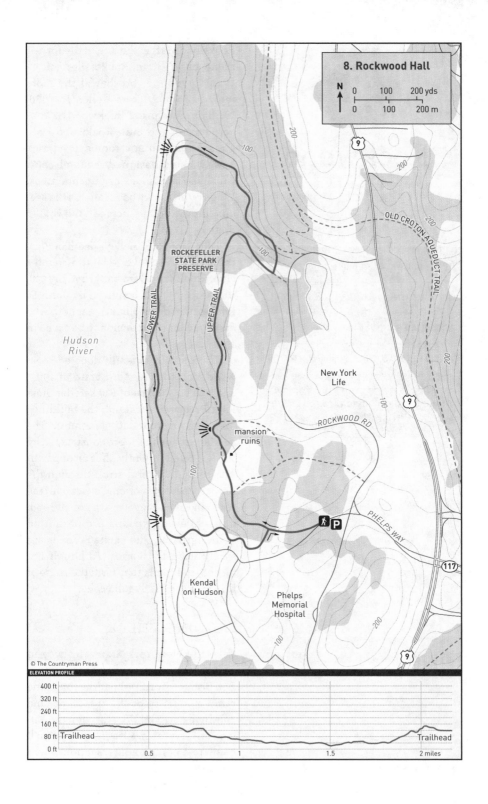

8. Rockwood Hall

N

| 0 | 100 | 200 yds |
| 0 | 100 | 200 m |

Old Croton Aqueduct Trail

Rockefeller State Park Preserve

Lower Trail

Upper Trail

Hudson River

New York Life

Rockwood Rd

mansion ruins

P

Phelps Way

117

Kendal on Hudson

Phelps Memorial Hospital

9

© The Countryman Press

ELEVATION PROFILE

| 400 ft |
| 320 ft |
| 240 ft |
| 160 ft |
| 80 ft |
| 0 ft |

Trailhead

0.5

1

1.5

2 miles

Trailhead

Thruway exit), immediately after crossing under NY 117, turn right at a sign for ROCKWOOD ROAD, and follow the ramp onto NY 117. After reaching a stop sign, continue ahead through an intersection, following the sign to KENDAL ON HUDSON. You'll pass an exit from a parking area on the left, then turn left at the entrance to the parking area.

THE HIKE

From the western end of the parking area, follow the crosswalk across the paved entrance road. Bear right onto a paved road (closed to traffic) and continue uphill on a gravel road. At a kiosk at the top of the climb, bear right onto another road, surfaced with paving stones, soon reaching a spectacular viewpoint over the Hudson River.

After passing a huge weeping beech tree, a path diverges to the right, but continue ahead, passing stone foundation walls to the right. These walls are all that remains of William Rockefeller's enormous mansion. As you approach the highest point along the road, the views of the Hudson River broaden, and you can see the Tappan Zee Bridge to the left, beyond the Kendal on Hudson retirement community.

You may hear the sound of trains directly below you. Metro-North's Hudson Line runs along the east shore of the river, and you can clearly hear (but not see) the passing trains (you'll be able to see them later on in the hike).

ALONG THE LOWER TRAIL

VIEW OF THE HUDSON RIVER FROM THE UPPER TRAIL

After taking in the view, continue ahead along the road, which descends in a sweeping curve, bordered by stone walls. At the next intersection, turn left. Almost immediately, you'll reach a Y-intersection. Here, you should take the right fork, following the sign for the UPPER TRAIL. You're now proceeding along a paving-stone road that climbs very gently, soon passing a grassy field on the right.

The road crosses another wooded area and descends to an open expanse, with grassy areas on both sides. Continue along the road, which passes a viewpoint over the Hudson River at the end of the grassy area, curves sharply to the right, and reenters the woods.

in close succession. Continue to follow the road, which parallels the brook, until you approach the shore of the Hudson River (at a sign for the LOWER TRAIL).

Just ahead, you'll come to a north-facing viewpoint over the river, with Croton Point jutting out into the river in the distance. The railroad tracks are now visible below, and you may see a Metro-North or Amtrak train zoom by. Continue along the gravel road, which now heads south, with a grassy slope on the left and the river on the right. Benches have been placed along the trail, inviting you to pause and take in the views.

After passing a huge oak tree on the left, you'll come to a fork. Here, you should bear right (following the sign for the LOWER TRAIL) and continue heading south along the river. Soon, you'll see stone walls above a grassy slope to the left. These walls mark the site of the Rockefeller mansion that you passed by earlier on the hike.

At the southern end of the Rockwood Hall property (marked by a number of evergreen trees), there are panoramic views up and down the Hudson River. A bench has been placed here, and you may wish to pause once more to enjoy the views.

Continue along the gravel road, which bears left and begins to head east. At the next intersection, a path to the right leads into the Kendal on Hudson property, but you should continue ahead on the gravel road, which winds uphill. Upon reaching another path which heads into Kendal on Hudson, bear left and continue uphill on the gravel road, now bordered on the right by boulders and a stone wall. When you reach the kiosk, bear right and head down to the parking area where the hike began.

Before reaching the end of the gravel road at a locked gate, turn left at a blue signpost for the Brook Trail and follow it downhill, bearing left at the fork. At the base of the descent, turn left onto a gravel road which proceeds through a ravine studded with rhododendron, crossing four bridges over the brook

Old Croton Aqueduct State Historic Park— Tarrytown to Yonkers

TOTAL DISTANCE: 9 miles

WALKING TIME: 5 hours

ELEVATION GAIN: 357 feet

MAPS: USGS 7.5' White Plains, Nyack, and Yonkers. A detailed color map containing historical comments on the aqueduct and nearby features of interest can be purchased from Friends of the Old Croton Aqueduct, Inc. (www.aqueduct.org).

TRAILHEAD GPS COORDINATES: N 41°04' 00.5" W 73°51' 37.1"

Originally known as Old Croton Trailway State Park, the Old Croton Aqueduct State Historic Park (OCA) extends a total distance of 26.2 miles from the New Croton Dam to the Westchester County/New York City line. The park encompasses the northern portion of the 41-mile aqueduct route, opened in 1842 to provide fresh water to New York City. Its acquisition in 1968 by New York State enabled one of the great engineering feats of the nineteenth century to be converted into a linear park. Construction of the aqueduct and the Croton reservoir and dam began in 1837 and was carried out largely by Irish immigrant labor. The gravity-fed tube, modeled on principles used by the Romans, maintained a steady gradient of 13 inches per mile over its entire length.

When water first flowed through the tube in 1842, it was predicted that the aqueduct would be adequate to supply New York City's water for another 100 years. Plentiful water encouraged the growth of the city, but the establishment of new industries, as well as the increased popularity of flush toilets and baths, rendered the old aqueduct inadequate to supply the water needs of the city's inhabitants. Construction of the New Croton Aqueduct, three times the size and a few miles to the east, began in 1885, and the new aqueduct was put into service in 1890. In the twentieth century, the Catskill and Delaware Aqueducts were also constructed. In 1955, the Old Croton Aqueduct was taken out of service, but the northernmost 3-mile section of the aqueduct was brought back into service in 1987 to supply the town of Ossining with water.

Because the water conduit is usually only a few feet under the surface, no buildings could be constructed over the masonry tunnel, thus making

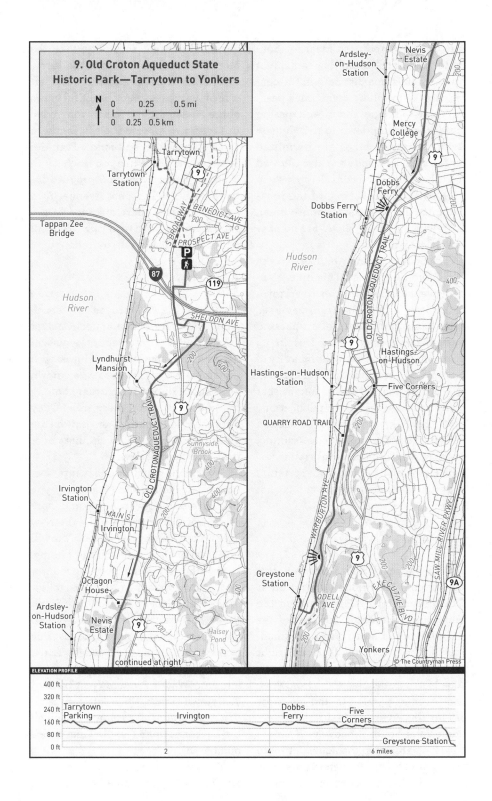

9. Old Croton Aqueduct State Historic Park—Tarrytown to Yonkers

N

| 0 | 0.25 | 0.5 mi |
| 0 | 0.25 | 0.5 km |

Tarrytown

9

Tarrytown Station

Tappan Zee Bridge

BENEDICT AVE

S BROADWAY

200

PROSPECT AVE

P

87

119

SHELDON AVE

Hudson River

Lyndhurst Mansion

OLD CROTON AQUEDUCT TRAIL

200

400

9

Sunnyside Brook

400

400

Irvington Station

MAIN ST

Irvington

200

Octagon House

Ardsley-on-Hudson Station

Nevis Estate

9

400

Halsey Pond

continued at right

Ardsley-on-Hudson Station

Nevis Estate

Mercy College

9

Dobbs Ferry

Dobbs Ferry Station

Hudson River

400

OLD CROTON AQUEDUCT TRAIL

200

9

Hastings-on-Hudson

Hastings-on-Hudson Station

Five Corners

QUARRY ROAD TRAIL

200

WARBURTON AVE

Greystone Station

9

ODELL AVE

EXECUTIVE BLVD

200

SAW MILL RIVER PKWY

9A

200

Yonkers

© The Countryman Press

ELEVATION PROFILE

| 400 ft |
| 320 ft |
| 240 ft | Tarrytown Parking | | Dobbs Ferry | Five Corners |
| 160 ft | | Irvington |
| 80 ft |
| 0 ft | | 2 | 4 | Greystone Station |
| | | | | 6 miles |

this unobstructed path ideal for non-motorized recreation. The aqueduct route, often with a dirt path in the center, is easy to follow, sometimes passing close to homes and often crossing streams running down to the Hudson River. Mountain bikes are permitted on the trail, and dogs are also allowed if leashed. Please be considerate as you walk by backyards. Most of the route is unmarked, although there are green posts with the letters "OCA" at a number of road crossings.

The book contains two hikes on the Old Croton Aqueduct. This hike, Hike #9, covers the section from Tarrytown to Yonkers, where the trail traverses suburban communities, often passing by the backyards of homes. Despite its proximity to civilization, the majority of the trail follows a quiet, secluded route. One special feature of this hike is that both ends are accessible by public transportation. Hike #10 covers the section from the New Croton Dam to Ossining, which passes through more pristine terrain. However, no public transportation is available at the northern end of that hike.

GETTING THERE

Take the New York State Thruway across the Tappan Zee Bridge and get off at Exit 9 (Tarrytown). At the top of the ramp, turn right onto South Broadway (US 9). Proceed north on South Broadway for about 0.4 mile, then turn right onto Prospect Avenue. You will note the aqueduct route heading south from Prospect Avenue, parallel to and just west of Martling Avenue (the first intersection east of South Broadway). There is a parking area atop the aqueduct route just south of Prospect Avenue; park here.

If coming by train from Grand Central Terminal in New York City, take the Metro-North Hudson Line to the Tarrytown Station. Be sure to sit on the left side of the train to enjoy beautiful views of the Hudson River! When you arrive in Tarrytown, proceed to the southern end of the station and follow Franklin Street up the hill. When you reach South Broadway, turn right and proceed for three blocks to Prospect Avenue. Turn left, continue a short distance to the aqueduct route, and turn right. You will return from the Greystone station.

THE HIKE

Begin the hike by proceeding south along the route of the aqueduct. Just before the next intersection, you will notice a chimney-like stone tower with the number "14." These towers, known as ventilators, were constructed along the aqueduct about every mile. They were equipped with an open grate on top and allowed fresh air to circulate over the water passing through.

When you reach the next intersection, White Plains Road (Route 119), you will have to detour from the aqueduct route, which is interrupted by the New York State Thruway just ahead. This will involve about half a mile of roadwalking, but it is the only detour you'll encounter on the entire hike. Turn right and follow White Plains Road for one block to South Broadway (Route 9), then turn left onto South Broadway, keeping to the east side of the street. Cross the bridge over the thruway and thruway ramp, then turn left onto Walter Avenue (just beyond Tarrytown Honda). Bear left onto Sheldon Avenue and follow it until you reach the aqueduct route (just beyond house number 81).

Turn right onto the aqueduct route. After crossing an embankment, you'll reach Gracemere (a private road), which is crossed on cobblestones. In a short distance, the aqueduct passes through gateposts in a stone wall and reaches South Broadway. Cross this busy street at the crosswalk and continue on a wide dirt path blocked off by wooden posts, entering the grounds of Lyndhurst, an American Gothic Revival "castle" built about 1840 and once owned by railroad magnate Jay Gould. Follow this dirt path through Lyndhurst. Soon after you leave the Lyndhurst property, you'll pass stone ventilator #15. The aqueduct now follows a high stone wall on the left.

In another half a mile or so, after crossing Sunnyside Brook on an embankment, you'll enter a quiet residential area. The aqueduct crosses several paved roads and follows a wide right of way past large, attractive homes. Then, about 2.5 miles from the start, you'll pass a parking area adjacent to a school and cross Main Street in Irvington. Continue ahead through a municipal parking area and immediately pass ventilator #16.

A short distance beyond, you'll cross a high embankment over Jewells Brook. After crossing two streets, you'll notice on the right the unusually shaped Octagon House, built in 1860. Next, the aqueduct passes through the Nevis Estate, now the property of Columbia University. The brick mansion with white columns on the right side of the trail was built by Colonel James Hamilton III, son of Alexander Hamilton, in 1835.

After passing ventilator #17, you'll proceed through the campus of Mercy College and then cross two more embankments. At the end of the second embankment, climb the steps to Cedar Street in Dobbs Ferry. Cross the street and continue ahead through a parking area. The Aqueduct now parallels Main

Street in Dobbs Ferry, with views over the Hudson River to the right.

In a few blocks, you'll reach an interpretive sign which explains the history and engineering of the aqueduct. The adjacent barn and garage are used as maintenance facilities. Across Walnut Street is the Overseer's House—a brick building, built in 1857, which formerly served as a residence and office for the aqueduct's caretakers. Several such structures were built along the aqueduct, but this is only one that remains. The building has been restored as a visitor center and park office (open to the public on weekend afternoons). Just

VENTILATOR #16 ALONG THE OLD CROTON AQUEDUCT

STONE-ARCH BRIDGE OVER QUARRY RAILWAY

beyond, the aqueduct crosses to the east side of Broadway and follows an embankment through a residential area, with more views over the Hudson River.

In another mile, the aqueduct—now in Hastings-on-Hudson—crosses back to the west side of Broadway at the Five Corners. Using the crosswalks provided, cross Chauncey Lane, Farragut Avenue, and Broadway. Turn left and cross the driveway of Grace Episcopal Church, then immediately turn right onto the aqueduct route at a green "OCA" post. After crossing another high embankment, you'll continue through a parking area and begin to parallel Aqueduct Lane on the right, with Draper Park on the left.

Soon, you'll notice on the left a sign, that reads QUARRY ROAD TRAIL. Here, a path descends and passes beneath the aqueduct. The aqueduct is supported by a stone-arch bridge, built in 1840 over a railway that served a former marble quarry to the east. It is worth taking this short side trail to get a view of this beautifully preserved stone-arch bridge.

Near the end of a long, uninterrupted stretch of the aqueduct, you'll pass ventilator #18. About half a mile later, after crossing another high embankment over a stream and a private road, you'll come to a particularly fine unobstructed view over the Hudson River and the Palisades. After passing the entrance to Lenoir Preserve and then a stone building on the left, you'll reach Odell Avenue, which crosses the aqueduct in the middle of a broad curve in the road.

Turn right and follow Odell Avenue downhill to Warburton Avenue, then descend through the park on steps to reach the Greystone Metro-North station. If you came by train from New York City, you should cross the overpass above the tracks and take a southbound train back to Grand Central Terminal.

If you drove your car to the start of the hike, you'll want to take a northbound train back to Tarrytown. Northbound trains to Tarrytown leave every hour—56 minutes past the hour on weekends (for schedules, go to www.mta.info). Be sure to sit on the left side of the train to enjoy beautiful views of the Hudson River! The train ride takes only 14 minutes. When you arrive in Tarrytown, proceed to the southern end of the station and follow Franklin Street up the hill. When you reach South Broadway, turn right and proceed for three blocks to Prospect Avenue. Turn left and continue for one block to the parking area where the hike began.

Old Croton Aqueduct State Historic Park—New Croton Dam to Ossining

TOTAL DISTANCE: 5.5 miles

WALKING TIME: 3 hours

ELEVATION GAIN: 466 feet

MAPS: USGS 7.5' Ossining; a detailed color map containing historical comments on the aqueduct and nearby features of interest can be purchased from Friends of the Old Croton Aqueduct, Inc. (www.aqueduct.org).

TRAILHEAD GPS COORDINATES: N 41° 13' 41" W 73° 51' 25.5"

The northern section of the Old Croton Aqueduct is the most pristine section of its 26.2-mile route through Westchester County. The first part of this hike traverses this section, where there is little evidence of suburban development. The second half of the hike goes through a more developed area, but it passes a number of historic features that add interest to the hike. The hike ends at the historic Double Arch bridge in Ossining, where you have the opportunity to learn about the history of the aqueduct at the Ossining Heritage Area Visitor Center.

GETTING THERE

A car shuttle is needed unless you wish to retrace your steps. Park one car where your hike will end in Ossining at the Ossining Heritage Area Visitor Center at 95 Broadway, just west of the junction of US 9 and NY 133 in Ossining (park in the lower parking lot on the north side of Broadway, adjacent to the entrance to the Sing Sing Kill Greenway). There are restrooms at the visitor center, as well as a museum (914-941-3189) with exhibits relating to the construction of the queduct. The visitor center is located in the Joseph C. Caputo Community Center of the village of Ossining and is usually open from 9:00 a.m. to 9:45 p.m., daily except Sunday.

Use a second car to reach the beginning of the hike by turning left out of the community center parking lot, then right onto US 9 at the light (only right turns are permitted here). Almost immediately turn right again onto Main Street, then quickly bear left onto Church Street (do not go down the hill on the right). Next, turn left (north) at the traffic light back onto US 9. Proceed north on US 9 for just over 3 miles. After

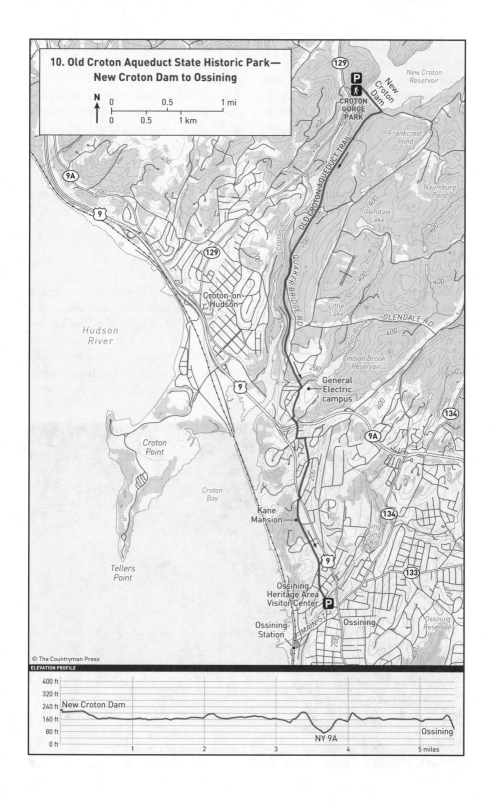

10. Old Croton Aqueduct State Historic Park—
New Croton Dam to Ossining

N
0   0.5   1 mi
0   0.5   1 km

129
CROTON GORGE PARK
New Croton Dam
New Croton Reservoir
Frankcrest Pond
Naumburg Pond
Glendale Lake
OLD CROTON AQUEDUCT TRAIL
QUAKER BRIDGE RD.
9A
9
200
400
129
Croton River
Croton-on-Hudson
Little Lake
GLENDALE RD.
Indian Brook
Indian Brook Reservoir
Hudson River
General Electric campus
9
9A
134
Croton Point
Kane Mansion
134
Sing Sing Kill
Croton Bay
9
133
Tellers Point
Ossining Heritage Area Visitor Center
Ossining
Ossining Reservoir
Ossining Station
MAIN ST.
Ossining

© The Countryman Press

ELEVATION PROFILE

400 ft
320 ft
240 ft   New Croton Dam
160 ft
80 ft   Ossining
0 ft
        1   2   3   NY 9A   4   5 miles

crossing the Croton River, take the second exit, following signs for NY 129. Turn right at the bottom of the ramp, continue past the next traffic light, then turn left at the second traffic light onto Maple Street, continuing to follow NY 129. Proceed ahead for 2.3 miles (the road becomes Grand Street), and watch for, but do not turn into, an entry road on the right that leads down to the Croton Gorge Park.

Take the first right beyond the entrance to Croton Gorge Park, which leads onto the access road for the New Croton Dam, known as Croton Dam Road. The road and dam are closed to vehicular traffic, but parking is permitted on the north side of the road before reaching the barricades that have been placed along it. If there is no room to park, go back to Croton Gorge Park, where ample parking is available (a parking fee is charged on weekends and holidays from May to December).

The southern end of the hike is reachable by train from Grand Central Terminal in New York City (take a Metro-North Hudson Line train to the Ossining station and follow Secor Road and Main Street uphill to the aqueduct route), but no public transportation is available at the northern end of the hike. For train information, go to www .mta.info.

THE HIKE

After parking, walk around the barriers which block vehicle access across the dam. Soon, you'll reach the New Croton Dam. As you walk across, take time to admire this beautiful stone structure and to look right (down into Croton Gorge Park) and left (across the Croton

NEW CROTON DAM

ROCK CUT ALONG THE OLD CROTON AQUEDUCT

Reservoir). More than 200 feet high, the dam was completed in 1907 and resulted in the original dam being submerged under a greatly enlarged reservoir.

On the far side of the dam, you'll walk around vehicle barricades, then turn right onto a gravel road, passing a "high voltage" area behind a chain-link fence. Soon, the road splits. The right fork continues down to Croton Gorge Park, but you should bear left, passing a sign for OLD CROTON AQUEDUCT STATE HISTORIC PARK. The tube is now immediately below.

Soon, the first ventilator comes into view. The path now becomes sandy, passing beneath power lines. A short distance beyond, you'll notice a stone house below on the right. The trail is now wide, with old stone walls both up to the left and down to the right. Through the trees, you'll get glimpses of the river below and of the ridge across the river.

Soon, you pass through a narrow rock cut. Note the drill marks on the surface of the rock.

Quaker Bridge Road East, reached in about a mile along the aqueduct, is the first road crossing. Continue straight across and around another gate to arrive at the second ventilator. Most of these ventilators were placed roughly 1 mile apart. After crossing Quaker Bridge Road, the aqueduct parallels that road, which is above on the left. Down a steep hill on the right is the Croton River. You'll next pass a kiosk for the Old Croton Aqueduct State Park on the right, with benches that afford you the opportunity to take a short rest. Just beyond, a trail on the right leads down to the river. After paralleling another old stone wall, you'll reach the third ventilator. A short distance beyond, you'll recross Quaker Bridge Road.

After walking on an embankment—a narrow ridge with steep slopes on both sides—you'll reach the end of the section of the aqueduct that carries water to Ossining and pass a small building on the left that houses a pump to move the water up to the town's treatment plant. Immediately ahead is the campus of General Electric's John F. Welch Leadership Development Center. The campus has been built over the aqueduct route, so it is necessary to take a detour. Turn right onto the paved road and watch for a green post, with the letters "OCA" on its side, between the entrance to the General Electric campus and Fowler Avenue. Turn left here onto a footpath that skirts the campus, with a chain-link fence on your left. Continue to follow the fence as it turns left, right, and left again, eventually emerging onto paved Shady Lane Farm Road.

Turn right onto this road, head down to Old Albany Post Road and turn left, immediately crossing under a bridge carrying NY 9A. On the west side of Old Albany Post Road, there are two historic buildings—the former Crotonville one-room schoolhouse and a former church. The old schoolhouse is now the Parker Bale American Legion Post #1597. Just beyond, you'll notice a face carved into a tree stump, and then you'll come to the old church, built in 1897.

Take the next left onto Ogden Road and head uphill, almost to the crest of the road, until you see another green OCA post on the north side. Turn right here onto the southbound aqueduct route. The brown building on the left just ahead is now used as a maintenance facility for the aqueduct, which continues across an embankment between backyards of homes. You have now walked nearly 4 miles.

After passing the fourth ventilator, you'll climb on a rough, steep path. At the top, you'll cross Piping Rock Drive and proceed steeply down the other side to a delightful grassy section, then cross another embankment.

In a short distance, you'll reach US 9, passing a sign on the left for the Old Croton Aqueduct. Cross this busy road using the pedestrian crossing. Next, continue down a paved driveway toward a chain-link fence and turn left onto a footpath. Soon the aqueduct emerges onto a wide grassy expanse, with townhouses on both sides. Between the townhouses on the right is the historic Kane Mansion, built in the Gothic Revival style in 1843. Beyond the townhouse development, you'll cross Beach Road. At almost 5 miles into the hike, you'll reach a large rectangular stone building. This structure was built as a weir (see below) when the aqueduct was constructed in 1842, but in 1882 was replaced by a weir in Ossining.

After passing a fire station of the village of Ossining on the right, you'll cross Snowden Avenue diagonally to the right and continue on the aqueduct route. After crossing two streets, Van Wyck and North Malcolm, you'll walk up a paved path with a children's playground on the left. Admire the gorgeous maple tree whose roots penetrate the tube 40 feet down, and walk down the concrete steps to the right of this venerable giant. Cross Ann Street to approach the Waste Weir, built in 1882. This weir was constructed to allow the flow of water through the tube to be controlled when inspection or maintenance was required farther south in the tube. A huge solid-cast-iron gate was dropped, diverting the water into the Sing Sing Kill. This weir chamber was one of a series that made it possible to drain the entire aqueduct. The mechanism was

DOUBLE ARCH BRIDGE OVER THE SING SING KILL

also used to spill off, or "waste," water in times of flood.

Cross the bridge over the Sing Sing Kill, and walk down to the viewing platform to see the double-arch bridge over the Sing Sing Kill. These bridges are one of the most prominent features of the Old Croton Aqueduct. The upper bridge, known as the Aqueduct Bridge, was completed in 1839 and passes over the lower bridge, the Broadway Bridge. The lower bridge was originally made of wood and was rebuilt with stone in the 1860s.

Before returning to your car, you may wish to visit the museum at the Ossining Heritage Area Visitor Center. You should also take the time to explore the Sing Sing Kill Greenway, which begins from the parking lot where you left the first car. A handicapped-accessible concrete walkway descends into the scenic gorge of the Sing Sing Kill, where you cross under the double-arch bridge. The walkway continues along the bottom of the gorge for a third of a mile. At the end of the walkway, concrete steps lead up to Central Avenue. You can either climb the steps and head left on Central Avenue to the aqueduct route, then turn left onto the aqueduct to return to your car, or else retrace your steps through the gorge along the walkway.

11

Teatown Lake Loop

TOTAL DISTANCE: 2.4 miles

WALKING TIME: 2 hours

ELEVATION GAIN: 378 feet

MAPS: USGS 7.5' Ossining; Teatown map; NY–NJTC Westchester Trails map

TRAILHEAD GPS COORDINATES: N 41° 12' 40.5" W 73° 49' 38.5"

The 1,000-acre Teatown Lake Reservation (now known as Teatown), Westchester County's largest private nature preserve, has much to interest visitors. In addition to approximately 15 miles of marked hiking trails, Teatown has three lakes, a scenic gorge, cascading streams, hardwood swamps, mixed forests, meadows, and laurel groves.

Teatown Lake was created in 1923 when Gerard Swope Sr., president of the General Electric Company, built a dam on Bailey Brook. The preserve was established in 1963 when 190 acres surrounding the lake were donated by the Swope family. A nonprofit organization, Teatown depends on contributions to support its educational and land preservation efforts.

The Teatown Nature Center (open daily from 9:00 a.m. to 5:00 p.m., except certain holidays) has a small shop focused on nature items, educational exhibits, and rotating art exhibits. The center and an outdoor enclosed area house birds of prey, reptiles, amphibians, and mammals. Many have been rescued, and most are native to the area.

One special attraction of Teatown is the two-acre Wildflower Island, home to over 200 native and endangered species of wildflowers. It is reached by crossing a bridge from Wildflower Woods, a fenced-in, deer-free area, which (when complete) will feature native plants, trees, shrubs, and wildflowers. Guided tours of Wildflower Island led by experienced volunteers are offered from mid-April through September. To preregister, call 914-762-2912, ext. 110. A nominal fee is charged.

This hike circles Teatown Lake and passes the interesting Griffin Swamp.

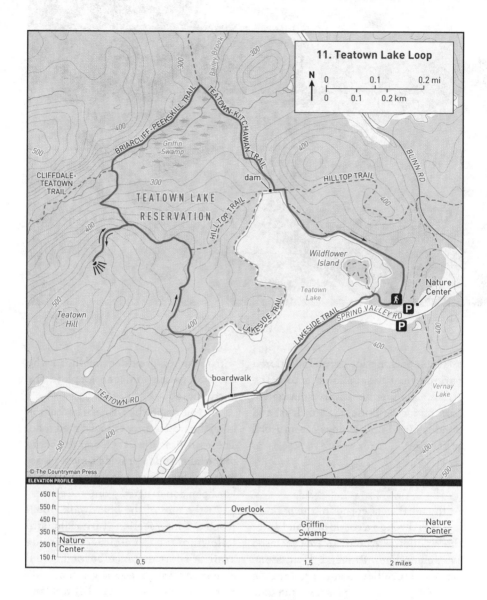

GETTING THERE

To reach the preserve from the Taconic State Parkway, take Exit 11 (NY 134, Ossining). Turn left at the bottom of the ramp (right, if coming from the north), proceed west for 0.3 mile, and turn right onto Spring Valley Road—a winding country road. In 0.6 mile, turn left at the fork (at the sign for the preserve). The parking lot for Teatown is on the right, just past the Nature Center building.

Alternatively, from US 9, turn right onto NY 133 in Ossining (left if approaching from the north) and in 0.2 mile turn left onto NY 134. In 3.9 miles, turn left onto Spring Valley Road, then left again for the preserve at the fork mentioned above.

TEATOWN LAKE

If the parking lot is full, additional parking may be available across the street. Non-members are charged a parking fee on Fridays, Saturdays, and Sundays (and on holidays), from April to October.

THE HIKE

At the northwest corner of the parking lot, pass through a rustic gate and enter the Wildflower Woods, an area enclosed to exclude deer. Proceed down stone steps and turn left, heading toward the lake. Bear right and pass a locked gate that leads to Wildflower Island (open only for guided tours), then bear right again and cross a curved boardwalk overlooking the lake, with the bridge to Wildflower Island on the right. The trail now bears right, passes through another rustic gate, and continues on a footpath parallel to the lake shore, crossing over exposed tree roots and traversing several small rock outcrops. The trail offers views over the lake,

with benches provided for those who wish to pause and contemplate the surroundings.

As you reach the western end of the lake, the trail approaches a paved road. The road runs directly along the shore of the lake, and to provide a more pleasant route for hikers, a floating boardwalk has been constructed along the shore.

At the end of the boardwalk, you'll reach a T-intersection. Turn right, still following the blue-blazed Lakeside Trail. A short distance beyond, you'll come to a Y-intersection by a stone wall. Here, you should take the left fork and continue on the orange-blazed Hilltop Trail (also the route of the green-blazed Briarcliff–Peekskill Trail), which parallels the stone wall on the right. Just ahead, the trail crosses a bridge over a stream and turns left to parallel it.

After turning right (away from the stream) and passing some interesting rock formations, the trail emerges onto a clearing for power lines. It turns left onto a grassy road, then turns right and crosses under the power lines. After traversing a short boardwalk, you'll reach a T-intersection. Here, the Hilltop Trail continues to the right, but you should turn left, continuing to follow the green-blazed Briarcliff–Peekskill Trail.

In 750 feet, you'll come to a junction where the white-blazed Teatown Hill Trail begins on the left. Turn left and follow this trail uphill to its terminus at a power line tower, which offers a broad southeast-facing view.

Retrace your steps to the Briarcliff–Peekskill Trail and turn left. The trail now begins a steady descent. After crossing a boardwalk at the base of the descent, you'll reach another T-intersection. Here, the yellow-blazed Cliffdale–Teatown Trail begins on the left, but you should turn right, continuing to follow the green-blazed Briarcliff–Peekskill Trail.

The trail now approaches the Griffin Swamp, crosses a wooden bridge over the inlet of the swamp, and turns right, following a footpath between the swamp

on the right and a rocky slope on the left. After passing a stone wall—made up of unusually large, rough stones—on the right, you'll reach a T-intersection. Here, the Briarcliff–Peekskill Trail turns left, but you should turn right, joining the Teatown–Kitchawan Trail (marked by purple and "TKT" blazes) which comes in from the left. After crossing the outlet of Griffin Swamp on a wooden bridge, the trail parallels a stream on the left, passing several cascades.

When you reach the dam of Teatown Lake, turn left and cross over the spillway. Just ahead, bear right at the next intersection (the route straight ahead is the orange-blazed Hilltop Trail). You're now once again following the blue-blazed Lakeside Trail, which follows the shore of scenic Teatown Lake, passing a gazebo (known as the "boathouse") on the right. Continue to follow the Lakeside Trail along the lake until you reach the Nature Center and the parking lot where the hike began.

ALONG THE LAKESIDE TRAIL

Vernay Lake/ Hidden Valley Loop

TOTAL DISTANCE: 2 miles

WALKING TIME: 1.5 hours

ELEVATION GAIN: 340 feet

MAPS: USGS 7.5' Ossining; Teatown map; NY–NJTC Westchester Trails map

TRAILHEAD GPS COORDINATES: N 41° 12' 40.5" W 73° 49' 38.5"

Although Teatown Lake is the centerpiece of the Teatown preserve, Teatown includes many other interesting features. This hike begins by descending to Vernay Lake, a recent addition to Teatown, and continues through the scenic Hidden Valley.

GETTING THERE

To reach the preserve from the Taconic State Parkway, take Exit 11 (NY 134, Ossining). Turn left at the bottom of the ramp (right, if coming from the north), proceed west for 0.3 mile, and turn right onto Spring Valley Road—a winding country road. In 0.6 mile, turn left at the fork (at the sign for the preserve). The parking lot for Teatown is on the right, just past the Nature Center building.

Alternatively, from US 9, turn right onto NY 133 in Ossining (left if approaching from the north) and in 0.2 mile turn left onto NY 134. In 3.9 miles, turn left onto Spring Valley Road, then left again for the preserve at the fork mentioned above.

If the parking lot is full, additional parking may be available across the street. Non-members are charged a parking fee on Fridays, Saturdays, and Sundays (and on holidays), from April to October.

THE HIKE

From the parking area, cross to the south side of Spring Valley Road, go through an opening in a stone wall, and immediately turn left. Bear right ahead, passing a kiosk on the left and a stone-lined pond on the right, and continue on the orange-blazed Twin Lakes Trail, which descends toward Vernay Lake on a gravel road. Near the base of the descent, the trail bears left, leaving the

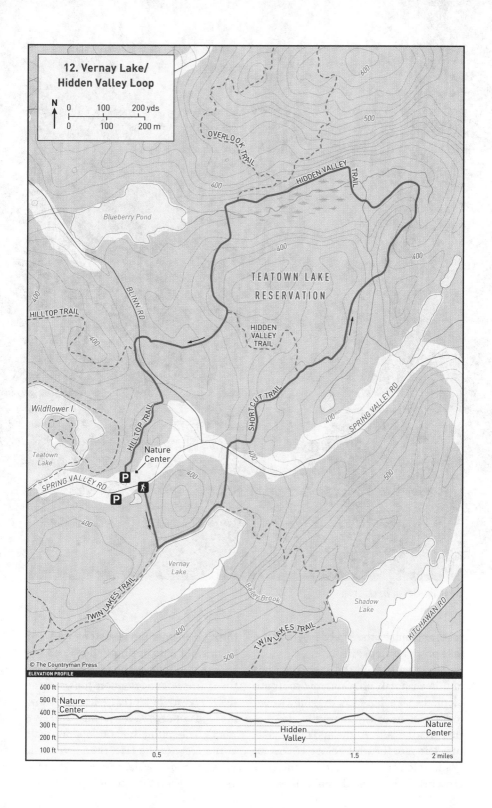

12. Vernay Lake/ Hidden Valley Loop

N

| 0 | 100 | 200 yds |
| 0 | 100 | 200 m |

OVERLOOK TRAIL

600

500

Blueberry Pond

HIDDEN VALLEY TRAIL

400

400

400

BLINN RD

HILLTOP TRAIL

400

TEATOWN LAKE
RESERVATION

HIDDEN
VALLEY
TRAIL

SHORTCUT TRAIL

SPRING VALLEY RD

400

500

Wildflower I.

HILLTOP TRAIL

Nature
Center

400

Teatown
Lake

P

SPRING VALLEY RD

P

400

400

Vernay
Lake

Bailey Brook

Shadow
Lake

KITCHAWAN RD

TWIN LAKES TRAIL

400

TWIN LAKES TRAIL

500

© The Countryman Press

ELEVATION PROFILE

| 600 ft |
500 ft	Nature
400 ft	Center
300 ft	Hidden
200 ft	Valley
100 ft

Nature
Center

0.5   1   1.5   2 miles

ALONG THE HIDDEN VALLEY TRAIL

road, and makes the final descent to the lake on stone steps.

When you reach the lake, turn left and head north on a narrow footpath along the lakeshore. On the right, a concrete dock affords panoramic views of this pristine lake. At the end of the lake, turn left onto the white-blazed Shortcut Trail, which climbs on a footpath. After crossing a grassy field, the trail passes through an opening in a stone wall and turns right onto Spring Valley Road.

The trail follows the road for 50 feet, then turns left and reenters the woods at the driveway of a private home (follow the sign CONNECTOR TO THE HIDDEN VALLEY TRAIL). The path climbs to a stone wall at the crest of the rise, then levels off. When the white-blazed trail ends at a T-intersection, turn right (uphill) onto

left and emerges into the Hidden Valley. You'll then cross a boardwalk over a wet area and recross the stream on a wooden bridge below attractive cascades. The trail immediately turns right, briefly paralleling the stream. It then crosses a boardwalk over a wetland (with abundant skunk cabbage in season), turns sharply left, and follows a path between the wetland on the left and a rocky slope on the right.

Near the end of the wetland, you'll reach a junction with the yellow-blazed Overlook Trail, which begins on the right. You should continue ahead on the red-blazed Hidden Valley Trail, which bears left, crosses a footbridge over the stream, and climbs out of the valley.

At the top of the climb, the trail passes through a gap in an old stone wall. After winding through an evergreen grove and crossing another stone wall, the path continues through an overgrown field, with signs on a post on the left. Turn right, following the sign to the NATURE CENTER, and continue along the red-blazed trail, descending through the field. At the base of the descent, the trail crosses a wooden boardwalk and passes through another stone wall. A short distance beyond, the trail intersects the paved Blinn Road, then turns left to parallel it.

Just ahead, the red-blazed Hidden Valley Trail ends at a junction with the orange-blazed Hilltop Trail. Continue ahead on the orange-blazed trail, paralleling Blinn Road. After passing the entrance to a dirt parking area, the trail climbs a little and soon emerges into a gravel parking area, with a red barn on the right. Continue ahead to the end of the trail at a kiosk behind the Nature Center. The parking lot where the hike began is on your right.

the red-blazed Hidden Valley Trail, which passes a huge rock outcrop on the right and soon begins a gradual descent.

After descending a little more steeply, the trail crosses a footbridge over a stream and bears left onto a woods road, which climbs briefly, then descends steadily. At the base of the descent, the trail curves sharply to the

13

Sylvan Glen Park Preserve

TOTAL DISTANCE: 3.6 miles

WALKING TIME: 2 hours

ELEVATION GAIN: 662 feet

MAPS: USGS 7.5' TK; NY–NJTC Sylvan Glen Park Preserve map (www.nynjtc.org/map/sylvan-glen-nature-preserve)

TRAILHEAD GPS COORDINATES: N 41°17' 59.1" W 73°51' 08.9"

Sylvan Glen Park Preserve is the site of a granite quarry that opened in 1895 and was abandoned in the fall of 1941, just before the advent of World War II. In its heyday, the quarry employed hundreds of workers, and its high-quality stone was used to construct such landmarks as the Cathedral of St. John the Divine in Manhattan and the approaches to the George Washington Bridge. Operations at the quarry were terminated rather abruptly, with the result that much of the machinery was left behind and still may be seen today.

The property was acquired by the town of Yorktown in 1981, and trails were established by the Yorktown Land Trust. Since then, additional trails have been built by volunteers of the New York–New Jersey Trail Conference and the Westchester Mountain Biking Association. The trails in this 408-acre park are blazed with colored plastic markers of the Town of Yorktown.

GETTING THERE

From the Taconic State Parkway, take the exit for US 202/NY 35 (Yorktown Heights). At the bottom of the ramp, head west on US 202/NY 35 (Crompond Road). Continue for 1.8 miles and turn right at a traffic light onto Lexington Avenue. In half a mile, turn right onto Morris Lane and follow it for 0.2 mile into the parking area for Sylvan Glen Park Preserve.

THE HIKE

From the kiosk at the end of the parking area, proceed ahead on the white-blazed Turtle Pond Trail, which follows a woods road, passing Turtle Pond on the right. After passing a fenced-in dog park on

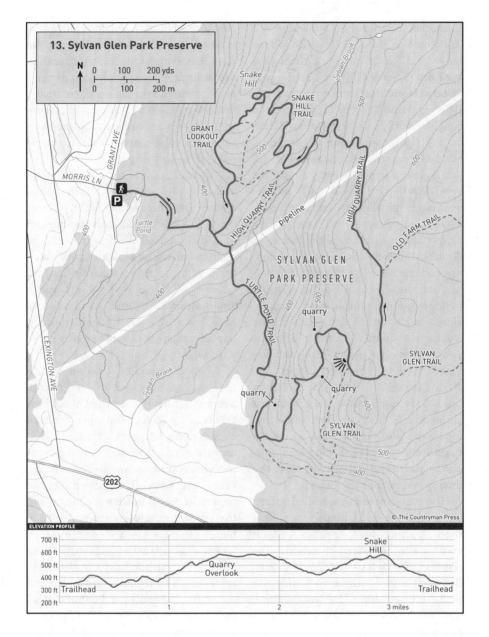

13. Sylvan Glen Park Preserve

ELEVATION PROFILE

the left, the trail bears right, then turns left and heads uphill.

At the top of the climb, the yellow-blazed Snake Hill Trail crosses. The Snake Hill Trail will be your return route, but for now, continue ahead on the white trail. Just ahead, the blue-blazed

High Quarry Trail begins on the left. Proceed ahead on the white-blazed Turtle Pond Trail, which bears right and crosses a gas pipeline.

On the other side of the pipeline clearing, the white-blazed trail reenters the woods and descends, passing the end of the yellow-blazed Snake Hill Trail on the right. Follow the white-blazed trail as it proceeds through a pine grove, crosses Sylvan Brook on a wooden footbridge, and begins to climb. After crossing another footbridge, the trail levels off, passes a stone foundation on the right, then resumes a gradual climb. As the trail once again levels off, you'll cross a rock causeway over a wet area. Just beyond, you'll notice numerous fragments of carved granite blocks on both sides of the trail. Interpretive signs relate the history of the Mohegan Granite Company, which installed modernized machinery in this area in 1925.

Just ahead, around a bend, you'll notice a driving range down to the right. Here, you should bear left, following the woods road uphill. In a short distance, you'll reach a junction where the blue-blazed High Quarry Trail begins. The High Quarry Trail proceeds ahead on the woods road, but you should turn right onto a footpath, continuing to follow the white blazes. You'll notice a rusted rail—a remnant of the narrow-gauge railroad that once served the quarry—embedded in the trail.

The trail passes a water-filled quarry pit on the left and widens to a woods road. A short distance ahead, you'll come to another intersection where the red-blazed Sylvan Glen Trail begins. Bear left and continue to follow the white blazes along the woods road, which climbs gradually, curving sharply to the left.

After passing a huge heap of discarded blocks of granite (note the drill marks in many of the rocks), the white-blazed Turtle Pond Trail ends at a T-intersection with the blue-blazed High Quarry Trail. Turn right and follow the blue trail steeply uphill, soon reaching the edge of a deep quarry pit.

Abandoned in 1941, the once-barren pit is now filled with trees and other vegetation. Remnants of the quarry operation are abundant here, including several cables that run through pulleys bolted into the rock. Take some time to explore these interesting artifacts, but be careful, as there is a steep drop from the edge of the quarry pit!

The trail passes under a rock bridge and bears left, leaving the rim of the quarry and descending slightly. Soon, it reaches a junction with the purple-blazed Hillside Trail. Here, you should continue on the blue-blazed trail, which turns sharply right, passing another quarry pit (filled with water) and a small stone shed (once used to store explosives). The trail goes through a gap in a stone wall and turns right to parallel it.

A short distance beyond, you'll reach a junction with the red-blazed Sylvan Glen Trail. Turn right and follow this trail for 40 feet, but when the trail curves to the left, bear right and follow an unmarked path to the right that leads to a viewpoint from an open rock ledge. From here, you can look down into the quarry, and you can also see the hills to the west. Again, use extreme caution here, as there is a very steep drop.

After taking in the view, return to the red-blazed trail and bear left, then continue ahead on the co-aligned blue and red trails. The trails head uphill and, as they level off, split. Bear left to stay on the blue trail, which continues along a level woods road.

Immediately after passing through a gap in a stone wall, the blue-blazed High Quarry Trail bears left. Just beyond, the green-blazed Old Farm Trail crosses. After passing through a gap in a high stone wall, the purple-blazed Hillside Trail begins on the left, but you should

DISCARDED GRANITE BLOCKS ALONG THE TRAIL

continue ahead on the blue-blazed trail, which descends on a footpath, soon reaching the wide gas pipeline clearing.

Cross the clearing and reenter the woods, continuing to follow the blue trail, which descends on switchbacks. At the base of the descent, the trail turns left to parallel a stream. Soon, it turns right, crosses the stream on large rocks below a small cascade, then turns left and continues to parallel the stream on the other side.

As the trail bears right, away from the stream, it reaches a junction with

CABLES RUNNING THROUGH PULLEYS BOLTED INTO THE ROCK

the yellow-blazed Snake Hill Trail. The blue-blazed High Quarry Trail turns left and joins the yellow trail, but you should bear right and follow the yellow blazes uphill on switchbacks. As you approach the top of the hill, you'll notice a triple-green blaze on the right. This short green-blazed trail makes a 300-foot loop around a huge pile of discarded granite blocks, a worthwhile detour.

After following this loop, return to the yellow-blazed Snake Hill Trail and turn right. The yellow trail continues to the top of the hill and descends slightly to end at a junction with the red-blazed Grant Lookout Trail. Turn right onto the red trail, which descends on a footpath, with some views through the trees to the right when there are no leaves on the trees (despite its name, there is no "lookout" on this trail).

In a short distance, you'll come to another quarry pit on the left, with many abandoned cut stone blocks. The red trail continues along a woods road (built to access the quarry) and ends at a T-intersection with the yellow-blazed Snake Hill Trail. Turn right and follow the yellow trail downhill to its end at the white-blazed Turtle Pond Trail. Then turn right onto the white trail and follow it back to the parking area where the hike began (be sure to bear right at the fork at the bottom of the hill).

Anthony's Nose/Camp Smith Trail

TOTAL DISTANCE: 4.2 miles

WALKING TIME: 4 hours

ELEVATION GAIN: 1,781 feet

MAPS: USGS 7.5' Peekskill; NY–NJTC East Hudson Trails #101

TRAILHEAD GPS COORDINATES: N 41° 19' 19" W 73° 58' 33.5"

The Camp Smith Trail is a strenuous hike, and it is one of the few hikes in this book that requires two cars for a shuttle. But it is also one of the most spectacular hikes in the book, as it offers a panorama of views of the Hudson River and the mountains of Harriman-Bear Mountain State Parks on the west side of the river. The broadest and best views are from Anthony's Nose, at the northwest corner of Westchester County, but views continue throughout the hike, each one different from the others. You'll want to allow sufficient time to appreciate these fantastic views, and the time allotted for this hike takes this into account.

This scenic trail was "a long time a-coming." Camp Smith, a military installation of the New York National Guard in Cortlandt Manor, was acquired by the state from 1885 through the mid-1920s. Until 1992, public entry was officially prohibited, but hikers would often climb via the Appalachian Trail (AT) to Anthony's Nose, which offers a fabulous view of the Hudson River.

In 1992, efforts by the Greenway Conservancy of Hudson River Valley resulted in Camp Smith granting permission to build a 4-mile trail through its property, from the toll house at the eastern end of the Bear Mountain Bridge approach road to the bridge itself. Constructed by volunteers from the New York–New Jersey Trail Conference, with the assistance of the New York National Guard's Challenge Program for high-school dropouts, the trail was completed in 1995. The trail route (including a 50-foot strip of land extending east of the trail and the land between the trail and the Hudson River) is now part of Hudson Highlands State Park Preserve.

This hike, as described, requires two cars. If you have only one car, possible out-and-back hikes are described in the

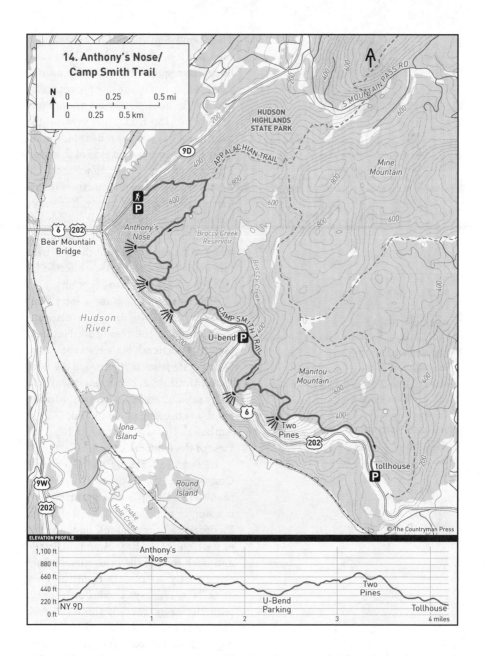

Other Hiking Options section at the end of the hike description.

GETTING THERE

Leave one car on US 6 at the tollhouse, 2.6 miles east of the Bear Mountain Bridge (or 0.7 mile west of the Camp Smith entrance). Then drive the second car toward the bridge (but don't cross it) and turn right onto NY 9D. Park along the shoulder of NY 9D, just north of the bridge (the best place to park is on a wide shoulder on the east side of the road, about 0.1 mile north of the Westchester-Putnam county line). If no parking can be found along the shoulder, consider an out-and-back hike from one of the two US 6 parking areas noted below.

THE HIKE

The white-blazed Appalachian Trail (AT) leaves NY 9D just north of the sign for the Westchester-Putnam county line. Follow the AT as it climbs steeply uphill. There are several level spots where you can take a break, but for the most part, the climb is unrelenting.

After about half an hour of hiking and 500 feet of elevation gain, you'll reach a wide woods road 0.6 mile from the start. The AT turns left along the road, but you should turn rightonto the blue-blazed Camp Smith Trail, which you'll be following for the remainder of the hike. The trail is marked with both blue plastic discs of the Taconic Park Region and blue paint blazes.

At first, the trail continues uphill along the wide woods road, sections of which have been eroded to the bedrock, but it soon levels off and passes a small pond on the left. You'll notice some side trails that depart to the right. These unofficial trails lead to viewpoints, but you'll soon reach the best of them all, so you should proceed ahead on the main trail.

After climbing a little more, you'll arrive at a T-intersection. The marked trail turns left here, but you should turn right onto a wide unmarked path and head toward the rock face of Anthony's Nose. This is the most expansive viewpoint on the hike, and it often attracts a crowd (especially on weekends). It is an excellent place to watch raptors, including the peregrine falcons that nest on the Bear Mountain Bridge.

To your left (southwest), across the river, you can see Harriman-Bear Mountain State Parks, where Bald and Dunderberg Mountains and the Timp

BEAR MOUNTAIN BRIDGE FROM ANTHONY'S NOSE

BEAR MOUNTAIN FROM ANTHONY'S NOSE

dominate. Directly across the river is the Bear Mountain Inn complex, which includes Hessian Lake, an ice skating rink, and a merry-go-round. The Perkins Memorial Tower on Bear Mountain is in front of you, and you may catch the glint of cars on the Perkins Memorial Drive that leads to the top of the mountain. The bald, rocky summit of Popolopen Torne is just beyond the Bear Mountain Bridge. Fort Montgomery is to the right of the bridge, with the United States Military Academy at West Point just barely visible to the north. On the east side of the river are Canada and Sugarloaf Hills. There are rail lines on both sides, and trains pass by frequently (Metro-North and Amtrak passenger trains use the tracks on the east side of the river; CSX freight trains use the tracks on the west side). You'll probably also see boats in the river—both pleasure boats (in the summer) and commercial ships and barges (the river is navigable by large vessels all the way to Albany).

So who was this Anthony with his magnificent nose? His identity is the subject of much folklore and speculation, but no one really knows. Early maps refer to this geological feature as Saint Anthony's Nose. Washington Irving spun his own humorous tale in the early 1800s. One version of the tale recounts that when Henry Hudson sailed up the river later to be named for him, he had an Italian cook aboard named Anthony who, it was said, had previously lived with local Native Americans. When Henry Hudson spotted the cliffs, he asked aloud, "What's that?!" One of his crew immediately responded, "Don't know, sir, but you should ask Anthony. Anthony knows." One thing is certain: It was named long before the time of Revolutionary War General "Mad Anthony" Wayne.

Now return to the marked trail and proceed ahead, following the blue blazes. A short scramble brings you up to a rock outcrop with a US Geological Survey benchmark that marks the summit of Anthony's Nose. There is a south-facing view over the Hudson River from here, but it is a limited one, with trees obscuring the views in all other directions.

The Camp Smith Trail now begins a steady descent on a footpath. After descending about 250 feet in elevation, you'll reach a rock outcrop with a view over Bear Mountain and the Bear Mountain Bridge. The trail turns left and levels off, passing a wetland on the left. It then climbs to another viewpoint atop a rock outcrop, from which both Iona Island and Bear Mountain can be seen.

The trail now bears left and heads inland, crossing an intermittent stream in a gully. It joins a woods road, level at first, but soon the road begins a steady descent (with its surface badly eroded). It crosses a stream and continues downhill, with the sounds of traffic on US 6 becoming more distinct. Finally, you'll approach a bend in the road (known as the "U-Bend"), where you can both see and hear the traffic. A short distance beyond, you'll cross Broccy Creek on rocks and reach a kiosk. The midpoint parking area (with spaces for six to eight cars) is just to the right. You have now descended about 550 vertical feet from the summit.

The Camp Smith Trail continues ahead, then turns sharply left and begins a steady ascent. The trail gradually moves away from the road, and the noise of the traffic decreases and then disappears altogether. After reaching the crest of the rise, the trail begins to descend, soon coming to a sharp bend. Here, just to the right of the trail, there is a panoramic viewpoint from a rock ledge. Iona Island may be seen on the left, with Bear Mountain to its right. For the first time, you can see the massive Anthony's Nose—which you just climbed—on the east side of the river.

The Camp Smith Trail now turns away from the river and begins to climb. As it levels off, it passes a south-facing viewpoint on the right, with the dominant

structure downriver the Wheelabrator Westchester plant at Charles Point, which produces electricity from household and business waste. After passing another viewpoint over Iona Island, the trail again heads inland.

Soon, you'll notice a massive jumble of rocks ahead. The trail ascends this steep section on switchbacks built by a volunteer trail crew. The trail route was carefully designed to minimize erosion and make the trail safe and enjoyable. At the top, you'll reach a viewpoint over the river.

The trail now descends a little, coming out at the "Two Pines" viewpoint, marked by two pitch pines near the edge. (Since the viewpoint was named, additional pitch pines have sprouted, although the original two pines are noticeably the largest.) Across the river are Dunderberg Mountain and the wetlands of Iona Island (a noted bird habitat), and downstream you can see the domes of the Indian Point nuclear power facility. On the opposite shore, farther downstream, the sharp outline of Hook Mountain (Hike #23) protrudes into the river.

After climbing a little, the Camp Smith Trail descends rather steeply. As the descent moderates, you'll come out at the top of a large sloping rock face, with a view over the river. Just a few minutes farther along the trail, you'll reach another rock outcrop with a broad south-facing view. You can see the city of Peekskill on the left, with the Wheelabrator and Indian Point plants to its right. You can also clearly see the railroad tracks on both sides of the river.

The next trail section has the steepest descent on the hike. Take your time to traverse this section—you'll need to use both your feet and your hands to descend safely. The steep section ends

IONA ISLAND AND DUNDERBERG MOUNTAIN FROM ANTHONY'S NOSE

with a set of stone steps, and then the trail levels off. After crossing an intermittent stream, it continues to descend, but at a much more moderate pace. At the base of the descent, you'll see the road directly ahead, and you might think that you're at the end of the hike— but the trail heads back into the woods and once again begins to ascend.

After passing an imposing cliff on the left, you'll reach the height of land, with a view of Dunderberg Mountain across the river. The view is partially blocked by trees, but it's the last view on the hike. The trail now descends and soon emerges on the grassy lawn of the Bear Mountain Toll House, where you left the first car. This stone structure was built to collect tolls from motorists when the Bear Mountain Bridge and the approach road, operated privately by the Harriman family, were first opened in 1924. When the state acquired the bridge in 1940, the tollhouse was abandoned. In the early 1990s, it was threatened with demolition, and the opening of the Camp Smith Trail helped galvanize support to preserve this historic

structure. It was restored as a visitor center in 2002 and features a small gift shop open weekends in season. A portable toilet is available.

OTHER HIKING OPTIONS

For a shorter two-car hike, parking is also available at a U-bend on US 6, 2.1 miles west of the Camp Smith entry or 1.1 miles east of the bridge. You also might want to consider doing the hike in the opposite direction (starting at the tollhouse and ending on NY 9D). Hiking in this direction has the advantage that the views become more impressive as you head north, ending at the most spectacular one.

Should you have only one car available, start from any one of the three parking areas noted above, and hike up and back to Anthony's Nose. From NY 9D, it's a 2.4-mile round-trip. From the tollhouse, it's a 7-mile round-trip, with the opportunity to savor the many views twice. From the U-bend, it's a 2.9-mile round-trip, with an elevation gain of 600 to 700 feet.

II.

THE EAST HUDSON HIGHLANDS

Introduction to the East Hudson Area

State parks on the east side of the Hudson River are managed by the Taconic Park Commission, a state agency with offices in Staatsburg. From the precipitous cliffs of Breakneck Ridge to the more gentle uplands of Fahnestock, the extensive number of hiking choices available offer wonderful recreational opportunities.

FAHNESTOCK STATE PARK

Located adjacent to the NY 301 and the Taconic State Parkway, this 16,000-acre park features lakes and rolling terrain. In the summer, the park offers swimming, boating, and picnicking. In the winter, a cross-country ski center, known as Fahnestock Winter Park, grooms about 10 miles of trails near the swimming area. The park also has many miles of trails that can take you far from the crowds that regularly enjoy the more developed facilities. Although not as mountainous as parkland closer to the Hudson, the varied terrain makes for peaceful excursions into the woodlands. Bow hunting is allowed in season, and some trails are open to mountain bikes and horses.

The park has its roots in the 1929 gift of 2,400 acres by Dr. Ernest Fahnestock in memory of his brother, Clarence. It was significantly expanded in the 1960s and the 1990s.

Much of the land that now forms the park was purchased by Adolphe Philipse in 1691 and established as the Philipse Grant six years later by King William III. The vast and rugged wilderness surrounding the interior range of hills could not be farmed and thus never had many settlers. Only the 8-mile-long vein of iron ore that follows the ridgeline of the hills to the south managed to attract settlers—and then not until after 1800. The early miners regarded these dark woods with foreboding; because they have not been logged for many years, the woods probably look now very much as they did then.

The mines in the park once provided iron ore to the West Point Foundry at Cold Spring, where the ore was turned into Parrott artillery for the Union Army. The bed of the railroad built in 1862 to carry the ore from the mines is now a hiking trail.

Thanks to the purchase of 4,400 acres in 1991 and 1995 by the Open Space Institute, the park was able to significantly expand its trail system. In 1996, the New York–New Jersey Trail Conference opened a 22-mile network of trails in what was then known as the Hubbard-Perkins Conservation Area, including two trails that connect to the main area of Fahnestock State Park. The park office phone is 845-225-7207.

HUDSON HIGHLANDS STATE PARK PRESERVE

"Eastward a high chain of mountains whose sides were covered with woods up to no more than half of their height. The summits, however, were quite barren; for I suppose nothing would grow there on account of the great degree of heat, dryness, and the violence of the wind to which that part was exposed." Thus, the Swedish botanist Peter Kalm observed the Hudson Highlands on the east side of the Hudson River in 1749. One highlight of his trip was his discovery and the first botanical description of the American mountain laurel, *Kalmia latifolia*, a shrub that grows on every slope from the Ramapos to the Shawangunks and whose blooms make walking here and everywhere in southern New York in late May and early June so special.

Hudson Highlands State Park Preserve consists of over 7,400 acres along the Hudson River in Westchester, Putnam, and southern Dutchess Counties. It includes a 1,000-acre tract on the Fishkill Ridge that was acquired by Scenic Hudson beginning in 1992. Standing as the northern gateway to the Highlands, the area's rocky outcrops offer panoramic views of the Hudson River and the Catskill Mountains.

The most impressive section of the park straddles the Putnam–Dutchess boundary north of NY 301 and protects a rugged, scenic area. Bull Hill, the aptly named Breakneck Ridge, and the impressive Sugarloaf Mountain (not to be confused with the nearby Sugarloaf Hill, located farther south) rise steeply above the Hudson and provide numerous challenging climbs and spectacular views.

Hudson Highlands State Park Preserve is managed by the office of Fahnestock State Park. Bow hunting is allowed in season.

Both Hudson Highlands State Park Preserve and Fahnestock State Park are traversed by the Appalachian Trail, which also follows its own protected corridor, owned by the National Park Service.

OTHER PARKS IN THE EAST HUDSON AREA

Although Hudson Highlands State Park Preserve and Fahnestock State Park account for the vast majority of preserved parkland in the East Hudson area, there are a number of smaller parks and preserves in the area that offer hiking opportunities. The 137-acre Manitou Point Preserve, described in Hike #15, features a particularly scenic trail that runs along the Hudson River. Other parks and preserves in the East Hudson area with hiking trails not described in this book include Manitoga, Garrison School Forest, and Glenclyffe.

15

Manitou Point Preserve

TOTAL DISTANCE: 3.1 miles	

WALKING TIME: 2 hours

ELEVATION GAIN: 522 feet

MAPS: USGS 7.5′ Peekskill; NY–NJTC East Hudson Trails #101

TRAILHEAD GPS COORDINATES: N 41°20′ 16.6″ W 73°57′ 30.2″

Manitou Point Preserve is the site of the country home of Edward Livingston, a descendant of Philip Livingston, who signed the Declaration of Independence. The mansion, completed in 1897, was designed in the Colonial Revival style by the noted architect George Frederick Pelham. In 1990, the property was acquired by the Open Space Institute and Scenic Hudson. It was sold to a private owner in 2013, subject to an access easement that allows the public to hike on the trails and woods roads that traverse the property. The mansion and its surrounding land are off-limits to the public.

The most notable feature of this hike is the section of the blue-blazed River Trail that runs atop a bluff along the Hudson River, offering outstanding views. In places, there is a steep drop from the trail to the river, so this hike is not recommended if the trail is covered with snow or ice.

GETTING THERE

From the east end of the Bear Mountain Bridge, head north on NY 9D for 1.7 miles and turn left into the parking area for the preserve at a small sign for the MANITOU POINT NATURE PRESERVE. The parking area is 750 feet north of the intersection of NY 9D with South Mountain Pass.

Train Directions
Take the Metro-North Hudson Line to Manitou station (only limited service is provided, primarily on weekends; see www.mta.info). From the station, proceed east on Manitou Station Road for 0.1 mile until you see on the left two stone pillars with a white gate. Go around the gate and turn left onto a dirt

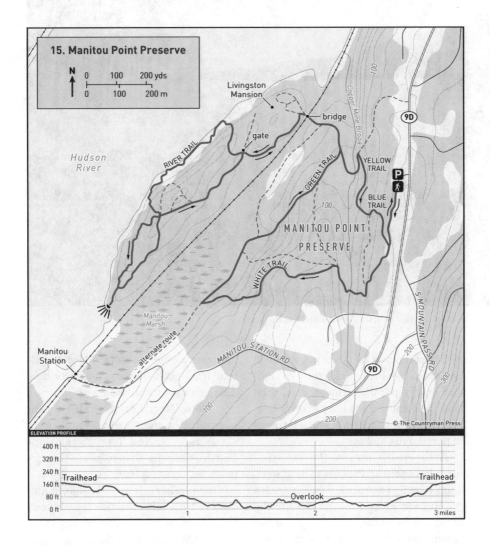

15. Manitou Point Preserve

ELEVATION PROFILE

road that runs along the southeast edge of Manitou Marsh. In 0.3 mile, the white trail begins on the right. Continue along the dirt road until you reach the start of the green trail (on the right) and follow the hike description, beginning with the third paragraph of the text. To return to the train station, when you reach the intersection of the blue trail with the white trail (last paragraph of description), turn right onto the white trail and follow it to its terminus on the dirt road. Turn left on the dirt road, follow it back to Manitou Station Road, then turn right on Manitou Station Road and proceed back to the station.

THE HIKE

From the kiosk just below the parking area, head south on the white trail, which parallels NY 9D. In a short distance, a blue trail begins on the right, but continue ahead on the white trail. In a quarter mile, the white trail bears right, away from the road, and descends

VIEW OF THE HUDSON RIVER FROM THE RIVER TRAIL

rather steeply into a ravine, where it crosses a stream on rocks. It turns right and briefly parallels the stream, then bears left and climbs out of the ravine. The trail now bears right and continues to parallel the stream.

At the crest of the rise, the white trail turns left again and begins to head west. Soon, it begins a gradual descent toward the Hudson River, running close to the southern boundary of the preserve. About two-thirds of a mile from the start, after paralleling an old stone wall, the white trail ends at a dirt road. Turn right and proceed north on the road, passing the Manitou Marsh on the left.

Soon, you'll notice an orange-blazed trail and then a wide green-blazed trail on the right. Turn right onto the green-blazed trail, which climbs gradually on a woods road to the crest of a rise, then descends. After passing a pink-blazed trail on the right, the green-blazed trail ends at a dirt road. Turn left and follow the road downhill.

Bear right at the next intersection and cross over the Metro-North railroad tracks on a wide stone-arch bridge. This is an active railroad, and you may see Metro-North or Amtrak passenger trains on their way to Poughkeepsie, Albany, or New York. To the right (north), the cone-shaped hill in the distance is Sugarloaf Hill.

On the other side of the bridge, immediately turn left onto the blue-blazed River Trail, which parallels the railroad tracks. On the right is the historic Livingston Mansion (the mansion and its grounds are not open to the public), and on the left (across the tracks), you can see the ruins of an old brick building. Soon, the trail curves right, away from the tracks, and reaches a dirt road.

Cross the road and continue on the blue-blazed trail, which climbs over a rise, then descends on switchbacks and stone steps to the shore of the Hudson River. The trail turns left onto a narrow footpath along a bluff overlooking the river, with panoramic views across the river. You may see a freight train on the

CSX tracks on the west bank of the river. Use caution, as there are steep drop-offs on the right. At one point, the trail crosses a wooden bridge over an area where the footpath had become eroded.

After following closely along the river for about a quarter mile, the trail turns left and steeply climbs rock steps. If you look back to the north, you can see Sugarloaf Hill above the trees. In a short distance, the trail bears left again and heads inland, soon reaching a complex junction, with a carriage road on the left and two branches of the blue-blazed River Trail on the right. Turn sharply right and follow the branch of the blue-blazed trail that runs closest to the river.

In another quarter mile (after bearing right at a fork), the blue-blazed trail ends at a south-facing viewpoint, with a stone bench. After taking in the view, retrace your steps on the blue-blazed trail for 200 feet, then bear sharply right at a trail junction. You're now following the inland branch of the blue-blazed River Trail, which leads to the complex junction you encountered earlier in the hike. Turn right onto the carriage road (still following the blue blazes), which curves to the left and heads north.

When you reach the next junction (the road ahead is blocked off with a gate), turn right and retrace your steps on the blue-blazed trail to the bridge over the railroad. Turn right again, cross the bridge, and follow the dirt road uphill.

After crossing a stream, the road curves to the left and then to the right. Just beyond the curve to the right, turn right onto a yellow-blazed trail and follow it uphill to a junction with a blue-blazed trail. Turn left onto the blue-blazed trail, and follow it to a white-blazed trail. Turn left onto the white-blazed trail and follow it a short distance to the parking area where the hike began.

SUGARLOAF HILL FROM THE RIVER TRAIL

16

Osborn Loop/ Sugarloaf Hill

TOTAL DISTANCE: 7 miles

WALKING TIME: 4.5 hours

ELEVATION GAIN: 1,589 feet

MAPS: USGS 7.5' Peekskill; NY–NJTC East Hudson Trails #101

TRAILHEAD GPS COORDINATES: N 41° 21' 02" W 73° 55' 34.5"

The Hudson Valley is rich in Revolutionary War history. The Beverly Robinson House, built by the Philipse family in 1758 on part of the Philipse Patent near Sugarloaf South, was confiscated and used as headquarters by Generals Israel Putnam and Samuel Holden Parsons in 1778 and 1779. In 1780, the house was used by General Benedict Arnold as his headquarters, and it was used as a military hospital during Arnold's command of West Point. Aboard the British ship *Vulture*, loyalist Beverly Robinson plotted with Benedict Arnold and Major John Andre to deliver West Point to the British. When Arnold learned that Andre had been captured and that the discovery of his treason was imminent, he fled from the house down a path to the river and then downriver on the *Vulture*; General Washington arrived only an hour or so later.

The Osborn Preserve, a 1,000-acre section of Hudson Highlands State Park, was established when William Henry Osborn II donated the land around Sugarloaf Hill in 1974. His grandfather, president of the Illinois Central Railroad, had assembled the property for a summer home in the 1880s. The charming home, just north on Castle Rock, is privately owned. In the early 1980s, the National Park Service purchased adjacent property along the ridge to reroute the Appalachian Trail (AT) onto protected land. Many of the preserve's trails are easy-to-follow carriageways and old roads and are suitable for novice hikers.

This moderate hike, with one rather steep ascent at the start, is largely on old carriage roads, and occasionally equestrians are encountered. The highlight is a climb of Sugarloaf Hill—a name derived from the cone shape in which sugar was sold in Colonial times.

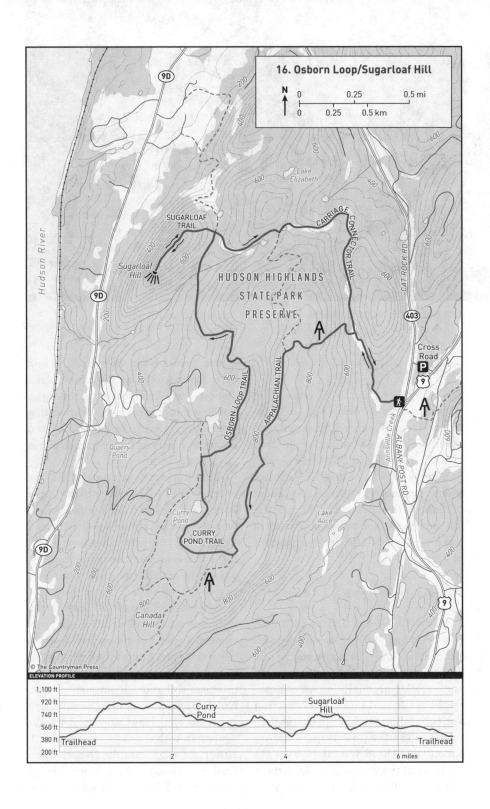

16. Osborn Loop/Sugarloaf Hill

N

0   0.25   0.5 mi

0   0.25   0.5 km

Lake Elizabeth

SUGARLOAF TRAIL

CARRIAGE CONNECTOR TRAIL

Sugarloaf Hill

Hudson River

HUDSON HIGHLANDS STATE PARK PRESERVE

CAT ROCK RD

Cross Road

OSBORN LOOP TRAIL

APPALACHIAN TRAIL

Annsville Creek

ALBANY POST RD

Quarry Pond

Curry Pond

CURRY POND TRAIL

Lake Alice

Canada Hill

© The Countryman Press

ELEVATION PROFILE

1,100 ft
920 ft
740 ft
560 ft
380 ft — Trailhead
200 ft

Curry Pond

Sugarloaf Hill

Trailhead

2   4   6 miles

OLD STONE WALL ALONG THE OSBORN LOOP TRAIL

GETTING THERE

The hike begins on the AT crossing of US 9 at its junction with NY 403 in Graymoor, Putnam County. This junction is 3.8 miles north of the major junction of US 9, US 202, and US 6 in Peekskill. Parking is available along Cross Road, which connects NY 403 with US 9, about 0.1 mile north of the trail crossing at the junction (there is abundant poison ivy in this area, so be careful when getting out of your car).

THE HIKE

From the junction of US 9 and NY 403, head west on the AT, crossing a field on puncheons, then passing through a gap in a stone wall. Soon, the trail turns right and ascends gradually on an old carriage road. In half a mile, after crossing a stream, follow the white blazes as they turn uphill and begin a steeper climb on a footpath. (Ahead, the carriage road is the route of the yellow-blazed Carriage Connector Trail, which will be your return route.) Near the top of the hill, turn sharply left, as the blue-blazed Osborn Loop Trail leaves to the right. You now join another carriage road, this one relatively level. You have now hiked for about a mile and have gained about 500 feet in elevation.

Continue south along the AT for another mile to a junction with the Curry Pond Trail, marked by a triple-yellow blaze. Turn right onto the yellow-blazed Curry Pond Trail, which heads downhill through dense mountain laurel thickets, passing interesting rock outcrops along the way.

After crossing its inlet stream, the trail reaches Curry Pond. Your impression will depend on the recent weather; the pond is just a big swamp during low water, but small wildlife abounds at this peaceful and seldom-visited spot. Another five minutes of walking brings you to the end of the Curry Pond Trail at a junction with the Osborn Loop Trail. Turn right and follow the Osborn Loop Trail, which soon turns right, leaving the carriage road. The path crosses several small streams, bears left, and climbs along an old stone wall. At the top of the climb, the trail bears right, with views to the left through the trees over the Hudson River 700 feet below.

The Osborn Loop Trail now begins a switchback descent of 150 vertical feet before resuming its northerly course. It passes through an area that was devastated by severe localized storms on May 15, 2018. You'll descend to cross a small stream, then climb to an intersection with the red-blazed Sugarloaf Trail at the height of the land.

You'll return to this intersection, but for now turn left and follow the red-blazed trail, which ascends about 220 vertical feet to the summit of Sugarloaf Hill. The trail climbs steeply, follows the crest of the narrow ridge (passing a west-facing viewpoint created by the May 2018 storms), and then descends slightly to reach one of the best viewpoints over the Hudson River: Anthony's Nose, Bear Mountain, and Dunderberg Mountain frame the Bear Mountain Bridge. This is a good spot for a break. You should be able to spot the interesting patch of prickly pear cactus on the warmer south-facing slope.

After enjoying the spectacular views from the summit of Sugarloaf Hill, retrace your steps to the intersection with the Osborn Loop Trail. Continue straight ahead, following the blue-blazed Osborn Loop Trail along a wide carriage road. Soon, you'll pass a large gazebo, rebuilt in the late 1990s by equestrian users of the area. After passing a small pond with a stone dam on the right, the blue-blazed Osborn Loop Trail makes a sharp right turn, but you should continue ahead on the carriage road, now following the yellow blazes of the Carriage Connector Trail. The trail soon turns sharply right and levels off, making walking easy.

When the Carriage Connector Trail ends at a junction with the white-blazed AT, continue ahead along the carriage road, now following the white blazes. Retrace your steps along the AT until you reach the intersection of NY 403 and US 9, then turn left and continue to Cross Road, where you parked your car.

PRICKLY PEAR CACTUS ON SUGARLOAF HILL

Breakneck Ridge/ Undercliff Loop

TOTAL DISTANCE: 7.5 miles

WALKING TIME: 6 hours

ELEVATION GAIN: 2,273 feet

MAPS: USGS 7.5' West Point; NY–NJTC East Hudson Trails #102

TRAILHEAD GPS COORDINATES: N 41° 25' 36" W 73° 57' 56"

Hudson Highlands State Park Preserve had its inception in 1938, when 177 acres was donated to the state by the Hudson River Conservation Society. Land acquisition continued and resulted in the creation of one of the most spectacular hiking venues in the state, with its acreage now encompassing over 8,700 acres. Here, the Hudson River becomes narrow and winding as it curls between Breakneck Point and Storm King, with towering cliffs on both sides. The construction in 1916 of the Storm King Highway (now NY 218) around the steep slopes of Storm King Mountain on the west side of the river was a remarkable engineering feat, as was the tunnel blasted through bedrock in 1912 to carry the waters of the Catskill Aqueduct 1,100 feet beneath the river. The handsome Bear Mountain Bridge was conceived in 1922 and opened in 1924, but in spite of its technological success, the suspension bridge was a financial failure for its private owners.

Climbing the Breakneck Ridge Trail from NY 9D to the top of the ridge is one of the most popular hiking adventures in the Hudson Highlands, in large part due to the strenuous effort encountered while scrambling up the very steep face. However, the hike described does not follow this portion of the Breakneck Ridge Trail, which is overused and can be dangerous in certain weather conditions. The route of this hike takes the walker on the newer Undercliff Trail, constructed by volunteers of the New York–New Jersey Trail Conference in 1997, which has comparable views, and then follows the upper section of the Breakneck Ridge Trail. The going is moderately strenuous, with two sections of boulder scrambling on the Undercliff Trail, so be sure to allow sufficient time to enjoy the outing.

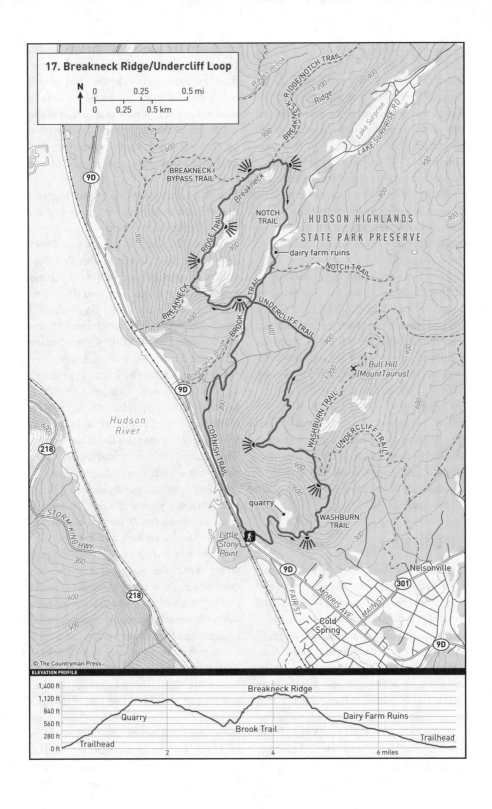

17. Breakneck Ridge/Undercliff Loop

N
0   0.25   0.5 mi
0   0.25   0.5 km

9D

BREAKNECK
BYPASS TRAIL

Wades Brook

BREAKNECK RIDGE/NOTCH TRAIL

1,200
Ridge

900

Lake Surprise

LAKE SURPRISE RD

900

Breakneck

NOTCH
TRAIL

RIDGE TRAIL

HUDSON HIGHLANDS

STATE PARK PRESERVE

BREAKNECK

900

dairy farm ruins

NOTCH TRAIL

TRAIL

UNDERCLIFF TRAIL

900

600

Breakneck Brook BROOK TRAIL

300

Bull Hill
(Mount Taurus)

1,200

WASHBURN TRAIL

UNDERCLIFF TRAIL

600

Hudson
River

CORNISH TRAIL

300

218

900

900

600

STORM KING HWY

300

quarry

WASHBURN
TRAIL

300

600

218

Little
Stony
Point

9D

300

Nelsonville

301

900

FAIR ST

MORRIS AVE

MAIN ST

9D

Cold
Spring

9D

© The Countryman Press

ELEVATION PROFILE

1,400 ft		Breakneck Ridge	
1,120 ft			
840 ft	Quarry		Dairy Farm Ruins
560 ft		Brook Trail	
280 ft	Trailhead		Trailhead
0 ft		2	4	6 miles

GETTING THERE

Drive 0.6 mile north on NY 9D from its junction with NY 301 in the village of Cold Spring to a small parking area on the east side of the road. Another small parking area is available on the west side of NY 9D, where a bridge gives access over the railroad tracks onto Little Stony Point (with a short loop trail). The trailhead can also be reached from the north by driving south on NY 9D approximately 2 miles from the Breakneck Ridge tunnel.

For hikers without a car, the east side of the Hudson River can be reached using Metro-North's Hudson Line, which offers hourly service from Grand Central Terminal in New York City to the Cold Spring station. For more information on train schedules, go to www.mta .info. The walk from the train station to the Washburn trailhead is 0.8 mile. Turn left at Fair Street, across the street from the village hall. When Fair Street ends at NY 9D, turn left onto a trail that parallels NY 9D to the west. The trailhead (on the east side of the road) is a short distance ahead.

THE HIKE

From the northern end of the parking area on the east side of the road, proceed north on the white-blazed Washburn Trail. In 100 feet, you'll reach a junction with the blue-blazed Cornish Trail, which continues straight ahead. The Cornish Trail will be your return route, but for now bear right and continue to follow the Washburn Trail uphill along an old road once used to access a quarry.

In half a mile, you'll reach the site of the quarry, which was opened in 1931 by the Hudson River Stone Corporation and closed in 1967. It is now growing in

with grasses and small trees, though remnants of an old circular road on the quarry floor are still visible. Just before reaching the quarry, the white blazes lead sharply right and skirt around the south end of the quarry rim. On the way, you'll see old pieces of iron piping and cables that remain as evidence of the past operation.

The trail resumes its climb, leaving the eroded quarry road and going up over a hump on the ridge to the right. Soon, you'll reach a panoramic viewpoint over the Hudson River. You now continue uphill, and after climbing another 400 vertical feet, you'll come to another viewpoint. The village of Cold Spring and Constitution Island to the south—along with West Point, Butter Hill, and Storm King across the river (with its gash for the highway)—make up the panorama. During the Revolutionary War, the Hudson River was chained from Constitution Island to West Point to deter the British advance. The heavy iron chain laid in 1778 was never breached. The trail continues to climb steeply and soon reaches a junction with the yellow-blazed Undercliff Trail at about 1,000 feet in elevation. You've now hiked for 1.4 miles.

Turn left onto the Undercliff Trail, which soon emerges on a rock slab overlooking the quarry on the left. At the right-hand end of this viewpoint, the trail meanders around a large glacial erratic—the first of several in the area.

Your first opportunity to see Breakneck Ridge arrives after 0.35 mile on the Undercliff Trail. Upon reaching the far end of the shoulder, the trail emerges on a rock outcrop with a sweeping view to the north. Breakneck Ridge, with its highway and railroad tunnels, is the ragged ridge to the north; Storm King is directly across the river. In clear

RUINS OF THE CORNISH DAIRY FARM

weather, the view includes the Shawangunks and the Catskills.

The Undercliff Trail now turns sharply right and begins to head in a northeast direction. After crossing a stream, it descends on switchbacks to reach the stone foundations of a woods road that was never completed. The trail turns right and proceeds along the road, which soon acquires a dirt-and-gravel surface, crossing a stream on a one-log bridge. After bending to the left, the trail resumes its steady descent, soon beginning to parallel a stream.

A short distance beyond, the Undercliff Trail turns right, crosses the stream, and reaches a wide woods road—the route of the red-blazed Brook Trail. You'll be returning on the Brook Trail, but the hike continues along the yellow-blazed Undercliff Trail. (If you'd like to cut the hike short, turn left onto the Brook Trail, then bear left onto the blue-blazed Cornish Trail and continue down to NY 9D.)

The Undercliff Trail now briefly turns left onto the woods road, then turns right, crosses Breakneck Brook on a bridge, and soon reaches the most rugged and exciting part of the hike. Follow yellow blazes up a boulder field to the base of a cliff wall, and just as it looks as if the trail leads over the cliff edge in front, make a left turn downhill away from the cliff wall. Turn right to begin a switchback climb around and through large boulders, passing under cliffs on the way to the notch. In three-quarters of a mile from the bridge over the Breakneck Brook, you'll reach the end of the Undercliff Trail. Turn right onto the white-blazed Breakneck Ridge Trail.

The Breakneck Ridge Trail follows an undulating footpath along the ridge, which takes you up and down over several false summits. The Hudson River and the Newburgh-Beacon Bridge are visible to the left when the leaves are off the trees, and on your right you'll be able to look down on Lake Surprise and its camp. Along the way, watch for an attractive wetland filled with cattails on the right.

When you reach a junction with the

BREAKNECK RIDGE FROM THE UNDERCLIFF TRAIL

red-blazed Breakneck Bypass Trail, which begins on the left at a large boulder, continue ahead on the white-blazed Breakneck Ridge Trail. A short distance beyond, the trail climbs to a small rocky knob. This is the end of the climbing for the hike; the rest of the way is downhill.

After leaving this high point, watch carefully for the junction with the blue-blazed Notch Trail halfway down a steep, rocky descent. Turn right onto the Notch Trail (if you start to follow both white and blue blazes, you've gone too far). The trail descends steeply along the side of the hill, then turns right onto a woods road and levels off.

Soon, you'll pass a dam and several derelict buildings. These ruins are the remnants of a dairy farm once operated by family named Cornish. The Notch Trail bears left and passes these ruins. A short distance beyond, the Notch Trail turns sharply left, but you should continue ahead (parallel to Breakneck Brook), now following the red-blazed Brook Trail.

In 0.2 mile, you'll come to the wooden bridge on the Undercliff Trail that you crossed earlier on the hike, but you should proceed straight ahead, continuing to follow the red blazes of the Brook Trail. Breakneck Brook is on the right, and more remnants from the past—a small concrete building and a dam—line its course.

A short distance beyond, you'll reach a fork. Bear left, leaving the Brook Trail, and begin to follow the blue-blazed Cornish Trail, which soon crosses the route of the Catskill Aqueduct. The trail follows an old road down to NY 9D, swinging first right and then left, and passing a cement-and-stone water tank and the ruins of the mansion of the estate of Edward G. Cornish, chairman of the board of the National Lead Company, who lived here during the 1920s. The mansion was destroyed by fire in 1956.

The road, now paved, continues to descend toward the river. Down to the right, the Metro-North railroad tracks and NY 9D can be seen. Turn sharply left just before the concrete pillars at NY 9D and continue along the Cornish Trail, which now follows a footpath, for another five minutes back to your car.

18

Fishkill Ridge

TOTAL DISTANCE: 7 miles

WALKING TIME: 5 hours

ELEVATION GAIN: 2,112 feet

MAPS: USGS 7.5' West Point; USGS 7.5' Wappingers Falls; NY–NJTC East Hudson Trails #102

TRAILHEAD GPS COORDINATES: N 41° 29' 17.5" W 73° 54' 31"

The land traversed by this hike along the Fishkill Ridge was purchased in 1992–93 by the Scenic Hudson Land Trust with funding from the Lila Acheson and DeWitt Wallace Fund, established by the founders of *Reader's Digest*. It was subsequently transferred to the State of New York and now forms a part of Hudson Highlands State Park Preserve.

Standing as the northern gateway to the famed Hudson Highlands, the area's rocky outcrops offer panoramic views of the Hudson River and the Catskill Mountains. Turkey vultures, eagles, hawks, and falcons soar high above the cliffs of this rugged 1,000-plus-acre site. This "lollipop-loop" hike includes a steep climb up (and back down), but the loop itself is moderate. Hunting is not allowed, but the start of the hike is near a private shooting preserve. Extra caution should be taken during big-game hunting season, usually mid-November through mid-December. Because of the steepness of the climb, this hike is also best saved for cooler days.

GETTING THERE

To reach the trailhead in North Highland, proceed north on US 9 from its junction with NY 301 for 3.3 miles and turn left onto Old Albany Post Road, a semicircle loop with two connections to US 9 some 0.4 mile apart. If you reach the Putnam–Dutchess County boundary (marked by a sign), you've gone 0.1 mile past the second connection. If coming from the north, use Exit 13 of I-84 and proceed south on US 9 for 2.6 miles to the junction on your right, 0.1 mile past the Putnam–Dutchess boundary.

Proceed along Old Albany Post Road, and park along the shoulder of the road. Parking is available adjacent to a bridge a short distance north of the trailhead.

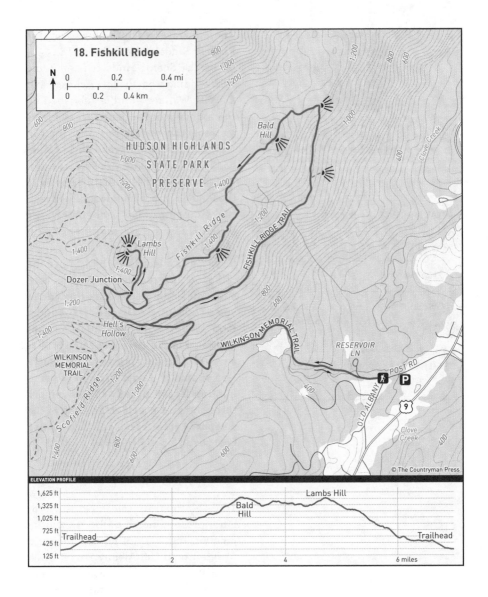

18. Fishkill Ridge

ELEVATION PROFILE

The trail itself starts at a junction with the private Reservoir Lane (open to hikers, but not to their vehicles).

THE HIKE

Walk to the junction with Reservoir Lane where the yellow-blazed Wilkinson Memorial Trail, named after a dedicated trail worker, begins. Walk up the dirt road, passing around a metal gate.

Soon afterward, the trail turns sharply left into the woods and begins a moderate climb.

The climb eases as the trail passes a dam and circles an unnamed pond that straddles the Putnam–Dutchess boundary. From here, there is a good view up to Hell's Hollow, the rugged gap between the ridges.

Soon, the serious 600-foot climb begins. Half of this climb is on woods roads, with switchbacks moderating the ascent, but other sections just go up—straight up.

As the Wilkinson Memorial Trail nears the ridgetop at almost 1,100 feet, it turns left onto a woods road. Here, the white-blazed Fishkill Ridge Trail begins on the right. The loop, which you will follow in a counterclockwise direction, begins here. You will return to this point before heading down the mountain. Turn right, leaving the Wilkinson Memorial Trail, and begin to follow the white-blazed Fishkill Ridge Trail.

Following a woods road, the Fishkill Ridge Trail begins by losing a little elevation and then starts to climb—first gradually, then more steeply. About 1.3 miles along the Fishkill Ridge Trail, it climbs steeply through an eroded section. When you get to this point, pay careful attention to the blazes—you will soon reach a sharp left turn, which is easily missed. If the grade moderates and you see no blazes, go back to be sure you have not missed this turn.

You're at about 1,300 feet elevation as the trail makes this left turn and climbs to the open summit of Bald Hill. The summit (elevation 1,500 feet) provides expansive views to the east, but as the trail begins to descend, there is an even better view from a rock outcrop just off the trail to the left. This overlook is a good place for a break.

Far to the south, an unusual view of a bend in the Hudson makes it look more like a large lake. The grassy area on the mountaintop ahead is Glynwood Farm in Fahnestock State Park (Hike #20). The skyline of New York City, as well as the tops of the towers of the George Washington Bridge, can be seen on a clear day.

About 15 more minutes along the trail is another fine 360-degree view

DOZER JUNCTION

that includes an unsightly quarry. As you continue walking, you'll pass more viewpoints, including one that includes Lake Valhalla to the south.

The trail now dips toward Hell's Hollow—you'll assume you're about to descend. However, steep drop-offs preclude a direct course. Instead, the trail bends right, climbs, and makes a short descent to a woods road.

Known by hikers as "Dozer Junction," this spot is the start of a blue-blazed connecting trail. As for the name, "Dozer Junction": To your left, down the woods road just a few yards, is an abandoned bulldozer. Hop on up. The backdrop makes for a fine photo, especially if one of you climbs into the driver's seat.

You'll soon return to this spot, but for now proceed across the road and continue to follow the white-blazed trail for a 10-minute, 120-foot climb to the summit of Lambs Hill (elevation 1,500 feet). The short climb is worth the effort, especially if you go a few yards beyond the summit, where the views really open up. Below, the Hudson stretches out in all its magnificence. The Newburgh–Beacon Bridge is to the northwest, with the Mid-Hudson Bridge

VIEW OF THE HUDSON RIVER AND THE CATSKILLS FROM LAMBS HILL

at Poughkeepsie visible farther up the river, and the high peaks of the Catskills on the horizon to the west. North and South Beacon Mountains, with their ubiquitous transmission towers and a reservoir between them, are just to the southwest. If you look to the right of North Beacon Mountain and across the Hudson, you may see a tower atop a rise on the far horizon. That's New Jersey's High Point Monument, more than 40 miles away.

Retrace your steps to Dozer Junction, turn right, and head downhill on the blue-blazed woods road past the bulldozer. Soon, you'll pass some iron ruins. Just beyond (but before a big washout cuts across the woods road), the blue trail turns sharply left and heads downhill toward the gap between two peaks. After only a minute (at a low point), the trail reaches a T-junction with another woods road. Turn left here, head slightly uphill, and bear left at a fork. Just ahead, you'll see the yellow blazes of the Wilkinson Memorial Trail. Continue straight ahead (not uphill), now following the yellow-blazed trail.

This section of the Wilkinson Memorial Trail follows both woods roads and narrow footpaths. At one point, it passes beneath a dramatic rock outcrop. In a quarter mile, you'll spot the three white blazes of the Fishkill Ridge Trail where you began the loop earlier in the hike.

Turn right, continuing to follow the yellow-blazed Wilkinson Memorial Trail, which heads steeply downhill. You're now retracing your steps, following the yellow blazes all the way back to Old Albany Post Road, where you left your car.

East Mountain/ Round Hill Loop

This hike follows less-used trails in the northwest corner of Fahnestock State Park in Putnam County. The old rock walls seen on your hike are remnants from when the land was cleared for farming. The area was also once used for iron mining, and roads and railroads were constructed to transport the iron ore and farm produce to the Hudson River and elsewhere. The route of this hike is mostly through hardwoods with limited views. It includes some moderate climbing and ends with a pleasant walk alongside an attractive stream.

TOTAL DISTANCE: 7.3 miles

WALKING TIME: 4.5 hours

ELEVATION GAIN: 1,578 feet

MAPS: USGS 7.5′ Oscawana Lake; NY–NJTC East Hudson Trails #103

TRAILHEAD GPS COORDINATES: N 41° 26′ 36″ W 73° 54′ 54″

GETTING THERE

From the intersection of NY 301 and US 9 just east of Cold Spring, proceed north on US 9 for 0.2 mile, then turn right onto a paved road at a brown sign for the HUB-BARD LODGE. Bear left at the fork, continue past a house on the left, and park along the right side of the road.

THE HIKE

Walk back along the paved road to a junction with a grassy road on the left. Turn left on the grassy road. Almost immediately, you'll reach a gate. A triple-white blaze on the gate marks the start of the white-blazed School Mountain Road, and a triple-blue blaze marks the start of the blue-blazed Fahnestock Trail.

Follow both blue markers and white markers along School Mountain Road—a multi-use woods road that makes for easy walking in a tranquil setting. In the next few minutes, the road crosses two streams—the first, on a wooden bridge, and the second, on a steel-plate bridge. In 0.4 mile, you'll notice two stone pillars on the left flanking a woods road

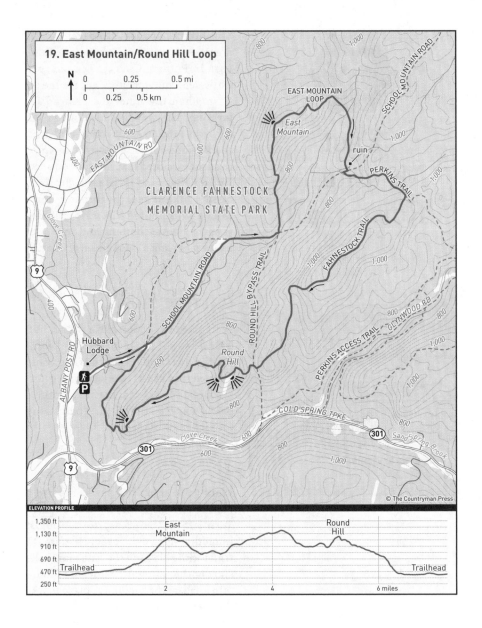

19. East Mountain/Round Hill Loop

EAST MOUNTAIN
LOOP

East
Mountain

ruin

PERKINS TRAIL

CLARENCE FAHNESTOCK
MEMORIAL STATE PARK

SCHOOL MOUNTAIN ROAD

EAST MOUNTAIN RD

Clove Creek

9

ROUND HILL BYPASS TRAIL

FAHNESTOCK TRAIL

GLYNWOOD RD

Hubbard
Lodge

Round
Hill

PERKINS ACCESS TRAIL

ALBANY POST RD

COLD SPRING TPKE

Clove Creek

301

Sand Spring Brook

301

9

© The Countryman Press

ELEVATION PROFILE

1,350 ft		East		Round	
1,130 ft		Mountain		Hill	
910 ft					
690 ft					
470 ft	Trailhead				Trailhead
250 ft		2	4	6 miles	

that leads to the site of the old Hubbard mansion. There used to be another steel-plate bridge here, but it was destroyed by Hurricane Irene in August 2011, and hikers now have to cross the stream on two I-beams. On the other side of the stream, the Fahnestock Trail—marked with blue disks—departs to the right. At the end of the hike, you'll return to this junction before retracing your steps on School Mountain Road.

Continue ahead on the white-blazed School Mountain Road, crossing two more steel-plate bridges. After a while, you'll begin a steady ascent between old rock walls. After crossing a wooden footbridge, you'll notice a triple-red blaze on the left which marks the start of the East

ABANDONED FARMHOUSE ALONG SCHOOL MOUNTAIN ROAD

Mountain Loop. Bear left onto the East Mountain Loop, leaving School Mountain Road, which heads to the right.

Recross the stream on another wooden footbridge and follow the red blazes uphill along a woods road, paralleling an old rock wall on your right. The footpath crosses another wall, then snakes upward to the summit of East Mountain, which offers a limited seasonal view of the Fishkill Ridge.

The East Mountain Loop now descends until it reaches a woods road, where it turns right onto the road and descends to cross a stream. Just before the stream crossing, the rusted iron wheels of an old farm wagon may be seen to the right of the trail. The trail now begins to ascend along the road, bordered by stone walls on each side.

After passing an abandoned farmhouse on the left, the East Mountain Loop ends at School Mountain Road.

Continue by turning right onto School Mountain Road, and you'll almost immediately cross a stream on rocks. On the left, you will see a triple-yellow blaze that marks the start of the Perkins Trail. If you wish to cut the hike short, continue ahead on School Mountain Road to your car, but if you wish to complete the entire loop, turn left onto the yellow-blazed Perkins Trail.

The trail climbs, sometimes on rocks, along a cascading stream. In about half a mile, it arrives at a junction with the blue-blazed Fahnestock Trail. Turn right onto the Fahnestock Trail, now following only blue blazes. The Fahnestock Trail proceeds to climb, then descends into a valley, where it briefly joins the green-blazed Round Hill Bypass Trail. Continue along the Fahnestock Trail as it turns left and begins a steep climb of Round Hill. At the top, the trail reaches an east-facing viewpoint over the hills of

STONE WALLS ALONG THE FAHNESTOCK TRAIL

Fahnestock State Park, with a communications tower on the right. The trail then descends a little to reach a southwest-facing viewpoint from a rock ledge on the left.

After descending some more on a winding path, the trail climbs out of a shallow ravine and continues to descend gradually along a cedar-studded ridge. Soon, you'll begin to hear traffic on US 9. About a mile from the summit, you'll reach a limited west-facing viewpoint amid red cedars, with Bull Hill (Mount Taurus) in the distance. You'll also be able to see the junction of US 9 with NY 301, only a short distance below. This is the final viewpoint of the hike, so you might want to take a break and enjoy the view.

The Fahnestock Trail continues to descend rather steeply on switchbacks. At the base of the descent, the trail turns right onto a woods road which parallels a stream containing many moss-covered rocks. In 0.6 mile, you'll reach School Mountain Road at the junction noted earlier. Cross the I-beam bridge over the stream, turn left, and walk back to your car along School Mountain Road.

Jordan Pond/ Perkins Trail Loop

This hike goes by three scenic ponds—Jordan Pond, Beaver Pond, and an unnamed pond known to local residents as the "Big Pond." On the way, it passes through preserved farmlands that may remind you of walking in southern England. The section that runs along the cascading Clove Creek is particularly beautiful, and visiting this area in June, when the mountain laurel blooms, is especially rewarding. The hike follows portions of the Charcoal Burners Trail, the Fahnestock Trail, the Perkins Trail, and the Cabot Trail.

TOTAL DISTANCE: 7.2 miles

WALKING TIME: 4 hours

ELEVATION GAIN: 1,209 feet

MAPS: USGS 7.5' West Point; USGS 7.5' Oscawana Lake; NY–NJTC East Hudson Trails #103

TRAILHEAD GPS COORDINATES: N 41° 26' 36.5" W 73° 51' 36"

GETTING THERE

From the junction of NY 9D and NY 301 in Cold Spring, proceed east on NY 301. In 5 miles, Dennytown Road begins on the right. Continue for another 0.6 mile on NY 301 and look carefully for a trail crossing, marked by a brown wand on the south side of the road and a sign for the Charcoal Burners Trail on the north side. Park along the shoulder near the trail crossing. If coming from the east, the distance to the trailhead from the junction of NY 301 with the Taconic State Parkway is 2.9 miles.

THE HIKE

Cross to the north side of the road and proceed north on the red-blazed Charcoal Burners Trail (named for the men who felled trees in the area during the nineteenth century and carefully burned them to make charcoal). The trail briefly parallels the road, then bears left and heads into the woods. Soon, you'll reach the eastern end of the yellow-blazed Perkins Trail (named for the former owners of this land), but you should continue ahead on the red-blazed Charcoal Burners Trail. The relatively

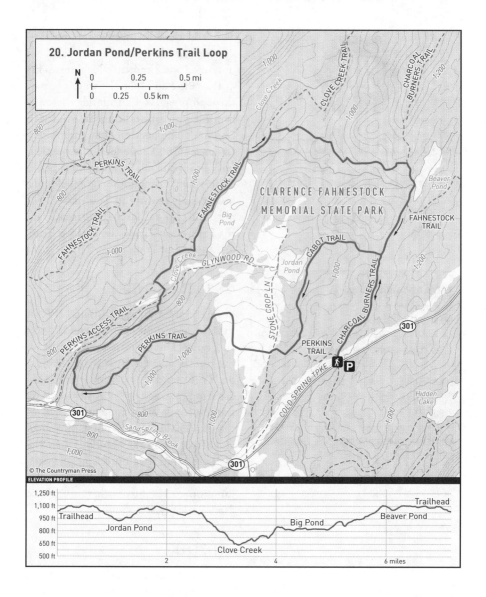

level trail passes through thickets of mountain laurel, with an understory of blueberry bushes.

In 0.6 mile, a cairn and a triple-white blaze mark the start of the Cabot Trail. Turn left and follow the Cabot Trail, which descends gradually, reaching Jordan Pond in 0.5 mile. After crossing the inlet of the pond, a short side trail leads down to the water. Here, a bench has been placed on a rock slab overlooking the pond—a great spot to take a break.

When you're ready to continue, return to the white-blazed Cabot Trail and turn right. The trail begins to ascend, soon passing a large rock outcrop on the left. After leveling off, the trail passes between old stone walls and emerges onto a clearing, with fir trees on the right. Here, the Cabot Trail ends, and you should continue ahead on

FIELD ALONG THE PERKINS TRAIL

the yellow-blazed Perkins Trail, which enters from the left. The Perkins Trail briefly follows a wide grassy road, then curves to the right.

Just beyond, you'll pass an unlocked gate, the first of several you'll encounter in this portion of the hike, which traverses private property and runs along several active fields. Please stay on the trail. Just ahead, the Perkins Trail turns left on a dirt road for about 150 feet, then turns right, passes a wooden gate, and begins to parallel an active field that attracts many butterflies, insects, and birds. Continue ahead, following a narrow corridor between a fence on the right and an old stone wall on the left, with views to the right over the ridge to the north. Soon, you'll pass a large horse barn on the left.

Beyond the barn, the trail follows a wide grassy path between two fences. It then turns right and continues along the right side of another large field. After descending for a short distance, the trail turns left onto a farm road that crosses the field (the turn is marked by a double yellow blaze on a post). A large pond may be seen below on the right. Continue along the farm road, which crosses two more fields. There are relatively few blazes in this section, so take care to follow the road across the fields. Bear right at the next fork (this turn is marked by a double blaze), and emerge onto another field. Here, the trail bears right, skirting the perimeter of the field on a grassy road. At the end of the field, the trail reenters the woods at a gap in a stone wall.

After reaching a limited viewpoint to the north and west from a rock outcrop, the trail begins a steady descent, passing some mountain laurel thickets along the way. Soon, you'll hear the sounds of traffic, as the trail comes close to NY 301. Near the base of the descent, the trail swings sharply to the right, heads away from the busy road, and begins to parallel the cascading Clove Creek. For a splendid half mile, the trail runs along this beautiful stream. The

JORDAN POND

trail then bears left, crosses the stream on a wooden bridge, crosses the private Glynwood Road (a dirt road), and climbs rather steeply to a grassy woods road.

The red-blazed Perkins Access Trail begins on the left, but you should turn right to continue along the yellow-blazed Perkins Trail, which follows the road. In a third of a mile, you'll come to a T-junction, where the yellow-blazed trail turns left. In another 150 feet, it reaches a junction with the blue-blazed Fahnestock Trail. The Perkins Trail turns left here, but you should bear right, leaving the Perkins Trail, and follow the blue-blazed Fahnestock Trail. A short distance ahead, you'll pass a large pond on the right, visible through the trees. Although the pond is unnamed, it is known to local residents as the "Big Pond."

Just beyond the northern end of the pond, the trail bears right, crosses the pond's inlet on a moss-covered cement bridge, and begins a steady climb on an eroded woods road. At the crest of the rise, follow the Fahnestock Trail as it turns right, leaving the woods road, and heads into the woods on a footpath (the white-blazed Clove Creek Trail, which begins here, continues ahead on the road). The Fahnestock Trail descends a switchback, climbs a rock outcrop, and continues to ascend more gently through mountain laurel and blueberries. Eventually, it turns right onto a woods road. The trail briefly turns left onto another woods road, then turns right and continues on a footpath through dense barberry bushes.

After a moderate climb, the blue-blazed Fahnestock Trail turns right onto a wide grassy woods road. A short distance beyond, the red-blazed Charcoal Burners Trail joins from the left. Continue ahead, now following both blue and red blazes, and descend to Beaver Pond. The trail briefly follows the shore, offering a panoramic view over this scenic pond.

The trail now turns right, descends to cross the outlet of the pond on a concrete bridge below the dam, then climbs through highbush blueberry bushes and dense mountain laurel thickets to reach another junction, where the two trails diverge. The blue-blazed Fahnestock Trail departs to the left, but you should continue ahead, now following only the red-blazed Charcoal Burners Trail. You'll pass the start of the white-blazed Cabot Trail on the right and retrace your steps on the red-blazed trail to NY 301, where the hike began.

Heart of Fahnestock

This pleasant woods walk passes peaceful lakes and lush swamps, and even uses a Civil War–era railroad bed. As you walk along, picture the rural communities that once dominated this region. Old stone walls, foundations, historic mine pits, and woods roads are all that remain of the active history of this now quiet area.

GETTING THERE

To reach the parking area on NY 301, take the Taconic State Parkway to the exit for NY 301 West (Cold Spring). Proceed west on NY 301 for 1.3 miles to a parking area on the north side of the road, on a small peninsula jutting into Canopus Lake. If this lot is full, a second parking area is located a short distance further west, at the Appalachian Trail (AT) crossing.

THE HIKE

Walk over to the other side of NY 301, and head west along the shoulder for a very short distance. You will notice, on the guardrail, a triple-blue blaze, which marks the start of the Three Lakes Trail. Climb over the guardrail and scramble down to the trail.

The Three Lakes Trail crosses an old paved road (known as the Philipstown Turnpike) that parallels NY 301 and heads into the woods, following a woods road. Rock cuts and piles of stone (called tailings) are evidence of mining activity in the area from the late 1700s through the late 1800s. The first mine you pass—identifiable only by its tailing pit—belonged to Richard Hopper, who opened it in 1820. The mine remained a small operation until the Civil War, when the heirs sold the mineral rights to Paul S. Forbes, the builder of the

---

TOTAL DISTANCE: 6.4 miles (3.5-mile alternate)

WALKING TIME: 3.5 hours (2-hour alternate)

ELEVATION GAIN: 876 feet

MAPS: USGS 7.5' Oscawana Lake; NY–NJTC East Hudson Trails #103

TRAILHEAD GPS COORDINATES: N 41° 27' 18.5" W 73° 50' 02"

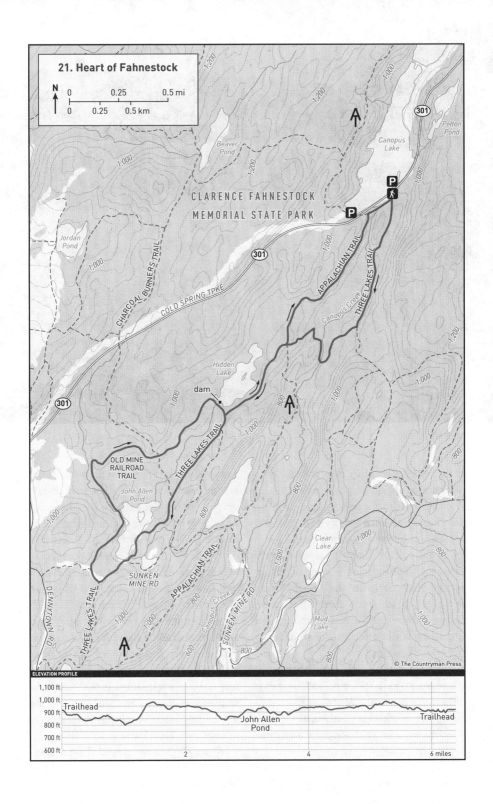

21. Heart of Fahnestock

N
0   0.25   0.5 mi
0   0.25   0.5 km

Beaver
Pond

Canopus
Lake

301

Pelton
Pond

CLARENCE FAHNESTOCK
MEMORIAL STATE PARK

Jordan
Pond

CHARCOAL BURNERS TRAIL

COLD SPRING TPKE

301

P

P

APPALACHIAN TRAIL

Canopus Creek

THREE LAKES TRAIL

301

Hidden
Lake

dam

THREE LAKES TRAIL

OLD MINE
RAILROAD
TRAIL

John Allen
Pond

Clear
Lake

SUNKEN
MINE RD

APPALACHIAN TRAIL

Canopus Creek

SUNKEN MINE RD

Mud
Lake

DENNYTOWN RD

THREE LAKES TRAIL

© The Countryman Press

ELEVATION PROFILE

1,100 ft
1,000 ft
900 ft   Trailhead
800 ft
700 ft
600 ft
                              John Allen
                                Pond
                                                            Trailhead

2   4   6 miles

JOHN ALLEN POND

railway. The mining operations were abandoned after the panic of 1873, and the surrounding land was acquired by Dr. Clarence Fahnestock in 1915 after a series of intervening land sales.

In half a mile, the trail passes a lovely marsh with an extensive stand of phragmites that rustle in the wind. There are many birds here, heard but often unseen. Soon the woods open up, and old stone walls offer evidence of long-gone settlements.

Remember, you are following the blue blazes, not just the obvious footway. There are several points on this hike when the marked trail abruptly leaves a woods road and turns onto a narrower footpath.

One such point comes about three-quarters of a mile into the hike,

as the blue trail turns right, leaving the woods road. If you notice green markers, you've passed the turn and are heading toward the Durland (formerly Clear Lake) Scout Reservation. Continue on the blue-blazed Three Lakes Trail, which passes fields of hay-scented fern and heads down to charming Canopus Creek (the outlet of Canopus Lake). A small, picturesque gorge just upstream is worth a short detour for a peek. The trail crosses the creek on large rock slabs and heads slightly north. It then turns sharply left and climbs through an impressive forest, certainly one of the more handsome second-growth forests in southern New York.

Soon the white-blazed AT crosses, but you should continue ahead on the blue-blazed Three Lakes Trail. You'll now pass through dense mountain laurel thickets. In a short distance, you'll approach the shore of Hidden Lake. At the southern end of the lake, a short unmarked trail on the right leads to the dam, which offers fine views. You may wish to take a short detour out to the dam, then return to the Three Lakes Trail.

For those wanting a shorter hike (so far, you've walked 2 miles), follow the blue blazes back the way you came to the junction with the white-blazed AT. Turn left at the junction and follow the AT for 0.9 mile back to NY 301, then turn right and follow the road to your car, a short distance away.

For those who wish to complete a longer hike, continue south on the Three Lakes Trail, which almost immediately reaches a junction with the yellow-blazed Old Mine Railroad Trail (which begins on the right). This will be your return route, but for now continue ahead on the blue-blazed Three Lakes Trail, which soon leaves the woods road it has been following and continues on a footpath.

About half a mile from the lake, you'll pass the southern terminus of the red-blazed Charcoal Burners Trail in the midst of a laurel grove. A short distance beyond, the trail passes the stone foundations of several buildings from John Allen's homestead. It then turns right and begins to follow an old mine railbed. Soon, it leaves the railbed and crosses a stream on rocks (to the right, the stone abutments of the mine railway are visible, but the bridge is gone).

The trail now arrives at the shore of beautiful John Allen Pond. It parallels the lakeshore for a short distance, reenters the woods, then crosses the outlet of the pond on rocks just below an old stone dam (now breached). It now climbs to the dirt Sunken Mine Road (also known as Sunk Mine Road). Turn right onto the road, passing the southern end of John Allen Pond on the right. In about 0.2 mile, the blue-blazed Three Lakes Trail leaves the road on the left, but you should continue ahead on the road. In another 500 feet, as the road bends to the left, the yellow-blazed Old Mine Railroad Trail begins on the right. Turn right and follow this wide trail, which gradually descends toward John Allen Pond. After approaching the pond, the trail crosses a small stream on rocks.

Note how well the trail is constructed and elevated. No, volunteers did not build this trail. They just used the features that give the trail its name—literally, an old mine-railroad bed.

During the Civil War, a narrow-gauge railroad was built to serve the iron mines in the area. However, the development of open-pit mines in the Midwest in the late 1800s brought these operations to an end. Starting a new life, much of the railbed was opened as a hiking trail in 1994, but in the early 2000s the northern section was closed as a result of constant beaver-caused flooding.

A few more minutes along, the marked trail makes a sharp right. Follow the blazed route, avoiding the woods road that branches left and leads to private land.

About 0.3 mile beyond John Allen Pond, follow the Old Mine Railroad Trail as it turns right, leaving the old railroad bed. Then, in another 0.3 mile, you'll cross the red-blazed Charcoal Burners Trail. Just beyond, look for a large glacial erratic. Doesn't it appear that two trees are supporting the rock?

Continue ahead on the yellow-blazed Old Mine Railroad Trail. Just before reaching Hidden Lake, the trail turns right and crosses the outlet of the lake

STONE ABUTMENT OF THE OLD MINE RAILROAD

below the dam on stepping stones. A short distance beyond, the Old Mine Railroad Trail ends at the blue-blazed Three Lakes Trail. You were here earlier in the hike.

Turn left and proceed north on the Three Lakes Trail for half a mile to the junction with the white-blazed AT, then turn left onto the AT and follow its white blazes along an old railbed. Here, the elevated roadway is as much as 15 feet above the surrounding land. The path continues through a rock cut and overlooks the marsh you passed near the start of the hike.

Soon, you'll begin to hear the sounds of the traffic on NY 301. Follow the AT up to the highway, and turn right to reach your car (or turn right onto a distinct woods road paralleling the highway that takes you back to the hike's starting point).

III.

ROCKLAND COUNTY AND HARRIMAN PARK

Introduction to the Ramapos: Harriman-Bear Mountain State Parks and Rockland County

The Ramapo Mountains extend from northern New Jersey into Rockland and Orange Counties. Their eroded slopes have risen above nearby seas for nearly 600 million years, making them among the oldest landmasses on the continent. These mountains are part of the Reading Prong, which extends from Reading, Pennsylvania, to the Hudson Highlands and north to the Green Mountains of Vermont. This Precambrian formation is the result of periods of intense folding and metamorphism of sediments deposited more than a billion years ago and of intrusions of magma that occurred several times in the Precambrian era. Although these forces leave a complicated picture for the geologist, later events, like the Ice Ages, are much clearer. The striations and polished rocks and the ubiquitous glacial erratics are obvious to the hiker on any walk through the Ramapos.

Whether the name "Ramapo" derives from a Native American name for the potholes that mark the Ramapo River or whether it comes from a Leni-Lenape word that means "place of slanting rock" is not known. The latter is certainly more descriptive, for the views of uplifted faces of various metamorphosed layers are a part of each hike.

HARRIMAN-BEAR MOUNTAIN STATE PARKS

Harriman-Bear Mountain State Parks span most of the Ramapos in New York State. Their origins are unusual. In 1908, the state proposed building a prison at Bear Mountain. Among the many who protested this desecration of beautiful and historic lands was Mary Harriman, widow of the railroad tycoon Edward Harriman, who offered to give the Palisades Interstate Park Commission (PIPC) 10,000 acres, the nucleus of the modern parks. In return, it was agreed that the commission's jurisdiction would be extended north along the Hudson and that the plans for the prison would be dropped. Subsequent gifts and purchases have expanded the park to its present 53,000 acres.

PIPC (often pronounced "pip see"), under the leadership of its president, George W. Perkins, and its general manager and chief engineer, Major William A. Welch, fostered much development, including roads, lakes, and children's camps. In 1910–11, a dock for steamboat excursions and a station on the West Shore Railroad were built at Bear Mountain, and the park officially opened for public use in the summer of 1913. By 1914, it was estimated that

ALONG THE BLUE DISC TRAIL ON BIG PINE HILL IN HAMMAN STATE PARK

more than 1 million people a year visited the park.

The Bear Mountain Inn was completed in 1915. It was constructed with huge boulders and chestnut logs, and at the time guests paid $4.50 per day for a room and three meals. Upstairs, the magnificent fireplace was constructed with stones from old walls.

During the Great Depression, which began in 1929 and continued through the 1930s, new roads, buildings, lakes, and camps were constructed in the parks by workers from the Temporary Emergency Relief Administration, the Works Progress Administration, and the Civilian Conservation Corps.

Although officially separate entities, the two contiguous parks are jointly administered and offer today's hikers more than 225 miles of marked trails. The present hiking trail system within the parks was the vision of early "trampers" belonging to walking clubs in New York City. During the summer of 1920, Major Welch, working with others, formed a permanent federation of hiking clubs known as the Palisades Interstate Park Trail Conference—the root of the present New York–New Jersey Trail Conference (NY–NJTC). Their first venture, the building of the Tuxedo–Jones Point Trail (now known as the Ramapo–Dunderberg Trail), enabled trampers to catch the ferry to New Jersey and the railway to Tuxedo on a Saturday afternoon, spend one night in the woods, and emerge in time to catch a train back to the city on Sunday evening. The first section of the

Appalachian Trail, which now extends for about 2,190 miles from Georgia to Maine, was opened from Arden to Bear Mountain in 1923.

By 1930, new trail building had largely come to an end, but quite soon "trail wars" broke out between competing outdoor clubs. Hiking groups accused one another of establishing their own trails and, even worse, of painting out blazes put on trees by rivals. In addition, individuals began to paint routes for their own use. Kerson Nurian was one of these culprits (Hike #27). It was at this time that trail maintenance standards were established under the guidance of the NY–NJTC. No new trail cutting was permitted without the permission of the group, and the willy-nilly proliferation of new trails ceased.

Today, Harriman-Bear Mountain State Parks are among the most popular hiking destinations for residents of the surrounding area. Although bus transportation is available to both sides of the parks, and the western side is also accessible by commuter trains, most visitors arrive by private automobiles. Especially on weekends and holidays, the parks often attract throngs of people who enjoy the activities in the more developed areas. However, even on busy weekends, you can escape these crowds if you choose to hike in less-used areas of the parks.

Most hikes in Harriman-Bear Mountain State Parks—including 10 hikes described in this book (Hikes #25 to #34)—involve loops that use segments of various trails. Sites of old farms, mines, cemeteries, and other signs of human habitation can often be found, and maps and guidebooks educate the walker. Much detailed history, specifically keyed to the trail system, can be found in *Harriman Trails: A Guide and History* by William J. Myles and Daniel Chazin.

Parking is permitted only in designated areas, and overnight backcountry camping is permitted only at designated shelters. Fires are allowed only at fireplaces at shelters.

OTHER STATE PARKS

From the New York–New Jersey boundary north to Haverstraw, a string of smaller parks is administered by PIPC. These parks provide a route for the Long Path along the Palisades cliffs. Tallman Mountain (Hike #22), Clausland Mountain (a county park), Blauvelt, Hook Mountain (Hike #23), the highly developed Rockland Lake, and High Tor (Hike #24) offer varied opportunities for walking and hiking, as well as more developed recreation, including swimming, tennis, and golf.

Tallman Mountain State Park

TOTAL DISTANCE: 4.3 miles

WALKING TIME: 2.5 hours

ELEVATION GAIN: 452 feet

MAPS: USGS 7.5' Nyack; NY–NJTC Hudson Palisades Trails #109

TRAILHEAD GPS COORDINATES: N 41°00' 55.7 W 73°54' 48.3"

Tallman Mountain State Park extends along the Palisades, overlooking the Hudson River and the Piermont Marsh. It has picnic areas, tennis courts, a running track and a swimming pool, all of which are located at the northern end of the park, just south of Piermont. The southern end of the park is undeveloped.

But if industrialists had their way, the park might look very different today. In the 1920s, a 171-acre parcel at the northern end of the park was owned by the Sparkill Realty Company, which leased the property to the Standard Trap Rock Company. Standard Trap Rock proposed to open the largest quarrying operation ever envisioned along this section of the river, and it began to construct a giant rock-crusher at the base of the cliffs. To prevent this defacement of the Palisades cliffs, the Palisades Interstate Park Commission appropriated the property in 1928, establishing Tallman Mountain State Park.

The 540 acres at the southern end of the park were purchased in 1923 by the Standard Oil Company, which actually constructed an oil tank "farm" on the property. Each tank was surrounded by an earthen berm to contain oil that might seep out of the tanks. The use of beautiful land along the Palisades for this purpose engendered much opposition, and eventually the "farm" was abandoned and the tanks removed. Thanks to the generous donation of funds by Commissioners Rockefeller, Perkins, and Harriman, the Palisades Interstate Park Commission acquired the property from the Standard Oil Company in 1942. Although the land has largely reverted to its natural state, the berms constructed by the Standard Oil Company still remain, and some of them are followed by this hike. Many of the depressions left when the oil tanks

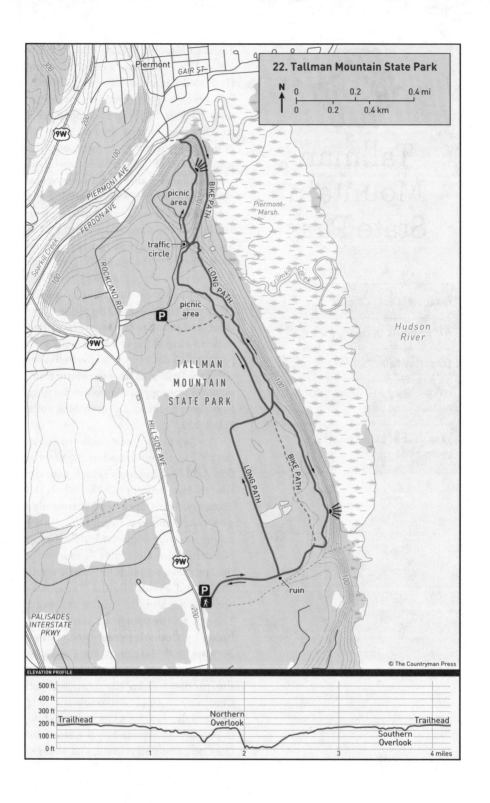

22. Tallman Mountain State Park

N
0   0.2   0.4 mi
0   0.2   0.4 km

Piermont

GAIR ST

9W

PIERMONT AVE

FERDON AVE

Sparkill Creek

ROCKLAND RD

9W

picnic area

BIKE PATH

Piermont Marsh

traffic circle

LONG PATH

picnic area

P

TALLMAN MOUNTAIN STATE PARK

Crumkill Creek

Hudson River

HILLSIDE AVE

LONG PATH

BIKE PATH

9W

P

ruin

PALISADES INTERSTATE PKWY

© The Countryman Press

ELEVATION PROFILE

500 ft
400 ft
300 ft
200 ft   Trailhead
100 ft
0 ft

Northern Overlook

Southern Overlook

Trailhead

1   2   3   4 miles

were removed have now become ponds or wetlands.

Besides offering the opportunity to see how the land was altered nearly a century ago by the oil tank "farm," the hike features panoramic views of the Piermont Marsh and the Hudson River from the Palisades cliffs. Most of the route is relatively level, but there is one steep downhill section where the trail descends on uneven stone steps, and caution must be exercised, especially if the steps are wet or covered with ice or snow.

GETTING THERE

Take the Palisades Interstate Parkway to Exit 4, and proceed north on US 9W for about 1 mile to the traffic light at the intersection of Oak Tree Road/Washington Spring Road. Continue north on US 9W for another quarter mile. After passing The Market on the right, turn right into a parking area on the east side of the road. A small sign identifies the parking area as part of Tallman Mountain State Park, but this sign is not easily seen from US 9W.

THE HIKE

From the parking area, proceed east on a level gravel road, following the aqua blazes of the Long Path. In 0.3 mile, you'll notice the ruins of a brick-and-concrete building on the right. Follow the Long Path as it turns left here, leaving the road. After crossing a wet area on plank bridging, the trail begins to run along a berm constructed by the Standard Oil Company in the 1920s. The trail follows the berm for about a third of a mile, passing a pond on the right and wetlands on either side. When the wide berm abruptly ends, the Long Path turns right onto a narrower berm which crosses another wet area.

About a mile from the start of the hike, the Long Path crosses a wide gravel road, the route of the Tallman Bike Path. This will be your return route, but for now you should continue ahead, following the aqua blazes of the Long Path. After crossing the road, the trail curves to the left and begins to head north along the top of the Palisades Escarpment, with views through the trees of the reed-covered Piermont Marsh directly below. After crossing a small stream, the trail follows an old road with a rough stone wall on the left.

In 0.35 mile from the Bike Path crossing, the Long Path bears right at a fork and descends to reach the south end of a picnic area. With a gated road visible on the left, the Long Path bears right again and soon passes a stone comfort station on the left (closed in the winter) and a large group of picnic tables. Just beyond, the trail bears right at a fork, descends a slope, and briefly continues ahead along a stone-lined road. The trail bears right, leaving the road, and continues to descend more steeply on a footpath and stone steps. Use caution here, as the steps are uneven and may be slippery. At the bottom of the steps, the trail turns sharply right and descends on a switchback.

The Long Path turns right at the base of the descent and crosses a stream on a wooden bridge. Just ahead, the park swimming pool is visible below on the right, with the Piermont Marsh and the Hudson River beyond. A bench has been placed here, and you might want to pause to enjoy the view.

When you're ready to continue, follow the Long Path as it turns sharply left and climbs a paved path to a traffic circle. The marked trail bears right and

PIERMONT AND HOOK MOUNTAIN FROM THE LONG PATH

crosses the park road leading down to the river. On the other side of the road, it goes up wooden steps and continues to climb rather steeply to the North Picnic Area. At the top, it turns right and follows the paved park road that runs close to the edge of the escarpment.

After passing a stone picnic shelter on the left, the Long Path reaches a viewpoint over the Hudson River from an open area on the right. The mile-long Piermont Pier (built by the Erie Railroad in 1838 as a terminus for its trains from the west) juts into the river to the north, with the Tappan Zee Bridge beyond. Piermont Marsh is directly below, and the villages of Irvington and Dobbs Ferry may be seen across the river.

Continue ahead along the paved road. In another 200 feet, as the road bends to the left, follow the aqua blazes which leave the road and continue ahead to a panoramic viewpoint. This one looks north along the Hudson, with the village of Piermont directly below and Hook Mountain jutting into the river in the distance. Benches have been placed here to encourage you to pause and enjoy the view. The Long Path now bears right and steeply descends to the river level on rough, uneven rock steps. Use caution here, especially when you reach the very steep section at the end of the descent.

At the bottom, leave the blazed Long Path and turn right onto an unmarked gravel road which curves to the right and begins to parallel the reeds of the Piermont Marsh. This is the Tallman Bike Path, which you will follow for most of the remainder of the hike. When the gravel road ends at a barrier of wooden posts, bear right and continue uphill on the paved park road. When you reach the traffic circle, turn left at the end of the guardrail and then immediately bear right onto an unmarked footpath that leads into the woods (do not turn left onto the paved path that descends to the left). Follow this unmarked path, which heads south, parallel to the park road. After crossing an open area, the unmarked path joins a moss-covered paved path that comes in from the left and soon ends at a park road that leads to the South Picnic Area.

Turn left onto this paved road, then bear right at the fork, following the green BIKE ROUTE sign. Continue along the road for about 500 feet. When you reach a barricade of wooden posts on your right, turn right onto another paved road, closed to vehicular traffic (but open to bicycles). The pavement ends at the top of the hill.

Continue ahead on the Bike Path (now unpaved) for another third of a mile. When you reach the location where the Long Path crosses the Bike Path, turn left onto this aqua-blazed trail. Continue for about 300 feet until you approach the cliff edge, and you'll notice an unmarked footpath that joins from the right. Turn right here and head south, with views of the Hudson River to the left through the trees. In about half a mile, you'll reach an open rock ledge on the left that affords spectacular views over the river, the Piermont Marsh below, and the Tappan Zee Bridge to the north.

After taking in the view, continue south along the unmarked trail. In about 500 feet, just before reaching a deep ravine, the trail turns right and begins to head west. Just beyond, bear right at a fork (be alert for this turn, which can easily be missed, as the left fork is more distinct). The unmarked trail soon ends at the gravel road followed by the Bike Path. Turn left onto this road and follow it back to the parking area where the hike began.

Hook Mountain

TOTAL DISTANCE: 12 miles (6-mile alternate)

WALKING TIME: 6.5 hours (3.5-hour alternate)

ELEVATION GAIN: 2,681 feet

MAPS: USGS 7.5' Haverstraw; USGS 7.5' Nyack; NY–NJTC Hudson Palisades Trails #110 and #111

TRAILHEAD GPS COORDINATES: N 41° 07' 14.5" W 73° 54' 41"

The towering cliffs of the Hook have awed travelers to southern New York State for centuries. Henry Hudson and the sailors who followed took note of this impressive headland as they made their way up the Hudson River. The cliffs created by the abandoned quarries further etch the skyline into sheer red-brown walls that appear to continue the Palisades. Whether walking to the high point in spring or fall to watch the hawk migration, or bicycling along the paths that hug the shores, you'll find much to enjoy in the parklands administered by the Palisades Interstate Park Commission that stretch from Nyack to Haverstraw on the Hudson's western shore.

The Long Path takes the high route from Nyack across the Hook and the hills called the Seven Sisters. You can make a 12-mile loop hike by first following the Long Path along the hills and then returning on the bike path along the shore of the Hudson, enjoying the best views of woods and water. If you want a shorter hike, you can choose a 6-mile loop by leaving the Long Path at Landing Road in Rockland Lake State Park and heading down to the bike path to return to Nyack Beach.

GETTING THERE

The hike begins at Nyack Beach State Park in Nyack, where a seasonal parking fee may be charged. To get there, take US 9W north to Nyack. Two blocks north of its intersection with NY 59 (Main Street), turn right onto High Avenue. Continue for one block and turn left onto North Midland Avenue. After approximately 1 mile, continue straight ahead as the main road curves to the left. Follow North Midland Avenue through the village of Upper Nyack until the road ends at the entrance to the Marydell Faith and

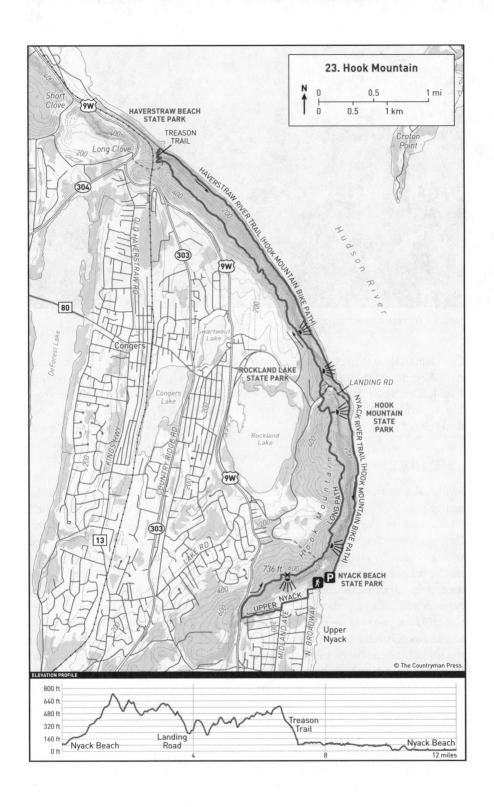

23. Hook Mountain

N

| 0 | 0.5 | 1 mi |
| 0 | 0.5 | 1 km |

Short Clove

9W

HAVERSTRAW BEACH STATE PARK

TREASON TRAIL

Croton Point

Long Clove

400

200

304

HAVERSTRAW RIVER TRAIL [HOOK MOUNTAIN BIKE PATH]

OLD HAVERSTRAW RD

303

9W

80

Hudson River

200

Congers

Swartwout Lake

DeForest Lake

ROCKLAND LAKE STATE PARK

LANDING RD

HOOK MOUNTAIN STATE PARK

Congers Lake

Rockland Lake

NYACK RIVER TRAIL [HOOK MOUNTAIN BIKE PATH]

KINGS HWY

COUNTRY RIDGE RD

9W

200

Long Path

Hook Mountain

200

303

13

LAKE RD

200

400

736 ft.

600

NYACK BEACH STATE PARK

P

UPPER NYACK

MIDLAND AVE

N. BROADWAY

Upper Nyack

© The Countryman Press

ELEVATION PROFILE

800 ft
640 ft
480 ft
320 ft
160 ft
0 ft

Nyack Beach

Landing Road

Treason Trail

Nyack Beach

4

8

12 miles

CROTON POINT FROM HOOK MOUNTAIN

Life Center, then turn right onto Larchdale Avenue. At the next intersection, turn left onto North Broadway and follow it into Nyack Beach State Park. Continue ahead to the parking area.

THE HIKE

Walk back to the tollbooth, and on a utility pole you'll see the three blazes which mark the start of the white-blazed Upper Nyack Trail. Follow this trail, which begins by running along paved roads. It heads south on North Broadway, then turns right onto Larchdale Avenue and follows it to its end. Note the cliffs on your right—that's the top of the Hook, where you're headed. At the end of Larchdale Avenue, the trail turns left onto North Midland Avenue and in 300 feet (after passing a private road on the right) turns right, this time into the woods. As you climb, you'll begin to hear the sounds of traffic on the busy US 9W just above you. (NOTE: As of September 2018, there are plans to relocate the Upper Nyack Trail off of the paved roads and onto a route that follows the base of the cliffs, traversing lands recently acquired by the park from the Marydell Center. You should follow the white blazes of the Upper Nyack Trail even if its route differs from that described above.)

About a mile from your car, the Upper Nyack Trail ends at a junction with the aqua-blazed Long Path. Turn right, and head north on the Long Path, which follows the (thankfully) never-completed Tweed Boulevard, part of an 1870s scheme by cohorts of the infamous Boss Tweed to build a road from Nyack across Hook Mountain to Rockland Lake—complete with a hotel on the summit.

After following the Long Path for three-quarters of a mile, you'll reach the top of the Hook, with views south toward New York City and north to Rockland Lake. Beyond the quarry lies the massif of Dunderberg that ends in the Timp. Farther north and on the other side of the river lies the ragged contour of Breakneck Ridge leading up toward South Beacon Mountain. The

Hudson River, wide here at Tappan Bay, is pinched to the north by Croton Point. Farther north it opens out into its widest segment at Haverstraw Bay before entering the narrows of the Hudson Highlands.

You are standing on the 736-foot peak of the Verdrietege, or tedious headland—so called by early Dutch sailors who struggled to sail upwind around it. But the landscape at your feet is not what the Dutch sailors saw, and the history of that landscape accounts for a good portion of the preservation movement that resulted in the parks now lining the Hudson's shores.

The diabase of the Palisades, which is volcanic in origin, surfaces here through the base of Triassic sandstone and shale. Quarries along the river to the south were active in the nineteenth century, and the columnar cliffs of the Hook were quarried extensively in the 1870s and 1880s, with the introduction of dynamite and heavy earthmoving equipment. The basalt columns were crushed to obtain traprock for macadam roads and, later in the 1890s, for concrete for New York City buildings. Angered at first only by the ear-shattering explosions heard up and down both sides of the river, residents of both New York and New Jersey began to speak out against the quarries. It was not until 1894 that a well-organized group opposed the visual desecration of the cliffs caused by the quarrying.

Finally, in 1900, after several years of legislative debate fueled by the argument that "preservation would largely benefit those who enjoyed the view from the New York side of the Hudson," a study commission report was accepted. It called for a permanent interstate park commission and the acquisition of land along the Palisades for recreational purposes. The Palisades

CEMETERY ALONG THE LONG PATH

ALONG THE HAVERSTRAW RIVER TRAIL

Interstate Park Commission was established in 1900 pursuant to an interstate compact signed by governors Theodore Roosevelt of New York and Foster M. Voorhees of New Jersey. With both private and public funds, the Commission began by acquiring lands from the top of the cliff face down to the river, and continued by adding cliff-top lands north to Nyack. Hook Mountain itself remained threatened until it was acquired by the Commission in 1911.

The trail continues straight ahead, descending from the summit and following the narrow and sinuous ridge of the mountain, with more views over the river to the south and east. In another 0.3 mile, at the base of a descent, a yellow-blazed trail leaves to the left. Continue ahead on the Long Path, which now begins to climb again. A short distance ahead, you'll reach a series of panoramic

viewpoints to the right of the trail, with Nyack Beach State Park visible directly below.

After continuing along the ridge for a short distance, the trail turns sharply left and begins a steady descent. Soon, it reaches a switchback in an old road and joins the road as it curves to the right. The Long Path follows the road as it descends gently along the western side of the ridge, then levels off.

At one point, the river is again visible through the trees on the right. Just beyond, the road bears left and ascends gently. You'll be amazed at the amount of rock work that was used to support this road! After reaching the crest of the rise, the road begins to descend, passing an interesting wide stone wall on the left. The road climbs a knoll, then begins a steady descent.

When you reach a sharp switchback

turn to the left, you'll notice a well-defined side trail that heads to the right. Follow this trail uphill to another viewpoint, undoubtedly one of the best of the day, with Croton Point jutting out into the river and Ossining visible across it. This is a good place to observe the clues to the second major industry of the region's past—clues that are much less obvious than those of the quarries. Along the shore below are the remains of old docks, the successors to Slaughter's Landing, a settlement begun in 1711 by John Slaughter from Rockland Lake. An ice business was started at Rockland Lake in 1831 when Moses G. Leonard impressed New York City hoteliers with the cleanliness and purity of the lake's ice. In 1855, the business became the Knickerbocker Ice Company, the largest in New York, employing as many as 1,000 men. Ice was cut from the lake and stored for shipment south to New York City. It was moved from the lake via an endless conveyor cable to the landings, where three pairs of tracks led across the docks, whose ruins are now guarded by an old lighthouse. Loads of 400 tons were carried south on barges.

Return to the Long Path and follow it as it curves sharply to the left and descends on a rocky, eroded section of the road. The trail soon turns right, leaving the old road, and continues on a footpath, passing a stone foundation on the left. After descending very steeply on a rocky footpath, the trail bears right, skirting old moss-covered concrete foundations, and reaches paved Landing Road.

If you want to follow the 6-mile hike, turn right on the paved road and follow it downhill, passing a stone cabin (a private residence). A short distance ahead, you'll reach a junction with the Nyack River Trail (also known as the Hook Mountain Bike Path), which joins from the left. Paint markings on a rock at the junction indicate that the distance from here to Nyack Beach State Park is 1.5 miles. Proceed ahead and follow the bike path south for 1.5 miles back to your car.

For those who wish to follow the 12-mile hike, which traverses the full length of the ridge, the Long Path continues across the road and into the woods, soon passing an early nineteenth-century cemetery. Beyond the cemetery, the climb steepens. As the grade moderates and the trail bends to the left, there is an unobstructed viewpoint over the Hudson River to the right of the trail. Just beyond, you'll be amazed to see Dutchman's breeches blooming in spring only a short distance from the prickly pear cactus that seems to enjoy this dry location.

The trail now begins a steady descent. Toward the base of the descent, as the trail bends to the left, you'll come to another unobstructed viewpoint over the river. Croton Point Park juts out into the river to the left, and the Village of Ossining is on the right. Directly below you is the site of a quarry. The drop to river level is quite steep, so caution should be exercised when approaching the edge.

At the base of the descent, you'll notice an overgrown area surrounded by a chain-link fence on the right. The trail now resumes its ascent, soon beginning to parallel a stone wall on the left, with tennis courts beyond the stone wall. At the end of the stone wall, where the trail bears left and continues to ascend, a vague, unmarked path leads ahead to a viewpoint over the river from the top of another abandoned quarry.

For the next half mile, the Long Path continues ahead along the ridge over undulating terrain, with views through the trees on both sides of the ridge. To the left, the park's Championship Golf Course is visible. After reaching an open area at the crest of the ridge, with west-facing views obscured by trees, the trail begins a rather steep descent, then bends left and soon again begins a gradual ascent. For the next mile, the trail follows the relatively level ridgeline, with some minor ups and downs, and with many views through the trees.

After reaching the highest point on this section of Hook Mountain, the trail begins to descend. In a short distance, you'll reach a three-way trail intersection. Here, the Long Path turns left, while the white-blazed Treason Trail begins on the right. This trail provides a connector to the bike path. You have walked about 3 miles from Landing Road, and your trek from the Hook across the hills of the Seven Sisters—and surely twice that number of small knobs and crests—has taken about four and a half hours.

Turn right and follow the white-blazed Treason Trail, which descends toward the river. Soon, the Treason Trail bears left and begins a steeper descent on switchbacks. Directly below you is the West Shore Railroad, built in 1883 and now operated by CSX. The railroad tunnels through the mountain, and the north portal of the tunnel is only about 150 feet from the trail. Many freight trains pass through the tunnel daily, and you may see and/or hear a train as you descend along the white-blazed trail.

As you approach the river, you'll pass a ruined stone structure on the right. This structure was probably used to store explosives when the quarries were active. Just beyond, the white-blazed Treason Trail ends at the Haverstraw River Trail (also known as Hook Mountain Bike Path), which is paved at this point. An abandoned stone building is adjacent to the intersection. This building was constructed by the park and used for administrative purposes when swimming was allowed at Haverstraw beach. A short distance to the north is Treason Rock (for which the Treason Trail is named). Here, Major John Andre is believed to have met the traitor Benedict Arnold.

Turn right and follow the bike path, which continues south along the river as a wide gravel path on a shelf about 80 feet above the water level, with views over the river. Bicyclists, joggers, and pedestrians will join you for the return trip, but the pleasant route is wide enough to accommodate all of these varied users.

After about 2 miles of pleasant walking, you'll notice two more old quarries on the right. To the left, at the end of the second quarry, an abandoned road leads down to the river. This is the site of Rockland Landing North. Just beyond, on the right, is another vandalized stone building surrounded by cedar trees.

Beyond the ruined stone building, the site of yet another, even larger, quarry is visible on the right. This area was once landscaped as part of the park development, and you can see the former backstop of a softball field overgrown by vegetation.

In another half mile, the bike path descends rather steeply to the river level (this portion of the path is paved). You're now at the site of Rockland Landing South, where ice from Rockland Lake was once shipped to New York City by boat. You'll pass some more abandoned buildings and see wooden pilings in the river—the remains of former docks. Continue south along the bike path (now known as the Nyack River Trail) for another 1.5 miles to Nyack Beach State Park, where you parked your car.

The Tors, High and Low

High Tor is one of Rockland County's most conspicuous landmarks. Rising 800 feet above the Hudson River, with a broad view of the surrounding area, the peak of High Tor has served as both signal and sentinel. During the Revolutionary War, beacons were placed on the mountain to alert the Americans of a possible British attack. In Celtic lore, "high tor" is a place in which to commune with the gods, "tor" being a gateway.

The Maxwell Anderson play *High Tor* (1937) signaled the beginning of a campaign to protect the mountain from quarrying. The end result was the acquisition and transfer to the Palisades Interstate Park Commission (PIPC) of 564 acres in 1943. In 1995, Scenic Hudson purchased a 54-acre former vineyard on the south face of the mountain, which has since been transferred to PIPC.

TOTAL DISTANCE: 6 miles

WALKING TIME: 4 hours

ELEVATION GAIN: 1,722 feet

MAPS: USGS 7.5' Haverstraw, NY–NJTC Hudson Palisades Trails #111 and #112

TRAILHEAD GPS COORDINATES: N 41° 10' 35" W 73° 57' 43.5"

GETTING THERE

Take the Palisades Interstate Parkway to Exit 10 (North Middletown Road). At the end of the ramp, turn right onto Germonds Road. In 0.7 mile, turn left onto NY 304. In 3.8 miles, turn left onto Ridge Road (County Route 23) and follow it for 0.9 mile to its end at Old Route 304 (County Route 90). Park in the grassy area at the southwest corner of the intersection. Parking is also available along Parliament Drive (the first side street off Ridge Road, heading south from Old Route 304).

THE HIKE

Hike west along Old Route 304 for a short distance, passing four utility poles along the road. The route is marked with the aqua blazes of the Long Path, which

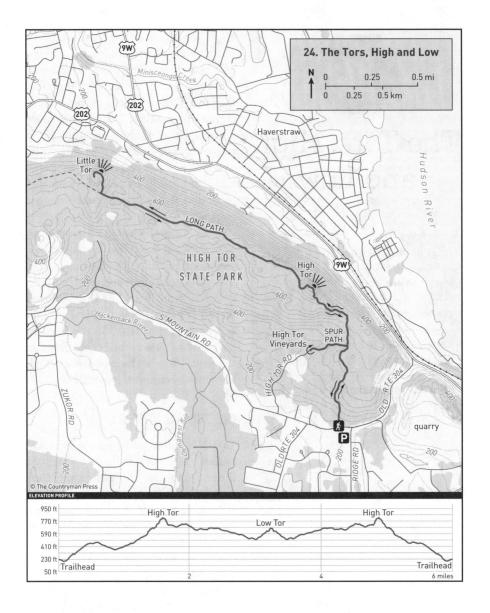

turns into the woods opposite house number 330.

After leaving the road, the Long Path crosses several wet areas on puncheons and soon begins a moderate climb on a rocky footpath. A short distance beyond, the trail bears left, crosses a stream on a wooden bridge, briefly levels off, then continues to climb. In half a mile, after gaining about 250 feet in elevation, the trail bears left and levels off again. It descends a little to reach a junction with the white-blazed Spur Path, which begins on the left (the junction is marked by two signposts and a triple white blaze on the left). Turn left and follow this quarter-mile side trail that leads gently down to the site of the historic High Tor Vineyards, passing a small pond along the way.

Return to the main trail and make a left on the Long Path, which now resumes a gradual climb. In another third of a mile, the Long Path reaches the crest of the ridge. To the right, you can see the Hudson River through the trees. An unmarked woods road proceeds ahead, but you should turn sharply left, continuing to follow the aqua blazes of the Long Path.

After a short gentle uphill stretch, you'll reach the base of a steep talus slope. The trail now begins a steep climb of High Tor. The grade moderates as the trail skirts a rocky knob on the left and descends a little into a ravine, but the climb soon resumes, with a number of steep sections. After passing through a grassy area, you'll emerge onto the summit of High Tor, having climbed over 600 vertical feet from the start of the hike.

Although the summit is only 832 feet high, the 360-degree view is truly superb. Lake DeForest (a reservoir), the skyline of New York City, and even part of Newark are visible to the south. The two round domes to the north are reactors of the Indian Point nuclear power plant. To the northwest are the rolling summits of Harriman State Park. Forested areas of Rockland County and northern New Jersey spread out to the west. Below you is Haverstraw, with its active waterfront. The long curved mountain along the shore of the Hudson River is Hook Mountain, another PIPC-protected park (see Hike #23). An aircraft beacon was once located on the summit, and the anchors of the beacon are still visible.

Linger if you wish, but the hike is not over. Carry on to Little Tor (aka Low Tor) by continuing on the Long Path as it heads downhill, away from the river. The trail makes a short, steep descent, then

LAKE DEFOREST FROM HIGH TOR

VIEW FROM HIGH TOR

turns right onto a fire road that runs just below the crest of the ridge. There are numerous opportunities to take a short bushwhack up to the crest for a fine view.

After 1.4 miles along the fire road, a gravel road crosses the trail. To the right, a white-blazed side trail leads up to Little Tor and its fine view. Haverstraw is some 700 feet below. You're more likely to have company here as it's just a 1-mile walk to Central Highway, which crosses the ridge to the west.

Hike back the way you came. You may wish to take another break on High Tor.

25

Ramapo Torne

TOTAL DISTANCE: 4.8 miles

WALKING TIME: 4 hours

ELEVATION GAIN: 1,422 feet

MAPS: USGS 7.5' Sloatsburg; NY–NJTC
Harriman-Bear Mountain Trails #118

TRAILHEAD GPS COORDINATES: N 41° 10'
26" W 74° 10' 07.5"

The southern end of Harriman State Park, accessed from the Reeves Meadow parking area off Seven Lakes Drive, is one of the most popular areas in the park. But the large majority of these visitors head up toward Pine Meadow Lake. This hike, which follows a less-used route, can take you away from the crowds and provide you with a feeling of remoteness. The many ups and downs will ensure a rewarding workout, and you'll be afforded plenty of fine views. Unless you're hiking on a weekday, be sure to start this hike early, as the Reeves Meadow parking area is often full by 9 a.m. on weekends.

GETTING THERE

Take the New York Thruway (I-87) to Exit 15A and proceed north on NY 17 for 2.7 miles, through and past the village of Sloatsburg, to a traffic light. Turn right onto Seven Lakes Drive and continue for 1.5 miles into the park. This loop hike starts at the parking area adjacent to the Reeves Meadow Visitor Center (open seasonally on weekends). Overflow parking is available across the road or along the shoulder (pay careful attention to the signs that prohibit parking in some areas).

THE HIKE

From the parking area, proceed into a field on the southwest side of the visitor center, where a brown post indicates the route of the Pine Meadow Trail, marked with a red dot on a white background. Turn right and follow the Pine Meadow Trail, heading southwest (back toward NY 17). In about a quarter mile, you'll come to a junction with the blue-on-white-blazed Seven Hills Trail. Turn left

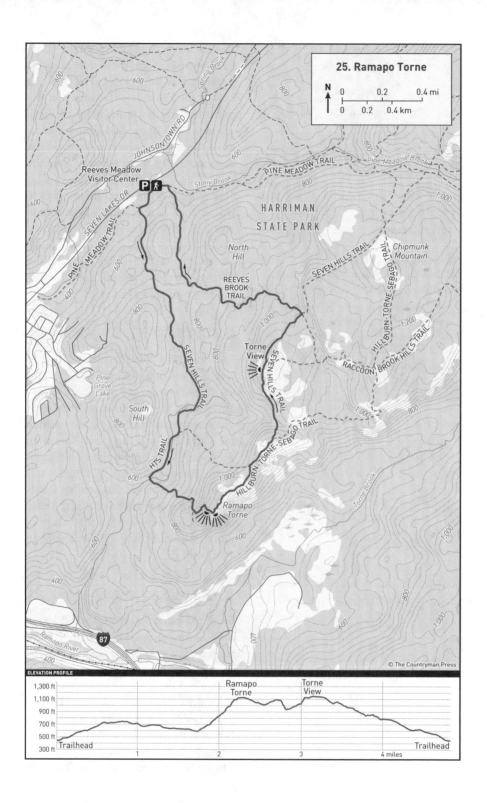

25. Ramapo Torne

N

| 0 | 0.2 | 0.4 mi |
| 0 | 0.2 | 0.4 km |

Spring Brook

600

600

800

800

JOHNSONTOWN RD

PINE MEADOW TRAIL

Pine Meadow Brook

1,000

Reeves Meadow
Visitor Center

Stony Brook

600

PINE MEADOW TRAIL

SEVEN LAKES DR

HARRIMAN

STATE PARK

SEVEN HILLS TRAIL

Chipmunk
Mountain

North
Hill

600

REEVES
BROOK
TRAIL

1,200

1,000

800

HILLBURN-TORNE-SEBAGO TRAIL

800

800

SEVEN HILLS TRAIL

Torne
View

RACCOON BROOK HILLS TRAIL

1,000

Pine
Grove
Lake

SEVEN HILLS TRAIL

800

South
Hill

800

HTS TRAIL

600

1,000

HILLBURN-TORNE-SEBAGO TRAIL

Torne Brook

1,000

Ramapo
Torne

600

800

600

800

1,000

400

Ramapo River

87

400

600

800

1,000

© The Countryman Press

ELEVATION PROFILE

1,300 ft			Ramapo Torne		Torne View		
1,100 ft							
900 ft							
700 ft							
500 ft							
300 ft	Trailhead	1		2		3	4 miles	Trailhead

TORNE VIEW

onto the Seven Hills Trail, which starts a long uphill climb of varying pitches.

The trail meanders through the woods, following several woods roads for part of the way. Remember to follow the blazes, which can sometimes unexpectedly diverge from a more obvious route that you might expect to follow.

About 1.65 miles from the start, you'll reach a T-junction with a woods road. Here, the Seven Hills Trail turns sharply left, but you should turn right, now following the orange blazes of the Hillburn-Torne-Sebago (HTS) Trail, which begins here. This is the former route of the "Old Red" Trail—an informal route up the Ramapo Torne which became an official trail in 2007.

The HTS Trail follows a level woods road for 0.3 mile, then turns left at a cairn, crosses a stream, and climbs rather steeply on a woods road. After gaining about 300 feet in elevation, the trail turns sharply left and climbs very steeply over rocks, emerging at a viewpoint to the southwest. It bears left and soon climbs some more to a rock ledge, just below the summit of Ramapo Torne.

Here, on a clear day, you can look south to the New York City skyline, west across the almost unbroken Sterling Forest State Park lands, and even north toward the Shawangunks and the Catskills. Below lies the unattractive Torne Valley, a former landfill, which now features electric power lines and a substation. To the south, the tall black building with the pointed top is a Sheraton hotel built on the site of the former Ford Mahwah Assembly Plant that closed in 1980.

Proceed ahead along the ridge of the Ramapo Torne, following the HTS Trail to another junction with the Seven Hills Trail, and continue straight ahead on a footpath marked with both blue-on-white and orange blazes. After a short

LANDFILL IN TORNE VALLEY

climb onto an interesting rock outcrop, the two trails split. Bear left and follow the blue-on-white blazes of the Seven Hills Trail, which begins a steep but attractive descent. Be careful here, especially if it's wet or icy.

Before long, you'll begin your climb to Torne View, another terrific spot. While the views here are slightly less expansive than at the previous overlook, there is little development to mar the vista. Just beyond, you may notice a junction with the black-on-white-blazed Raccoon Brook Hills Trail (the blazes are painted on the rocks), but continue ahead on the blue-on-white-blazed Seven Hills Trail, which descends to a valley, then crosses a small hill to a second valley. Here, just before reaching the bottom, you'll reach a junction with the white-blazed Reeves Brook Trail.

Turn left here and follow the white blazes downhill, steeply in places, for the last 1.4 miles of the hike. The woods are mostly open, but there are interesting rock outcrops along the way. For most of the way, you'll parallel Reeves Brook, and if the water level is high, you may notice some lovely cascades in the stream. Finally, you'll reach a junction with the red-on-white-blazed Pine Meadow Trail. Turn left, and almost immediately you'll see the visitor center ahead and be back at your car.

26

Breakneck Mountain Loop

TOTAL DISTANCE: 6.9 miles	

TOTAL DISTANCE: 6.9 miles

WALKING TIME: 4 hours

ELEVATION GAIN: 1,495 feet

MAPS: USGS 7.5' Thiells; NY–NJTC Harriman-Bear Mountain Trails #118

TRAILHEAD GPS COORDINATES: N 41° 11' 06" W 74° 04' 29"

This hike uses the Tuxedo–Mount Ivy, Breakneck Mountain, Suffern–Bear Mountain, and Red Arrow Trails to make a "lollipop-loop" hike (out and back on the same trail with a loop in the middle). The terrain is almost entirely through deep woods, with part of the route passing through dense stands of mountain laurel and traversing open rock slabs. Except at the start, the climbing is gentle, and the route makes for a leisurely saunter in a peaceful atmosphere embellished by birdsong. Rocky footing at the beginning and the end may pose a slight challenge to the inexperienced hiker.

GETTING THERE

From the Palisades Interstate Parkway, take Exit 13 (US 202/Suffern/Haverstraw). Turn right at the bottom of the ramp onto US 202 West, and proceed for 1.7 miles to a junction with NY 306. Turn right onto NY 306, then right again at the stop sign just ahead. In 0.2 mile, turn left onto Mountain Road (at a sign for RAMAQUOIS), then, in another 0.2 mile, turn left again onto Diltzes Lane. Continue on Diltzes Lane for 0.2 mile and, just before the overhead power lines cross the paved road, turn right into a gravel parking area with a sign indicating that parking for hikers is available.

THE HIKE

Toward the rear of the parking area, at a green gate that blocks off the power line access road, you'll notice a triple-red-dash-on-white blaze that marks the start of the Tuxedo-Mount Ivy Trail. Follow this trail uphill on a wide dirt road (used to access the nearby power lines). Bear right as you approach the power lines and continue along a dirt road, parallel to and below the power lines. Follow

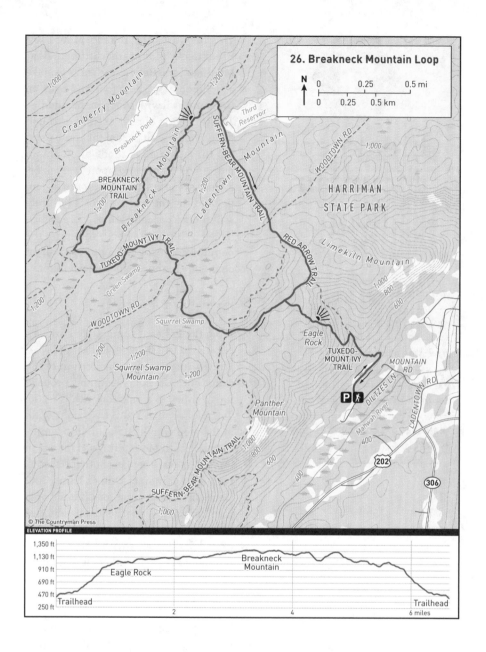

26. Breakneck Mountain Loop

N

| 0 | 0.25 | 0.5 mi |
| 0 | 0.25 | 0.5 km |

HARRIMAN
STATE PARK

ELEVATION PROFILE

the road for 0.2 mile, crossing two small streams. When the road bears left and crosses under the power lines, you'll come to a Y-junction, where you should take the left fork and head uphill. A short distance beyond, the Tuxedo–Mount Ivy Trail leaves the service road and makes a right turn into the woods.

Continuing ahead, the Tuxedo–Mount Ivy Trail ascends gradually on an old woods road, bordered for part of the way with rough stone walls. After crossing a stream on stepping-stones, the road becomes rockier. Watch carefully for a left turn and follow the red-on-white blazes as the trail leaves the road it has been following and continues to climb rather steeply on another old woods road. Near the top of the climb, the trail bears right and continues on a footpath.

Just below the summit of Eagle Rock, the trail reaches a viewpoint, with Limekiln Mountain visible across the valley to the north and the Hudson River to the east. The view is partially obscured by trees, but it is the only broad viewpoint on the entire hike. Beyond the viewpoint, the trail continues to climb, but much more gradually.

Soon, you'll reach a T-junction. The Red Arrow Trail, which will be your return route, begins on the right, but you should turn left to continue on the Tuxedo–Mount Ivy Trail, which now descends gently. After climbing a little, the Tuxedo–Mount Ivy Trail reaches a junction with the yellow-blazed Suffern–Bear Mountain Trail at the height of land. The junction is marked by an interesting rock outcrop on the right (a good place to take a break) and an old stone fireplace on the left. The Suffern–Bear Mountain Trail, as its name implies, runs for just over 23 miles from Suffern to Bear Mountain. Proposed in 1924 by Major William A. Welch, then general manager of the Palisades Interstate Park Commission, the Suffern–Bear Mountain Trail is the longest trail in the park.

The Tuxedo–Mount Ivy Trail now levels off and passes through dense mountain laurel thickets. In places, the laurels arch over the trail. After going through these delightful groves for half a mile, the trail reaches a T-junction with Woodtown Road, a woods road. Here the trail turns right onto the road, crosses a stream on a wooden footbridge, and immediately leaves the road, turning sharply left into the woods. The trail now follows another old woods road which climbs gradually and soon levels off.

After crossing another stream on rocks, you'll notice the Green Swamp

WEST POINTING ROCK

ALONG THE BREAKNECK MOUNTAIN TRAIL

to the left of the trail. Toward the end of the swamp, after a short climb, follow the Tuxedo–Mount Ivy Trail as it turns right, leaving the woods road it has been following. A short distance beyond, you'll reach another junction, where a triple-white blaze on a tree and the letters "BM" painted on a rock mark the start of the Breakneck Mountain Trail.

Turn right onto the Breakneck Mountain Trail.

Breakneck Mountain was once known locally as Knapp Mountain after the name of the original owner. This trail, too, was blazed at the suggestion of Major Welch in 1927. The trail proceeds northeast along the ridge of Breakneck Mountain, often emerging onto

cycles. As the trail approaches the northeastern end of Breakneck Pond, the pond can be glimpsed through the trees to the left.

In 1.5 miles, the Breakneck Mountain Trail ends at a junction with the yellow-blazed Suffern–Bear Mountain Trail. Do not turn left up the rocks, but continue straight ahead, following the yellow blazes downhill to the right toward the Third Reservoir (which can be glimpsed ahead through the trees). The Suffern–Bear Mountain Trail passes the western end of the reservoir, which makes for an appealing spot to rest. The water is tranquil and inviting, but swimming is forbidden. The Third Reservoir, built in 1951, is the most recently built of the three reservoirs constructed to serve the now-closed Letchworth Village State Developmental Center. Even with three reservoirs, Letchworth Village used to run out of water in dry years, and when this happened, a pipe was laid over Breakneck Mountain and water pumped out of Breakneck Pond.

The Suffern–Bear Mountain Trail now climbs over Ladentown Mountain and descends to Woodtown Road, crossing it and then a stream. You'll soon reach a junction with the Red Arrow Trail (the junction is marked by cairns). Turn left onto the Red Arrow Trail, which skirts the edge of a swamp and descends, passing old rock walls on the left and continuing through mountain laurel thickets. The trail bears right at a fork, then bears right again and continues uphill on a woods road.

Soon, you'll reach the end of the Red Arrow Trail, marked by a triple blaze. Turn left onto the Tuxedo–Mount Ivy Trail and follow it downhill to your car, now retracing the route you followed at the start of the hike.

open rock slabs. Soon, it passes West Pointing Rock, a 10-by-14-foot boulder with a sharp projection on its west side. Farther along the ridge, a particularly beautiful section traverses an open slab with large boulders left by the glacier that once covered this area. Notice the large cracks in the rock underfoot caused by winter's freeze-and-thaw

Nurian/ Appalachian Trail Loop

TOTAL DISTANCE: 7 miles

WALKING TIME: 4.5 hours

ELEVATION GAIN: 1,890 feet

MAPS: USGS 7.5' Sloatsburg; USGS 7.5' Monroe; NY–NJTC Harriman-Bear Mountain Trails #119

TRAILHEAD GPS COORDINATES: N 41° 15' 53" W 74° 09' 17.5"

This hike follows eight distinct trails— Arden–Surebridge, Stahahe Brook, Nurian, Dunning, White Bar, Ramapo– Dunderberg, Lichen, and Appalachian. You'll have the opportunity to clamber through massive rocks in an area called the Valley of Boulders (on the Nurian Trail) as well as to explore the fascinating rock formation known as the Lemon Squeezer on the Appalachian Trail (AT). You'll walk by the beautiful, secluded Green Pond and the larger but also very scenic Island Pond. There are over 30 lakes and ponds in Harriman State Park, but nearly all of them were either created or have been greatly altered by the construction of dams. Green and Island Ponds are among the very few that remain in their natural state.

GETTING THERE

From the Tuxedo railroad station, proceed north on NY 17 for 5.6 miles and turn right (east) onto Arden Valley Road at a sign for Harriman State Park. Cross over the New York State Thruway and make the next right into the Elk Pen parking area. If approaching from the north, take the New York State Thruway to Exit 16 (Harriman) and drive 4 miles south on NY 17 to reach the turn onto Arden Valley Road and the parking at the Elk Pen.

There once were approximately 60 elk penned here, hence the name for the parking area. The animals were brought from Yellowstone Park at the end of 1919, but they did not flourish; when their number gradually decreased, those remaining were sold in 1942.

THE HIKE

Begin the hike by heading east on the wide path through a grassy field toward the mountains, following the white

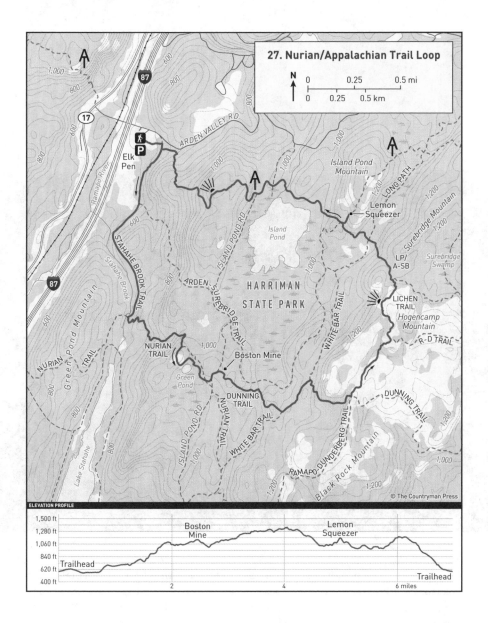

27. Nurian/Appalachian Trail Loop

N
0   0.25   0.5 mi
0   0.25   0.5 km

ELEVATION PROFILE

1,500 ft
1,280 ft   Boston   Lemon
1,060 ft   Mine   Squeezer
840 ft
620 ft   Trailhead
400 ft   Trailhead
                    2   4   6 miles

© The Countryman Press

blazes of the AT. At the end of the field, turn right onto a woods road known as the Arden Road (or the Old Arden Road). Just ahead, the AT turns left and begins to climb Green Pond Mountain, but you should continue ahead on the road, now following the Arden–Surebridge Trail, blazed with an inverted red triangle on a white background.

In 0.3 mile, the Arden–Surebridge Trail turns left, leaving Arden Road. Continue ahead on the road, now following the Stahahe Brook Trail, marked with red-stripe-on-white blazes. The route now is slightly uphill. As you begin to approach the New York State Thruway, the noise of traffic becomes increasingly intrusive.

GREEN POND

Soon, you'll reach Stahahe Brook. The road formerly crossed the brook on a substantial wooden bridge, but this bridge was washed away by Hurricane Irene in August 2011, and the park does not plan to rebuild it. Follow the red-stripe-on-white blazes, which turn left just before the brook and proceed into the woods on a footpath parallel to the brook.

In half a mile, the Stahahe Brook Trail ends at a junction with the white-blazed Nurian Trail, named after Kerson Nurian, who first blazed this trail in the 1920s. Nurian, who was born in Bulgaria and was employed as an electrical engineer at the Brooklyn Navy Yard, was one of the first trail builders in Harriman State Park. In the 1930s, however, Nurian often found himself in conflict with others who also blazed hiking trails in the park. At that time, there was little regulation of the creation of trails or of their blazing, and hikers felt free to build and name their own section of trail. This practice led to the "Great Trail War," which eventually resulted in the dispute being settled by the New York–New Jersey Trail Conference.

Turn left onto the Nurian Trail, following switchbacks uphill to the ravine of the outlet brook of Island Pond. This ravine, which features a number of huge rocks, is known as the Valley of Boulders.

Emerging from among these massive boulders, the trail descends slightly and then curves right, around the end of a long, sloping rock in a hemlock grove. Soon, you'll reach the start of the Dunning Trail, indicated by three yellow blazes on a tree to the right of the trail.

Turn right onto the Dunning Trail, which leads straight up a rocky pitch and then down toward the scenic Green Pond. The Dunning Trail follows the northern shore of this pristine pond, while the Nurian Trail follows a parallel (but very different) route only a short distance away.

Beyond the pond, the Nurian Trail joins the Dunning Trail from the left for a very short stretch, but departs to the right within 75 feet. Continue to follow the yellow blazes, and turn left when the Dunning Trail reaches Island Pond Road (a woods road). The trail now heads uphill. Watch carefully for a turn to the right that takes you to the Boston Mine—a large opening in the side of a hill that was last worked around 1880 and is now flooded. Ore from the mine was sent to the Clove Furnace at Arden, and many tailings remain in the area.

Turn right at the mine, and continue uphill. The trail undulates through hemlock and laurel and passes beneath a large rock outcrop. Half a mile from the Boston Mine, the White Bar Trail joins from the right. You should turn left, now following both yellow and white blazes. When the trails diverge in a quarter

mile, turn right and continue uphill on the yellow-blazed Dunning Trail.

After climbing rather steeply over a rise, the Dunning Trail descends a little to reach a junction with the red-dot-on-white-blazed Ramapo–Dunderberg Trail. The Ramapo–Dunderberg Trail was the first trail to be built by the New York hiking clubs in Harriman State Park. Originally blazed in 1920, its route was suggested by Major William A. Welch, the general manager of the park at the time. Turn left onto the Ramapo–Dunderberg Trail, which passes through an area where the scars of a forest fire are quite noticeable, soon crossing a huge open rock surface known as the Whaleback. The trail now steeply descends a rock face to cross a stream on a log bridge, then climbs to a junction with the blue-L-on-white-blazed Lichen Trail.

Turn left and follow the Lichen Trail, which ascends to a west-facing viewpoint over Island Pond, then descends to end at a junction with the co-aligned Long Path (aqua) and Arden–Surebridge Trail (inverted red triangle on white). Turn left and follow the joint route of these trails, which descend rather steeply. In 0.3 mile, you'll reach a junction where the White Bar Trail begins on the left and then the Long Path departs to the right. Continue ahead on the Arden–Surebridge Trail.

In another quarter mile, you'll reach a junction with the white-blazed AT. Just to the right on the AT is the Lemon Squeezer, where the trail is routed through a very narrow rock cleft. You should take a short detour to visit this fascinating feature, then return to the Arden–Surebridge Trail and turn right, briefly following both the Arden–Surebridge Trail and the AT.

When the trails diverge, leave the

ISLAND POND

Arden–Surebridge Trail and continue ahead on the white-blazed AT, which descends rather steeply and briefly joins an old woods road, known as the "Crooked Road," near the shore of Island Pond. Soon, the AT turns left and climbs a knoll, with a limited view of Island Pond on the left. After descending, it passes the rusted remains of a rotary gravel classifier and crosses a wooden bridge over a stone spillway. Built by the Civilian Conservation Corps (CCC) in the 1930s as part of a project to increase the size of Island Pond, it was never completed, and Island Pond is one of the few lakes in the park that remain in its natural state.

In another 500 feet, you'll cross a gravel road that leads from Arden Valley Road to Island Pond. Soon, the AT turns left onto Island Pond Road, but in another 400 feet, it turns right and begins a steep climb up Green Pond Mountain. Near the summit, rock outcrops to the right of the trail offer limited west-facing views.

The AT now descends the mountain on switchbacks. At the base of the descent, turn right onto Arden Road, still following the white blazes, and in 100 feet turn left and cross the meadow where you began your hike. Continue to the Elk Pen parking area and your car.

28

Rockhouse Mountain Loop

TOTAL DISTANCE: 7.5 miles (6-mile alternate)

WALKING TIME: 4 hours (3-hour alternate)

ELEVATION GAIN: 1,415 feet

MAPS: USGS 7.5' Thiells; USGS 7.5' Peekskill; NY–NJTC Harriman-Bear Mountain Trails #119

TRAILHEAD GPS COORDINATES: N 41° 15' 11" W 74° 03' 58"

This relatively easy "lollipop-loop" hike goes through central Harriman State Park, an area once rich with farms and mines going back to Colonial times. Circling but not climbing Rockhouse Mountain, the walking is easy, with just a few short climbs. However, a 7.5-mile hike can be a bit long for young children or beginning hikers. There are several interesting historic places to explore, so choose a nice day and start early. The hike is all on marked trails, except for a short section toward the end on an easy-to-follow woods road.

GETTING THERE

The road to the parking area is closed to vehicles in winter (December 1st through April 1st). However, an alternative year-round access, which also shortens the hike by 1.5 miles, is available as an option (see *Other Hiking Options*).

Take the Palisades Interstate Parkway to Exit 16 (Lake Welch). Proceed for half a mile to where the road splits. Bear right onto Tiorati Brook Road, and continue for 1.1 miles to a large parking area, just after a bridge, in a field on the right. You can also drive to the parking area from Tiorati Circle (see *Other Hiking Options* for directions to the circle). If coming from Tiorati Circle, the parking area is 2.4 miles south on Tiorati Brook Road, on your left.

THE HIKE

Cross to the other side of Tiorati Brook Road, and begin the hike by following the blue-blazed Beech Trail, which heads southwest. This is one of the newer trails in the park, blazed in 1972 (most trails in Harriman go back to the 1920s or 1930s). And though there are lots of beech trees along the route, it was really named after

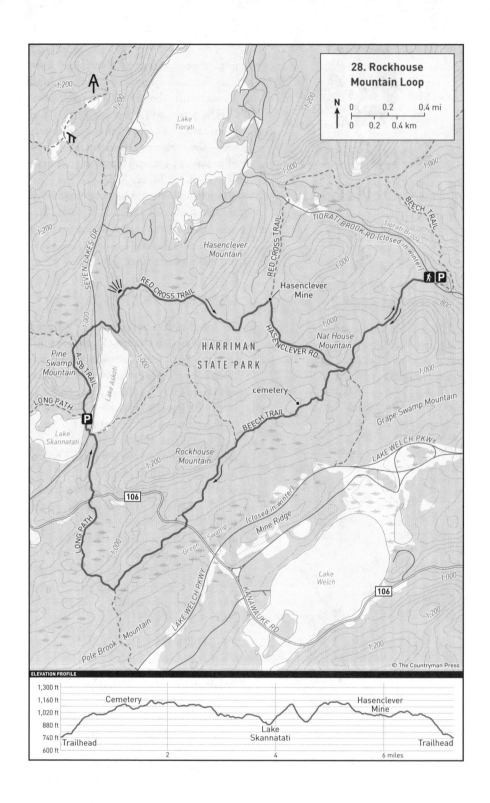

28. Rockhouse Mountain Loop

N

| 0 | 0.2 | 0.4 mi |
| 0 | 0.2 | 0.4 km |

Lake
Tiorati

BEECH TRAIL

TIORATI BROOK RD (closed in winter)

Tiorati Brook

RED CROSS TRAIL

Hasenclever
Mountain

Hasenclever
Mine

RED CROSS TRAIL

HASENCLEVER RD

Nat House
Mountain

SEVEN LAKES DR

HARRIMAN
STATE PARK

cemetery

Pine
Swamp
Mountain

A-SB TRAIL

Lake Askoti

Grape Swamp Mountain

LONG PATH

BEECH TRAIL

Lake
Skannatati

Rockhouse
Mountain

LAKE WELCH PKWY

106

LONG PATH

(closed in winter)
Mine Ridge

Green Swamp

Lake
Welch

106

LAKE WELCH PKWY

KANAWAUKE RD

Pole Brook Mountain

© The Countryman Press

ELEVATION PROFILE

1,300 ft			
1,160 ft	Cemetery		Hasenclever
1,020 ft			Mine
880 ft			
740 ft	Trailhead	Lake	Trailhead
600 ft		Skannatati	

2   4   6 miles

Art Beach, a tireless trail worker. The spelling was changed to circumvent a park policy against naming trails for living persons.

The trail follows a woods road, which soon reaches a fork. Bear right and continue along the trail, which now runs alongside a gully. Soon you'll enter an area filled with blueberry bushes and mountain laurel; observe how the old road was built up from the surrounding ground. After crossing a small stream, the trail begins a steady climb. You may notice a fine cascade just 0.3 mile from the start. Trail builders named it Arthur's Falls to honor a crew member.

After climbing just over 200 vertical feet, the trail reaches an intersection with the unmarked Hasenclever Road. Note this location because you will return here near the end of the hike. Continue ahead on the Beech Trail, which turns right, follows the road for only 15 feet, and then reenters the woods. The trail crosses another small stream and begins to climb again. You'll notice a change in vegetation as you near an old farmstead. Soon, you'll pass an old cemetery on your right. Cleaned and restored as an Eagle Scout project in 1990, the graves are from the Babcock, Youmans, and Jones families. Most of the readable inscriptions are from the mid- to late 1800s.

If you have the time and desire to explore the farm area, go back along the trail and look for a route through the barberry. In this area, you can find the remains of stone foundations and even an old root cellar. When you're ready to start hiking again, continue ahead on the blue-blazed Beech Trail, which levels off and passes a large glacial erratic on the left.

HASENCLEVER MINE

CEMETERY ON THE BEECH TRAIL

John Boyd Thacher State Park just south of Albany. You, however, are not going that far—at least not today.

The Long Path traverses a wet area and emerges into a pine plantation, probably planted by the Civilian Conservation Corps (CCC) in the 1930s. Once again you reach County Route 106. The trail turns right and follows the road for about 250 feet, then turns left and renters the woods just before a bend in the road. Soon, the trail turns left onto a woods road which leads down to Seven Lakes Drive. On the way, you'll cross under a telephone line, where you'll notice an abundance of sweet fern. Pull off a leaf and crush it in your fingers for a pleasant smell.

At Seven Lakes Drive, the trail turns right and crosses a bridge over the outlet of Lake Askoti (Mohegan for "this side"), then turns left and climbs down an embankment to reach a large parking area at Lake Skannatati (Mohegan for "the other side"). This parking area is an alternative place to start the hike, especially when Tiorati Brook Road is closed for the winter (see *Other Hiking Options*).

Bear right and walk to the northern end of the parking area. Here, the Long Path enters the woods, but you should bear right and continue on the Arden–Surebridge Trail (with blazes showing an inverted red triangle on white), which begins here. The Arden–Surebridge Trail climbs a shoulder of Pine Swamp Mountain and, in just under half a mile, reaches the trailhead of the Red Cross Trail (red cross on white background), which begins on the right.

A little over 2 miles from the start of the hike, the trail crosses County Route 106. Just before reaching this crossing, be alert for the marked route to bear left off the woods road and onto a narrower footpath. As you continue along, observe the attractive jumble of rocks to the right of the trail and the wonderful stand of mountain laurel, which in June will be ablaze with large white and pink blossoms.

About half a mile after crossing County Route 106, the Beech Trail ends at a junction with the aqua-blazed Long Path. Turn right onto the Long Path, a major long-distance trail, which currently extends over 300 miles from the George Washington Bridge north to

Turn right onto the Red Cross Trail, which heads down to recross Seven Lakes Drive. The trail soon passes by a large rock slab jutting into Lake Askoti, which is a good place to take a short break. You've now hiked 4.7 miles—more than half of the total distance of the hike. The Red Cross Trail now makes a short, steep climb to another viewpoint. At 1,100 feet above sea level, you can look back across the road toward Pine Swamp and Surebridge Mountains.

After crossing under a telephone line, the trail climbs a little, descends, and traverses some wet areas. It soon reaches a woods road and turns left to follow it. A short distance beyond, you'll reach a junction with another woods road, known as the Hasenclever Road. You are now at the center of the Hasenclever Mine complex. You'll know that you're here when you spot the rusted debris on the side of the trail and the large mine pits—one of which is large enough to swallow a truck.

In 1765, Peter Hasenclever, while traveling through the area, discovered a large deposit of iron ore. He immediately bought 1,000 acres, including most of Cedar Ponds (now Lake Tiorati). His intention was to construct a furnace, but he was recalled to England before it could be built. However, mine operations under a succession of owners continued on and off for almost 100 years. In the mid-1850s, one owner planned a railroad from the mine to the Hudson River at Stony Point. Though the railroad was never completed, the trench in which it was to run can still be seen, as can stone foundations and other remnants of the mining activity. At its peak, some 20 to 30 men worked in this area. The book *Iron Mine Trails* by Edward J. Lenik (published by the Trail Conference in 1996 and now available online as an e-book) provides an extensive history and guide for exploring this area in depth.

Turn right, leaving the Red Cross Trail, and follow the unmarked Hasenclever Road. Although not blazed, this wide woods road is easy to follow. (If you'd rather not follow an unmarked route—especially if you're worried about darkness or weather—an alternative route is to stay on the marked Red Cross Trail, which reaches the paved Tiorati Brook Road in little more than half a mile. Turn right and walk along the road for 1 mile back to your car.) Hasenclever Road soon crosses a bridge with concrete abutments and begins a gradual climb. In 0.7 mile, you'll reach a junction with the blue-blazed Beech Trail. Turn left onto the Beech Trail, and head back to the parking area, which you'll reach in three-quarters of a mile.

OTHER HIKING OPTIONS

During the winter months, when Tiorati Brook Road is closed—or for those wanting a shorter hike of 6 miles—begin the hike at the Lake Skannatati access just off Seven Lakes Drive. To reach this parking area, take the Palisades Interstate Parkway to Exit 18 and the Long Mountain Circle. Go around the circle to Seven Lakes Drive (not US 6). Head south on Seven Lakes Drive for 6.4 miles and turn right (downhill) into the Lake Skannatati parking area. Begin the loop hike on the Arden–Surebridge Trail, as noted in the text above, but when you reach the intersection of Hasenclever Road with the Beech Trail, turn right (rather than left) to continue on the route of the hike that will lead you back to the parking area at Lake Skannatati.

Iron Mines Loop

TOTAL DISTANCE: 8 miles

WALKING TIME: 5 hours

ELEVATION GAIN: 1,803 feet

MAPS: USGS 7.5' Monroe; USGS 7.5' Popolopen Lake; USGS 7.5' Thiells; USGS 7.5' Sloatsburg; NY–NJTC Harriman-Bear Mountain Trails #119

TRAILHEAD GPS COORDINATES: N 41° 14' 30" W 74° 06' 08"

Harriman State Park is full of historical walks, and this hike, which visits several of the region's nineteenth-century iron mines, blends good hiking with the annals of that time. Iron mining in the Ramapos actually dates back to 1742. At the onset of the Revolutionary War, the colonies were producing 14 percent of the world's iron, and they began exporting iron ore in 1817. Entrepreneurs were attracted not only by the iron ore of the Ramapo Hills, but by the nearby watercourses, needed to power the bellows for the furnaces, and by the heavily wooded slopes, whose timber yielded the necessary charcoal. Several nearby furnaces—including the Sterling Furnace near Sterling Lake, the Greenwood Furnace near the Ramapo River, the Queensboro Furnace, and the Forest of Dean Furnace—produced iron for guns during the American Revolution and the Civil War.

The mines varied in depth from 10 to 6,000 feet, the deepest being the Forest of Dean Mine (now located on the property of the United States Military Academy at West Point). Many of the mines are water-filled and dangerous. This walk takes you past a few of the mines that can be viewed safely from the trail.

The mines you'll walk past are in the Greenwood group, so called because their ore was smelted at the Greenwood Furnace at Arden. This and other furnaces are described in *Vanishing Ironworks of the Ramapos* by James M. Ransom, a book to read if you wish to delve deeply into the history of the area. The Greenwood Furnace was established about 1810 and supplied cannonballs to the American forces during the War of 1812. Robert Parrott acquired an interest in the furnace and surrounding lands in 1837, and he and his brother Peter managed the ironworks and became its

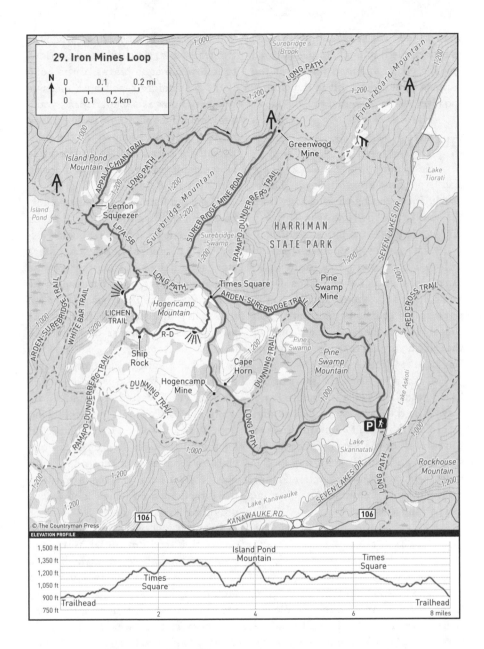

sole owners. With coal transported by the newly built Erie Railroad through the Ramapo Valley, the furnace's output increased until yearly production reached 5,000 tons of pig iron, destined for fine hardware and stoves. During the Civil War, the iron was used for the famous Parrott rifle, the most effective artillery weapon of the Union Army. This rifle was made at the West Point Foundry at Cold Spring under the direction of Robert Parrott. The ore supplied by the Greenwood, Surebridge, Pine Swamp, O'Neil, and Clove Mines was hauled to a kiln about half a mile above the Greenwood Furnace, where the ore was roasted to drive off sulfur, stamped to reduce the fragments to the size of a "pigeon's egg," and then smelted in the furnace, which was built in the charming glen beside the outlet of Echo Lake.

GETTING THERE

The mines loop starts at the Lake Skannatati parking area off Seven Lakes Drive. To reach this parking area from the south, take the New York Thruway (I-87) to Exit 15A and proceed north on NY 17 for 2.7 miles, through and past the village of Sloatsburg, to a traffic light. Turn right onto Seven Lakes Drive and continue for about 7.8 miles to the parking area for Lake Skannatati, on the left side of the road. The turnoff to the parking area is 0.7 mile beyond the Kanawauke Circle.

You can also reach the start of the hike via the Palisades Interstate Parkway. Take the Parkway to Exit 18 and go around the Long Mountain Circle to the turnoff for the Seven Lakes Drive. Continue on Seven Lakes Drive for 2.6 miles beyond the Tiorati Circle, and turn right (downhill) into the Lake Skannatati parking area.

THE HIKE

Two trails leave from the northwest corner of this parking area—the inverted-red-triangle-on-white-blazed Arden-Surebridge Trail, and the aqua-blazed Long Path. Follow the aqua blazes of the Long Path, which heads west and parallel to Lake Skannatati, and crosses an inlet stream near the northwest bay of the lake.

After climbing some more, the trail comes out on a woods road, the route of the yellow-blazed Dunning Trail. Turn left, briefly following both aqua and yellow blazes—but just ahead, when the two trails split, bear right and continue to follow the aqua blazes of the Long Path. Just before reaching a massive boulder (known as Cape Horn), you'll see remnants of nineteenth-century mining activity below to the left. Directly below the trail is a shaft of the Hogencamp Mine, which was active from 1870 to 1885.

The Long Path now begins to climb, passing a split boulder on a hill to the left. After a level section through a valley, the trail climbs slightly and passes stone foundations. A tramway from the Hogencamp Mine, used to transport the iron ore to a mine road, passed through this valley, and the stone foundations are probably remnants of structures built for the tramway.

The Long Path descends to a junction with the Arden–Surebridge Trail, marked with inverted-red-triangle-on-white blazes. Turn left, now following both aqua and red-on-white blazes. In another 100 feet, you'll reach a large glacial erratic on the right known as "Times Square." Trails or woods roads extend in five directions from Times Square, thus providing its nickname.

Bear left just beyond Times Square onto the red-dot-on-white-blazed Ramapo-Dunderberg Trail, which heads southwest. It steeply climbs Hogencamp Mountain through hemlocks. Toward the top, you'll come out on a rock outcrop in an area that was ravaged by fire in 1988. You'll pass wonderful rock clefts and climb some more over bare rocks with glacial striations, with panoramic south-facing views over rolling terrain.

After reaching the summit of Hogencamp Mountain (1,353 feet), the trail continues across the broad summit ridge. It then zigzags down to Ship Rock, so named because it looks like a

CAPE HORN

bottom-up prow of a boat. Just beyond, the trail makes a sharp right turn.

A short distance beyond, you'll notice a triple-blue-L-on-white blaze, which indicates the start of the Lichen Trail. Turn right and follow this picturesque trail, which proceeds through tall mountain laurel and hemlock, and over rock ledges. After passing a viewpoint to the northwest, the Lichen Trail drops sharply along an evergreen-covered hillside. At the base of the descent, it reaches an intersection with the co-aligned Arden–Surebridge Trail and Long Path, with inverted-red-triangle-on-white and aqua blazes. Turn left and follow the Arden–Surebridge Trail/Long Path, which passes a swamp on the right and heads down a pretty hemlock-covered hillside.

As the trail levels off at the bottom of the hill, it passes a wet area on the right and reaches another intersection. Here, the Long Path leaves to the right (northeast) and the White Bar Trail begins on the left. Continue ahead on the red-on-white-blazed Arden–Surebridge Trail,

the middle route, which crosses a small stream, follows it briefly, then begins to climb beside cliffs with massive rock formations. The hill to your right is recovering from the devastation of fires.

Soon, you'll notice a dramatic cleft at the edge of a cliff and reach a junction with the white-blazed Appalachian Trail (AT). Turn right, leaving the Arden–Surebridge Trail, and follow the white AT blazes, which lead under an overhanging rock and into a fascinating rock formation, aptly named the Lemon Squeezer. The trail climbs through a miniature chasm at the base of the cliff and then a steep rock face, where you will need to use both your hands and your feet. If the climb is too difficult, it is possible to bypass the steepest part by following a blue-blazed trail on the left.

After reaching the top of the Lemon Squeezer, the AT continues on a more moderate grade to the summit of Island Pond Mountain. Just north of the summit, you'll pass the ruins of a stone cabin built by Edward Harriman over a century ago.

HIKING THROUGH THE LEMON SQUEEZER

features, turn around and head south on Surebridge Mine Road, continuing past the junction with the AT. Soon, you'll pass a large swamp, where signs of mining abound; tailing piles are everywhere, and a few pits of the Surebridge Mine lie to the east of the road. The road follows a causeway built up of tailings and heads south across Surebridge Swamp. An arch of rhododendron shades the causeway, from which there are glimpses of twisted stumps and wildflowers in the sphagnum bog.

Near the south end of the swamp, the road climbs a little, and the co-aligned Arden–Surebridge Trail/Long Path joins from the left. Continue ahead, now following the inverted-red-triangle-on-white and aqua blazes along Surebridge Mine Road. Just ahead, you'll pass Times Square, where the red-dot-on-white-blazed Ramapo–Dunderberg Trail crosses and the Long Path leaves. Continue ahead on the Arden–Surebridge Trail, which begins a steady descent on an old mine road.

At the base of the descent, the yellow-blazed Dunning Trail begins on the right. Continue ahead on the Arden–Surebridge Trail, which crosses a stream. Just beyond, a large rectangular cut in the hillside to the left is a remnant of the Pine Swamp Mine, which operated from 1830 to 1880. You'll pass several other mine pits as you continue along the old mine road.

Just beyond these mine openings, the trail bears right and descends into the woods, passing a stone wall and stone foundations on the left. The Arden–Surebridge Trail now climbs around a shoulder of Pine Swamp Mountain and returns to the parking area at Lake Skannatati, where you left your car.

The AT descends from the summit and enters an attractive hemlock grove. After winding through the hemlocks, you'll reach a junction with the aqua-blazed Long Path, marked by a wooden signpost. Continue ahead on the AT, which soon parallels a stream, crosses it, then turns right and climbs over the ridge of Surebridge Mountain.

At the base of the descent, the AT crosses Surebridge Brook and turns left onto Surebridge Mine Road. A little farther along the road you'll notice a 100-foot-long, water-filled mine pit on the right, with an adjacent pile of tailings. This is the site of the Greenwood Mine, from which iron ore was extracted between 1838 and 1880. At the north end of the mine pit, you can see a drill mark in the rock face, and several rusted pipes are visible nearby.

After examining these interesting

Menomine Trail/Black Mountain

TOTAL DISTANCE: 4.5 miles

WALKING TIME: 3 hours

ELEVATION GAIN: 1,031 feet

MAPS: USGS 7.5' Popolopen Lake; NY-NJTC Harriman-Bear Mountain Trails #119

TRAILHEAD GPS COORDINATES: N 41° 17' 44" W 74° 03' 34.5"

In 1994, volunteers of the New York–New Jersey Trail Conference cleared and marked the Menomine Trail as a convenient connection between the Appalachian Trail (AT) and the Long Path. More importantly, it was the first marked trail to utilize the large Silvermine parking area that, unlike many others, is maintained (plowed) in winter.

This hike includes the 1,200-foot summit of Black Mountain. The route up the mountain features some lovely views, and the peak has an extensive view of the Hudson Valley down as far as the New York City skyline. The last part of the hike is not on a marked trail, but the route is pleasant and easy to follow (although it includes a short walk along Seven Lakes Drive).

GETTING THERE

To reach the Silvermine parking area, take the Palisades Interstate Parkway to Exit 18. Proceed almost all the way around the traffic circle to Seven Lakes Drive (westbound). The parking area is on your left, 1.4 miles along the road. A fee is usually charged from Memorial Day to Labor Day.

THE HIKE

Begin the hike on the yellow-blazed Menomine Trail by crossing the wide bridge at the bottom of the parking area and turning left on a dirt road, passing two small wooden outbuildings. After a short stretch through the woods, the trail begins to parallel the shore of Silvermine Lake.

Silvermine Lake has an interesting history. In the early 1900s, the area was called Bockey Swamp, "bockey" being a local term for the woven baskets used by charcoal burners. During

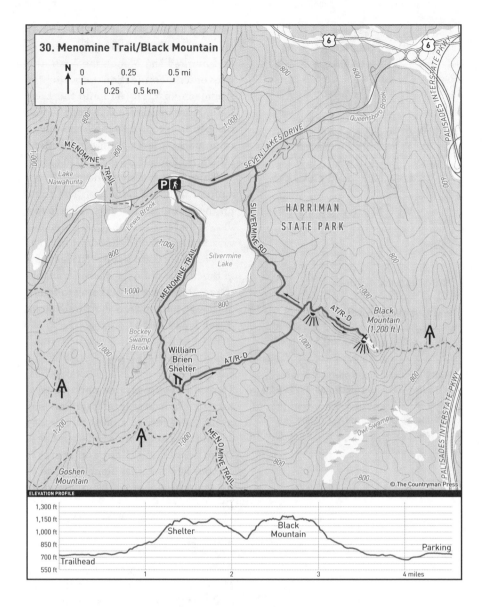

30. Menomine Trail/Black Mountain

the 1920s, beavers—which had just been reintroduced—built a dam, killing many trees. The park cleared the dead trees and planted rice, which they hoped would attract birds to the area. Instead, deer ate the rice. In 1934, the Civilian Conservation Corps (CCC) built a 600-foot dam, and the new lake was named Menomine (wild rice) by Major William A. Welch, the first general manager of the park. In 1936, a ski slope and rope tow were installed, and the area was named Silvermine after a legendary Spanish silver mine on Black Mountain. In 1942, a second ski slope was added, and in 1951 the lake was renamed Silvermine. The parking lot was enlarged in 1968, but the ski area was closed in 1986. The name Menomine was brought back to the area when the trail was dedicated in 1994.

After about 20 minutes of walking, the trail heads away from Silvermine Lake and begins a modest ascent on a woods road to a crest, where it makes a sharp left, crosses Bockey Swamp Brook (the inlet of the lake), and climbs rather steeply on a rocky woods road to the William Brien Memorial Shelter, 1.4 miles from the hike's start. Here, the Menomine Trail crosses the white-blazed AT, which is co-aligned with the red-dot-on-white-blazed Ramapo–Dunderberg Trail.

The William Brien Memorial Shelter, built in 1933, was later named for the first president of the New York Ramblers, a local hiking club. A short blue-blazed trail from the shelter leads to a well (all backcountry water should be treated before drinking). This area is popular with backpackers and long-distance AT hikers, as it is one of the few legal places to camp within the park.

From the shelter, look ahead about 100 feet to a boulder-covered hill. The AT and Ramapo–Dunderberg blazes will be clearly visible at the top. Continue ahead on the Menomine Trail for 50 feet, make a left onto the AT/Ramapo–Dunderberg Trail, and climb up the hill. The trail meanders along the top of the ridge through open hardwoods and, in about a mile, descends to a wide gravel road. Known as the Silvermine Road, it was built in 1934 as a fire road and will be the route you later use to complete this hike.

For now, cross the road and continue ahead on the AT/Ramapo–Dunderberg Trail as it climbs steeply up Black Mountain on a well-defined footpath. In about five minutes, you'll reach a good viewpoint from a rock outcrop over Silvermine Lake and the area you just traversed. Continue climbing more gently on the AT/Ramapo–Dunderberg Trail to the broad 1,200-foot summit of Black Mountain, which affords spectacular views over the Hudson River and

WILLIAM BRIEN MEMORIAL SHELTER

SILVERMINE LAKE FROM VIEWPOINT ON BLACK MOUNTAIN

the surrounding area. The small lake ahead of you is Owl Swamp. Farther afield, on the west bank of the river, are the dramatic shapes of the Tors (Hike #24) and Hook Mountain (Hike #23). On a clear day, the New York City skyline is visible on the horizon. You'll want to linger here for a while and take in the panoramic view.

When you're ready to continue, retrace your steps down the mountain back to the gravel Silvermine Road. Turn right, downhill, toward the lake.

The road is unmarked but very easy to follow. In 15 minutes, you'll pass by the dam (crossing is prohibited and unsafe), and five minutes later, you'll cross Queensboro Brook on a substantial bridge. Almost immediately after the bridge, two green-and-black-painted metal posts flank the road. Here, turn left and follow an unmarked trail about 100 feet to Seven Lakes Drive. Turn left and walk along the shoulder of the road for 0.4 mile back to the Silvermine parking area, where the hike began.

Anthony Wayne Loop

TOTAL DISTANCE: 5.5 miles

WALKING TIME: 4 hours

ELEVATION GAIN: 1,850 feet

MAPS: USGS 7.5' Popolopen Lake; NY–NJTC Harriman-Bear Mountain Trails #119

TRAILHEAD GPS COORDINATES: N 41° 17' 54" W 74° 01' 40"

This hike uses portions of several trails in Harriman State Park, including the Suffern–Bear Mountain Trail, the longest trail in the park. It features a wonderful ridge walk with extensive views both to the east and west. The hike begins at the Anthony Wayne Recreation Area, opened in 1955, where the huge parking area once served visitors to two large swimming pools. The pools were closed in 1988 and have since been demolished, leaving the parking area for use primarily by hikers.

GETTING THERE

Take the Palisades Interstate Parkway to Exit 17, and drive past the tollbooth to park in the first lot on the right-hand side. Parking is normally free, except when special events are held. For information, call the Palisades Interstate Park Commission at 845-786-2701.

THE HIKE

Walk back toward the tollbooth, turn left, and head toward two stone gateposts on the east side of the access road to the parking area. Signs on the metal barrier between the gateposts indicate that hiking trails start here. Our hike begins on the white-blazed Anthony Wayne Trail, which (like the recreation area) was named after the famous general "Mad Anthony" Wayne, who was believed to have marched with his men through the area in 1779 during the American Revolution. The Anthony Wayne Trail heads uphill on a gravel road (also marked with blue-on-white-diamond blazes as a bike trail), crosses a dirt road, and soon reaches a T-junction where the trail turns left. Look immediately to the left to find a triple-red-F-on-white blaze that marks the start of the

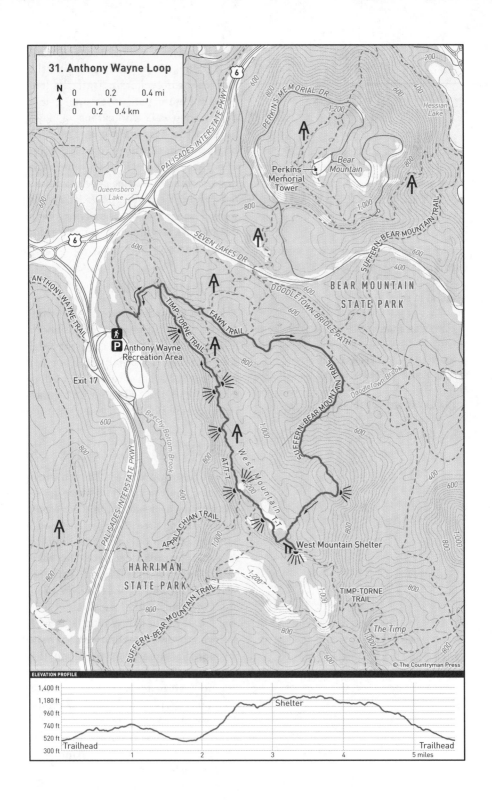

31. Anthony Wayne Loop

N
0   0.2   0.4 mi
0   0.2   0.4 km

Perkins Memorial Tower

Bear Mountain

Hessian Lake

PERKINS MEMORIAL DR

Queensboro Lake

SEVEN LAKES DR

BEAR MOUNTAIN STATE PARK

SUFFERN–BEAR MOUNTAIN TRAIL

DOODLETOWN BRIDLE PATH

ANTHONY WAYNE TRAIL

TIMP-TORNE TRAIL

FAWN TRAIL

Anthony Wayne Recreation Area

Exit 17

PALISADES INTERSTATE PKWY

Beechy Bottom Brook

SUFFERN–BEAR MOUNTAIN TRAIL

Doodletown Brook

A.T./T-T

West Mountain T-T

West Mountain Shelter

APPALACHIAN TRAIL

HARRIMAN STATE PARK

TIMP-TORNE TRAIL

The Timp

SUFFERN–BEAR MOUNTAIN TRAIL

© The Countryman Press

ELEVATION PROFILE

1,400 ft	
1,180 ft	Shelter
960 ft	
740 ft	
520 ft	
300 ft	Trailhead Trailhead

1   2   3   4   5 miles

WEST MOUNTAIN SHELTER

Fawn Trail. This trail was shown on the first park map produced in 1920 and was badly damaged by bulldozers making a fire lane during the fire of 1988.

After climbing a switchback and then ascending more gradually, the Fawn Trail meets the blue-blazed Timp-Torne Trail at the height of land. Take note here because the hike will bring you back to this junction later on. Ahead (if there are no leaves on the trees) is a good view of Bear Mountain and the Perkins Memorial Tower. Continue on the Fawn Trail, which crosses the Timp-Torne Trail and bears left. It goes gently downhill at first and continues through a peaceful hardwood forest. After crossing the Appalachian Trail (AT), the Fawn Trail proceeds through a shallow valley and follows a woods road to a junction with the Doodletown Bridle Path.

The hamlet called Doodletown was first inhabited by the Junes (or Jouvins), descendants of the French Huguenots, probably in 1762. There are a number of suggestions for the derivation of the name. One of the most interesting is that the British derided the settlers by playing the tune "Yankee Doodle" as they marched through town (although records show that it had already been named Doodletown by the time of the British arrival). It is believed that 300 people once lived in Doodletown, and for many years after the hamlet's abandonment in 1965, the school remained standing. Today, only foundations of the buildings can be discovered, sometimes covered by the nonnative barberry. The Doodletown Bridle Path, which circles the hamlet, was built in 1935 for use by horses and cross-country skiers, but its use by horses ended when the stables at Bear Mountain were demolished in 1961.

Continue to follow the Fawn Trail as it turns right and heads east along the Doodletown Bridle Path. It soon begins to descend, with a pretty stream below on the left. In about half a mile, the Fawn Trail ends, and the yellow-blazed

WEST-FACING VIEW FROM WEST MOUNTAIN

Suffern–Bear Mountain Trail comes in from the left. Continue along the Bridle Path, now following yellow blazes. In 750 feet, turn right, leaving the Bridle Path, and follow the yellow blazes of the Suffern–Bear Mountain Trail uphill on a rocky woods road. After the trail crosses the Doodlekill, the climb steepens. Soon after the trail bears left, leaving the woods road, it reaches a short, rocky climb over a talus slope, followed by a more gentle section. The Suffern–Bear Mountain Trail then passes through a small rock outcrop. Just off the trail

of Bear Mountain on the right. A short distance beyond, you'll reach a junction with the blue-blazed Timp-Torne Trail, which takes its name from two prominent summits in the Harriman-Bear Mountain State Parks: the Timp, which you have just seen (and will see again in a few minutes), and the Popolopen Torne, to the north. Turn left, following the blue blazes, and in about 500 feet you'll reach the West Mountain Shelter, built in 1928, with excellent views of the Timp and the Hudson River. This is a great place to take a break.

When you're ready to continue, retrace your steps back to the junction and turn left, now following both blue and yellow blazes. In 0.3 mile, the yellow-blazed Suffern–Bear Mountain Trail goes off to the left, and you continue ahead on the blue-blazed Timp-Torne Trail. Fire once consumed the area crossed by the trail, but now birch, cedar, and pines are thankfully making a comeback, and your route on the ridge is open to the sky.

In another 0.1 mile, the AT joins the Timp-Torne Trail at a junction marked with a wooden signpost. Your hike for the next 0.7 mile is along the spectacular west ridge of West Mountain, which offers many fine outlooks both to the west and to the east as the trails jog from one side of the ridge to the other, tempting you to linger.

The coaligned blue-and-white blazes lead over open flat rocks and up a short climb before reaching a fork where the two trails split. Bear left and follow the Timp-Torne Trail, which heads downhill over rock slabs, passes through an interesting cleft in a rock, and finally reaches the junction with the Fawn Trail where you were previously. Turn left and retrace your steps back to your car.

to the left, there is a limited view of the Timp and the Hudson River.

After descending into a hollow and continuing through a mountain laurel thicket, the trail climbs a talus slope and emerges in an open area, with a view

32

Popolopen Torne

TOTAL DISTANCE: 4.5 miles

WALKING TIME: 3.5 hours

ELEVATION GAIN: 1,608 feet

MAPS: USGS 7.5' Popolopen Lake; USGS 7.5' Peekskill; NY–NJTC Harriman-Bear Mountain Trails #119

TRAILHEAD GPS COORDINATES: N 41° 19' 26" W 73° 59' 16"

This loop hike traverses both sides of a spectacular gorge and scrambles up an exquisite peak with a breathtaking 360-degree view of West Point, Bear Mountain, and the Hudson River.

GETTING THERE

From the traffic circle on the west side of the Bear Mountain Bridge, proceed north on US 9W for 0.2 mile to the Fort Montgomery State Historic Site on the east side of the road. Free parking is available, but there is a small admission charge to enter the visitor center (845-446-2134), which has displays and an interesting historic film. Self-guided tours of the area are available.

THE HIKE

Begin the hike by walking back to US 9W, crossing the road, and heading south on a sidewalk over the Popolopen Viaduct (built in 1916 and widened in 1936). Just after the guardrail ends, you'll notice a triple-red-on-white blaze on a rock to the right, which marks the start of the Popolopen Gorge Trail. Turn right onto this trail, which soon begins to descend on a woods road, crossing under a power line on the way. At the base of the descent, it reaches the abutment of a former bridge over Popolopen Creek. Until the 140-foot-high Popolopen Viaduct was built in 1916, the iron bridge supported by this abutment—known as the Hell Hole Bridge—was the only way to cross the creek in this vicinity.

The Popolopen Gorge Trail now climbs on a footpath and begins to run parallel to the cascading Popolopen Creek. About half a mile from the site of the old bridge, watch carefully for a double blaze that marks a sharp left turn. The trail now climbs steeply on

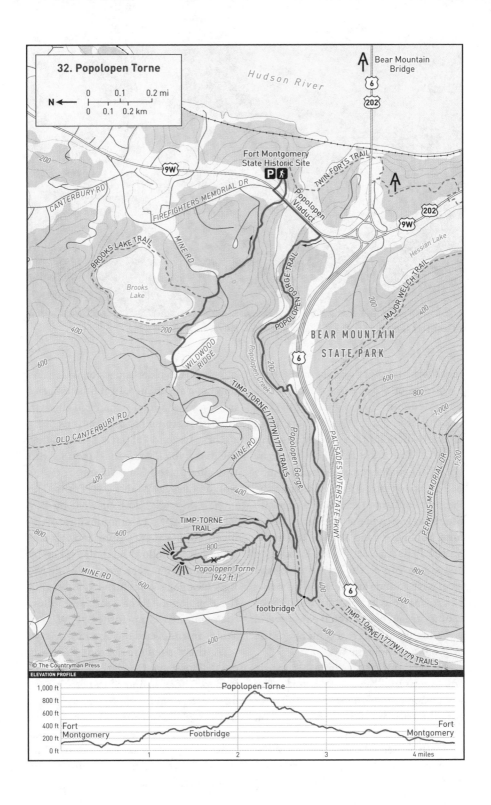

32. Popolopen Torne

N ← | 0   0.1   0.2 mi
      0   0.1   0.2 km

Hudson River

Bear Mountain
Bridge

6
202

Fort Montgomery
State Historic Site

9W

TWIN FORTS TRAIL

Popolopen
Viaduct

202

9W

CANTERBURY RD

FIREFIGHTERS MEMORIAL DR

BROOKS LAKE TRAIL

MINE RD

Brooks
Lake

Hessian Lake

MAJOR WELCH TRAIL

POPOLOPEN GORGE TRAIL

BEAR MOUNTAIN
STATE PARK

Popolopen Creek

WILDWOOD
RIDGE

6

200

TIMP-TORNE/1777W/1779 TRAILS

OLD CANTERBURY RD

MINE RD

Popolopen Gorge

PALISADES INTERSTATE PKWY

PERKINS MEMORIAL DR

TIMP-TORNE
TRAIL

Popolopen Torne
(942 ft.)

MINE RD

6

footbridge

TIMP-TORNE/1777W/1779 TRAILS

© The Countryman Press

ELEVATION PROFILE

		Popolopen Torne	
1,000 ft
800 ft
600 ft
400 ft Fort
200 ft Montgomery   Footbridge
0 ft

Fort
Montgomery

1   2   3   4 miles

VIEW OF BEAR MOUNTAIN BRIDGE AND HUDSON RIVER FROM THE POPOLOPEN TORNE

rock steps and switchbacks, and reaches a wide woods road—the route of the Bear Mountain Aqueduct, built in 1930 to bring water from Queensboro Lake to the Bear Mountain Inn, and rebuilt in 2012. You are now high above the gorge; the water roars below. You may get glimpses through the trees of the Popolopen Torne, across the creek to the right, which is the high point of the hike. You'll also hear and see the traffic on the Palisades Interstate Parkway—just above you on the left—but, for the most part, sounds of traffic will probably be drowned out by the thunderous, cascading stream below. You'll pass several large manhole covers, remnants of the original 1930 aqueduct.

After about half a mile along the aqueduct, you'll come to a fork. The wide woods road—the route of the 2012 aqueduct—bears left here, but you should continue straight ahead onto a footpath, which follows the route of the 1930 aqueduct. You'll pass more manhole covers and exposed sections of

pipe from the older aqueduct, which has now been abandoned. In another quarter mile, a woods road joins from the left, and the surrounding area flattens out.

Just beyond (about 1.5 miles into the hike), you'll come to a junction with the blue-blazed Timp-Torne Trail, as well as the 1777W and 1779 Trails. The latter two trails, both marked by Boy Scouts in 1975 to commemorate the bicentennial of the American Revolution, roughly follow the routes taken by British and American troops during the Revolutionary War. Turn right, leaving the Popolopen Gorge Trail, and follow the coaligned Timp-Torne/1777W/1779 Trails down toward the stream.

At the base of the descent, the trails cross Popolopen Creek on a truss footbridge. The crossing of the creek here has been a challenge for many years. Until 1998, hikers crossed on a wooden bridge a short distance upstream, but that bridge was washed away by Hurricane Floyd. In 2004, funding was obtained for a new truss footbridge that was installed by volunteers of the New York–New Jersey Trail Conference. This bridge was built much higher than the previous one and was designed to withstand flooding. But the ferocious Hurricane Irene in August 2011 washed it away. In 2013, a new bridge of similar design was procured by the park and installed by Trail Conference volunteers.

After crossing the bridge, the trails head uphill on stone steps and soon reach a woods road—the route of the West Point Aqueduct, built in 1906 to carry water from Queensboro Lake to the United States Military Academy at West Point. The trails turn right and follow the aqueduct. In 300 feet, be alert for a double-blue blaze which marks a sharp left turn. Turn left and follow the blue-blazed Timp-Torne Trail, which leaves the aqueduct and begins its climb of the Popolopen Torne (the 1777W and 1779 Trails continue ahead along the aqueduct).

The Timp-Torne Trail crosses the unpaved Fort Montgomery Road and the paved Mine Road and climbs steadily through the woods. Soon, it comes out on open rocks. You'll need both your hands and your feet to negotiate some of the steep climbs. Pay careful attention to the blazes, which indicate the twists and turns of the best route.

As you get higher and climb through this fascinating terrain, views open up. At first, you can see Bear Mountain and the Hudson River to the east. A little higher, the view broadens to include the magnificent Bear Mountain Bridge

WEST-FACING VIEW FROM THE POPOLOPEN TORNE

across the Hudson, built privately in 1924. It was the first vehicular bridge built over the Hudson south of Albany and, when built, it had the longest main suspension span in the world. The bridge was not profitable, and it was sold to New York State in 1940. Behind the bridge is Anthony's Nose, the location of another hike (Hike #14) in this book. As you approach the summit, a west-facing view over the hills of the West Point Military Reservation opens up (the Harriman Park–West Point boundary is only yards away).

The summit of the Popolopen Torne is marked by a stone monument honoring members of the United States armed forces. The stones making up the monument were carried by volunteers from the base of the mountain. The summit offers a magnificent 360-degree view, and you'll want to take a break to rest from the climb and enjoy the panoramic view.

The Timp-Torne Trail continues beyond the monument and passes two more viewpoints—first to the west, then to the east—before reentering the woods. After a short descent over rocks, the route down the mountain follows a graded trail and is not as steep as the climb up the mountain. The trail passes one final east-facing viewpoint from a rock ledge and descends through the woods to Mine Road, reaching it about 500 feet east of where you crossed the road on the way up. Turn left and follow the road a short distance to a small parking area on the right. Turn right at the parking area onto a dirt road and, in 100 feet, turn left onto a woods road that descends toward the Popolopen Gorge. When you reach the route of the aqueduct, turn left and rejoin the 1777W and 1779 Trails. For the rest of the hike, you'll be following three coaligned trails: Timp-Torne, 1777W, and 1779.

The trails continue along the aqueduct for the next 0.7 mile. At first the route is level, supported by a stone retaining wall on the right, but you'll encounter a short, steep climb, followed by an equally steep descent. After crossing a stream, the trails climb to the paved Mine Road. Turn right onto Mine Road (passing Wildwood Ridge, a dead-end street) and continue for about 500 feet, then turn left at a double blaze and reenter the woods. The trails now descend, with Brooks Lake visible on the left through the trees.

At the base of the descent, the red-on-white-blazed Brooks Lake Trail joins briefly, and the trails cross a wet area on puncheons. At the next intersection, follow the Timp-Torne/1777W/1779 Trails as they turn right onto a grassy woods road, which leads in a short distance back to the paved Mine Road. Turn left, follow the road for only 150 feet, then turn right and reenter the woods on a footpath. Bear left at a fork in the trail, and you'll soon emerge onto a wide turn on a paved road. Take the right fork and head slightly downhill for a short distance until you see a double blaze, where the trails turn right and reenter the woods. Follow the coaligned Timp-Torne, 1777W, and 1779 Trails under the Popolopen Viaduct to their terminus at the Fort Montgomery Historic Site, where the hike began.

Bear Mountain Loop

TOTAL DISTANCE: 4.2 miles

WALKING TIME: 3 hours

ELEVATION GAIN: 1,388 feet

MAPS: USGS 7.5' Peekskill; USGS 7.5' Oscawana Lake; NY–NJTC Harriman–Bear Mountain Trails #119

TRAILHEAD GPS COORDINATES: N 41° 18' 44" W 73° 59' 20"

This loop hike climbs Bear Mountain on the steep Major Welch Trail and descends on a newly rebuilt section of the Appalachian Trail (AT). The original route of the AT on Bear Mountain was completed in 1923, but the path has been relocated several times since then.

By 2000, the AT route up the east face of Bear Mountain had become eroded and unattractive. In light of heavy use of this section of the AT by day visitors to the Bear Mountain Inn, the Trail Conference decided that the trail should be relocated. The most attractive alternative required traversing an area of jumbled boulders to the northwest of the existing AT. To build a new trail through this area, the Trail Conference recruited professional trail builders to lead the construction effort and train hundreds of volunteers.

Construction of the new route up the east face of Bear Mountain began in 2006. By the time this relocation of the AT on the lower east face of the mountain was completed and opened in 2010, more than 800 individuals had volunteered over 30,000 hours of their time to construct this section of the AT, which features stone steps and crib walls. Construction required the same kind of masonry skills utilized by the Civilian Conservation Corps (CCC) in the 1930s to build roads, walls, and buildings in Harriman-Bear Mountain State Parks. Funding for the project was provided by the Trail Conference; the National Park Service; the Appalachian Trail Conservancy; the New York State Office of Parks, Recreation, and Historic Preservation; and the Palisades Interstate Park Commission. The relocated AT route on the upper east face of the mountain, from the Scenic Drive to the summit, was constructed largely by

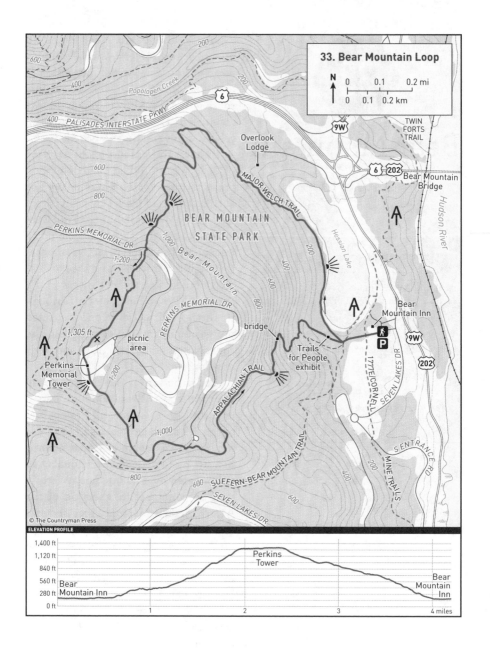

33. Bear Mountain Loop

N

0	0.1	0.2 mi
0	0.1	0.2 km

BEAR MOUNTAIN STATE PARK

Popolopen Creek

PALISADES INTERSTATE PKWY

PERKINS MEMORIAL DR

MAJOR WELCH TRAIL

Overlook Lodge

Bear Mountain

Hessian Lake

Hudson River

TWIN FORTS TRAIL

Bear Mountain Bridge

Bear Mountain Inn

1,305 ft.

Perkins Memorial Tower

picnic area

bridge

Trails for People exhibit

APPALACHIAN TRAIL

1777E (CORNELL)

SEVEN LAKES DR

S ENTRANCE RD

MINE TRAILS

SUFFERN-BEAR MOUNTAIN TRAIL

SEVEN LAKES DR

© The Countryman Press

ELEVATION PROFILE

1,400 ft				
1,120 ft		Perkins Tower		
840 ft				
560 ft	Bear			Bear Mountain Inn
280 ft	Mountain Inn			
0 ft	1	2	3	4 miles

AmeriCorps trail crews, working with volunteers, and was completed in the fall of 2018.

GETTING THERE

From the traffic circle on the west side of the Bear Mountain Bridge (at the north end of the Palisades Interstate Parkway), proceed south on US 9W for 0.4 mile, then bear right at the traffic light and follow the ramp to the Bear Mountain Inn. Park in the large parking lot adjacent to the inn. A parking fee is charged on weekends year-round, and daily from Memorial Day to Labor Day.

VIEW FROM THE SUMMIT OF BEAR MOUNTAIN

THE HIKE

From the parking area, proceed west (toward the mountain) on a paved path that runs along the south side of the Bear Mountain Inn. About 400 feet beyond the inn, you'll reach a junction of paved paths, marked by a trail sign. Turn right and follow the red-circle-on-white-blazed Major Welch Trail (named after the park's first general manager, who was instrumental in creating the extensive network of hiking trails in Harriman-Bear Mountain Parks). The Major Welch Trail proceeds north along a relatively level paved path, following the western shore of Hessian Lake and passing views of Anthony's Nose (across the river) and a tower of the Bear Mountain Bridge. In the 1700s, this lake was known as Lake Sinnipink, derived from a Native American name of the nearby Assinapink Creek. During the nineteenth century, blocks of ice were cut from the lake and shipped to New York City by the Knickerbocker Ice Company.

In about half a mile, near the northern end of the lake, the trail bears left and climbs stone steps. Soon the trail levels off, then climbs more gradually on a rocky footpath. After passing a water tank, above on the left, the trail descends slightly on a dirt road, then bears left and continues on a relatively level (but very rocky) footpath through dense mountain laurel. If there are no leaves on the trees, below and to the right you may notice the flat-roofed Overlook Lodge, part of the Bear Mountain Inn complex.

In another 0.3 mile, the trail bears left and resumes its climb of Bear Mountain. The ascent soon steepens, with the trail following a rocky footpath through mountain laurel. Within a short distance, the trail turns left onto a well-graded footpath with stone steps, constructed in 2014 by an AmeriCorps trail crew along with professional trail builders. In about 600 feet, the trail climbs a long flight of narrow stone steps wedged between large rocks (the stone steps

STONE STEPS ALONG THE MAJOR WELCH TRAIL

were constructed by the Jolly Rovers Trail Crew) and turns right at a large boulder, switching back toward the west.

At the end of the new trail section, the Major Welch Trail turns left and begins to climb several rock outcrops surrounded by mountain laurel. It then climbs a long rock outcrop studded with pitch pines, which affords a panoramic north-facing view. After climbing a little farther, the trail emerges onto another rock outcrop with an even broader view, including the Hudson River. Brooks Lake is visible directly ahead, and the Bear Mountain Bridge is on the right, with Anthony's Nose behind it.

The trail continues ahead, briefly leveling off but soon resuming its ascent. Soon, you'll climb stone steps and reach the paved Perkins Memorial Drive, an auto route to the top of Bear Mountain. Follow the trail as it crosses the road diagonally to the left, climbs stone steps, and continues to climb over more rock outcrops through mountain laurel.

After climbing another 150 vertical feet, you'll reach a T-junction with a well-graded gravel path. A blue-blazed trail begins on the right, but you should turn left to continue on the Major Welch Trail. This handicapped-accessible trail section, opened in 2011, was skillfully constructed by a team of experienced professional trail builders to blend into the environment while making it possible for all users to enjoy a hiking experience.

At the next intersection, turn left again, now joining the white-blazed Appalachian Trail (AT), which runs concurrently with the Major Welch Trail, following a level path across the summit ridge of Bear Mountain. In 0.2 mile, you'll pass a massive boulder on the left. Atop the boulder are the concrete foundations of a former fire tower (replaced in 1934 by the Perkins Memorial Tower). This boulder marks the actual summit of the mountain (1,305 feet).

Just beyond, the trail crosses the paved loop road around the summit and reaches the Perkins Memorial Tower (the Major Welch Trail ends here). Built in 1934 to honor the memory of George W. Perkins, the first President of the Palisades Interstate Park Commission, the tower was originally used as a weather station, then as a fire lookout. In 1992, the tower was renovated, and new exhibits were installed. The staircases leading to the top of the tower feature tiles that detail historical events and include interesting snippets of information, such as the cost of a meal at the Bear Mountain Inn in 1920. The tower is usually open to the public without charge whenever the Perkins Memorial Drive is open to traffic (the road is closed during the winter and when the weather is inclement).

Continue past the tower, recrossing the paved loop road, and proceed ahead to a broad south-facing viewpoint, with Dunderberg Mountain jutting into the Hudson River on the left. Several rustic benches have been placed in this area for hikers to rest. After enjoying the view and taking a break, head back toward the tower, but bear right onto the white-blazed AT. Follow the AT as it begins to descend the mountain on stone steps and continues on a well-graded footpath. As you descend to the Bear Mountain Inn, you'll traverse over 1,000 stone steps, with the footpath supported in places by stone crib walls.

In 0.6 mile from the summit, after passing several viewpoints, you'll reach an abandoned section of the Scenic Drive (formerly part of an automobile loop route around Bear Mountain). The AT crosses the drive and continues downhill. In another three-quarters of a mile, after passing a seasonal waterfall on the left, the trail curves to the left and reaches a panoramic viewpoint over Iona Island and the Hudson River. After descending a little farther, it crosses a 28-foot-long wooden bridge and begins to descend more steeply on stone steps through an area of jumbled boulders.

Toward the base of the descent, you'll come to a junction where a blue-blazed side trail begins on the right. Bear left (following an arrow pointing to the "inn") and continue to follow the AT, which descends more gradually. After passing a stone building known as the Spider Hill House on the right, the AT goes through the Trails for People exhibit, which gives the history of the AT and explains various methods of trail construction. Just beyond, the AT reaches the trail junction behind the Bear Mountain Inn. Continue ahead past the inn and retrace your steps to the parking area where the hike began.

Brooks Lake

TOTAL DISTANCE: 1 mile

WALKING TIME: 1 hour

ELEVATION GAIN: 192 feet

MAPS: USGS Peekskill; NY–NJTC
Harriman-Bear Mountain Trails #119

TRAILHEAD GPS COORDINATES: N 41° 19'
48.6" W 73° 59' 31.3"

If you're looking for a short, easy hike in Harriman–Bear Mountain State Parks, this is the hike for you. It circles Brooks Lake, in the northwest corner of the park, offering scenic views over the water.

Today, the lake offers the hiker a tranquil, quiet experience, but it wasn't always that way. When the park acquired Brooks Lake in 1918 from the heirs of Eliza Brooks, an aerial tramway crossed the southern end of the lake. This tramway was used to carry iron ore from the Forest of Dean Mine to the Hudson River, where it was transferred to boats or to trains on the West Shore Railroad at the site of the present-day Mine Dock Park. The Forest of Dean Mine, located several miles west of Fort Montgomery, was opened in the 1750s and was actively mined until 1931. It was subsequently acquired by the United States Government and is now part of the United States Military Reservation at West Point.

The red-square-on-white-blazed Brooks Lake Trail, the route of this hike, was blazed in 2004 at the suggestion of local residents.

GETTING THERE

From the traffic circle at the west end of the Bear Mountain Bridge, proceed north on US 9W, crossing the Popolopen Viaduct. Just beyond the northern end of the viaduct, turn left onto Firefighters Memorial Drive and continue downhill for 0.4 mile. At the base of the descent, turn left onto Mine Road, then immediately turn right into Brooks Park and continue to the parking area.

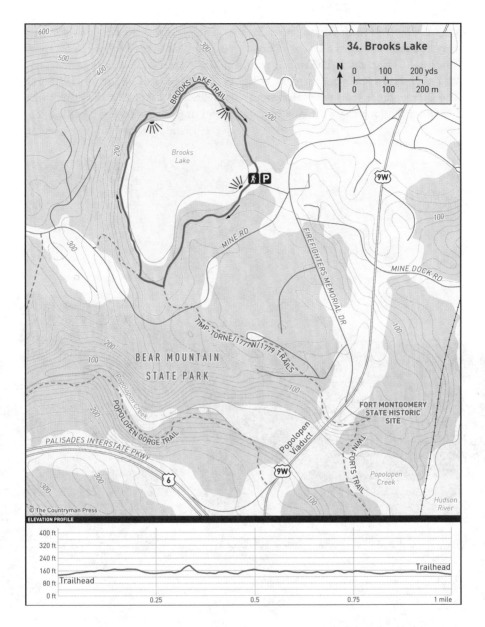

THE HIKE

For the entire hike, you'll be following the Brooks Lake Trail, with red square-on-white blazes. From the parking area, the trail heads south on a wide gravel road, passing a kiosk on the right. In 125 feet, the road ends at a viewpoint over the lake. Here, the trail turns left and continues on a narrower gravel road. In 0.2 mile, the trail makes a short but rather steep descent, passing an interesting rock outcrop and an abandoned stone-and-concrete building on the left. After climbing a little, the Brooks Lake Trail turns right, leaving the gravel road and joining the blue-blazed Timp-Torne Trail (also the route of the 1777W and

1779 Trails). The trails run together for only 100 feet, crossing a wet area on a boardwalk, after which the Timp-Torne, 1777W, and 1779 Trails depart to the left. The Brooks Lake Trail bears right and heads north along the west side of the lake.

The treadway now becomes a little rougher as the trail follows a footpath along a narrow shelf above the lake, crossing several rocky areas. Soon, you'll notice a strand of inch-thick wire rope lying across the trail, with a longer segment of rope hanging from an

BROOKS LAKE

TRAMWAY CABLE ACROSS THE BROOKS LAKE TRAIL

adjacent tree. This is a remnant of the cable used to suspend the tramway cars that carried iron ore over the lake to the Hudson River (see above). As you proceed along the lake, a number of east-facing views open up. The mountain visible in the background is Anthony's Nose, on the east side of the river.

At the northwest corner of the lake, 0.6 mile from the start, the trail crosses a stream on rocks and again curves to the right. Just beyond, there are several south-facing viewpoints over the lake, with Bear Mountain in the background. After proceeding south along the east side of the lake, the trail briefly parallels and then crosses an old woods road, lined on both sides with stone walls. Just beyond, the trail emerges onto a grassy field. It passes a wooden pavilion on the right, with more views over the lake, and descends to end at the parking area.

IV.
THE WEST HUDSON HILLS

Introduction to the
West Hudson Area

North and west of Harriman-Bear Mountain State Parks, New York's Orange County—known by hikers as the West Hudson area—has four distinct hiking areas: the privately owned Black Rock Forest and Schunemunk Mountain, Storm King, and Sterling Forest State Parks.

BLACK ROCK FOREST

Black Rock Forest is a 3,870-acre preserve dedicated to scientific research, education, and conservation of the natural ecosystem that once covered this entire region. Only 50 miles north of New York City, the area is home to numerous ponds, wetlands, and great biological diversity.

The land remains relatively pristine, thanks to the foresight of Dr. Ernest Stillman, who in 1949 established and endowed it as a Harvard University research forest. In 1989, after Harvard decided the tract was no longer needed for its programs, the land was acquired by the late philanthropist William Golden, who established the nonprofit Black Rock Forest Preserve.

Today, the forest is used as a field station by the Black Rock Forest Consortium, an alliance of more than 20 private and public educational and research institutions, including the New York–New Jersey Trail Conference (NY–NJTC). The consortium provides a center for research and teaching at all levels and serves as an information network linking students, researchers, teachers, administrators, and institutions.

Although scientific research is the primary purpose of the forest, public access is permitted to the hiking trails and woods roads in the forest. Hikers in the forest may notice distinctive plots of native trees, each with differing timber-management techniques. All but one of the ponds in the forest are part of water systems for nearby towns, so swimming is not permitted in these ponds. Public vehicular traffic is not permitted on the dirt roads that criss-cross the forest, but these roads are open to hikers. The forest is closed to the public during deer hunting season (mid-November through mid-December) and may also be closed during times of high fire danger. Call 845-534-4517 for information, or go to www.blackrockforest.org. Organized groups such as hiking clubs must call to preregister.

SCHUNEMUNK MOUNTAIN STATE PARK

Schunemunk Mountain sits in solitary splendor, its long, gently rounded form isolated from the Hudson Highlands and the Shawangunks as completely as its rocks are separated by the ages from their surroundings. Hikers will encounter light grayish and pinkish sandstones and shales, and will marvel at the unique conglomerate bedrock, commonly called puddingstone, while walking along either of the two distinct ridges. In many places, the bedrock has been ground down to a smooth surface by the movement of glaciers. The puddingstone is made up of different sizes of pink- and lavender-colored rocks as well as attractive white quartz pebbles.

The name Schunemunk is believed to mean "excellent fireplace" and was given to the Leni-Lenape Native American village once located on the northern part of the mountain, which is now a familiar sight to travelers on the adjacent New York State Thruway.

The northern half of the ridge was saved from development by Star Expansion Industries, the Ogden Family Foundation, and the Storm King Art Center, which, under the leadership of H. Peter Stern, formed the Mountainville Conservancy. In 1996, with the assistance of a grant from the Lila Acheson and DeWitt Wallace Foundation, the Open Space Institute acquired 2,100 acres of Schunemunk Mountain. In 2003, this property was acquired by the State of New York and became Schunemunk Mountain State Park, managed by the Palisades Interstate Park Commission. The Nature Conservancy owns an additional 389 acres.

The hiking-only trails are open from dawn to dusk. Hunting is not permitted, but violations are not uncommon, so many hikers avoid the mountain during deer season, mid-November through mid-December.

STORM KING STATE PARK

To the east of Black Rock Forest stands mighty Storm King Mountain (Hike #41). In 1922, Dr. Ernest Stillman donated 800 acres to the Palisades Interstate Park Commission to ensure the preservation of the scenic surroundings of the old Storm King Highway. Little did he know

that controversy would surround the mountain just four decades later when Consolidated Edison announced plans for a pumped storage power project that would have forever altered the area.

Prominent local citizens, the NY–NJTC, and The Nature Conservancy joined forces to fight the project. Along with others, they founded Scenic Hudson, Inc., the organization that still works today to preserve the Hudson Valley's natural heritage. The landmark legal battle that ensued—not finally settled until 1980—now forms the basis of the environmental law movement championed by organizations such as the Natural Resources Defense Council.

In the summer of 1999, the Storm King area was ravaged by a forest fire. It had been exceptionally dry, and the fire's heat went deep into the topsoil. To everyone's surprise, explosions followed. Long-forgotten unexploded shells detonated under the intense heat. This ordnance had apparently been fired well over a century ago to test cannons manufactured across the river at the West Point Foundry in Cold Spring. Fortunately, no one was injured. The park was closed, and a US Army Corps of Engineers cleanup began in 2000. The park was reopened to the public in 2003.

Except for hiking trails, the park is undeveloped. It is managed from the administration building at Bear Mountain. Seasonal deer hunting is permitted only in the section of the park west of US 9W.

STERLING FOREST STATE PARK

Sterling Forest is known for its role in the early mining and smelting industry. Many historic mines and the remains of two nineteenth-century furnaces are found on the property, one visited on Hikes #35 and #36. During the Revolutionary War, the ironmasters at Sterling forged a 500-yard-long chain that was stretched across the Hudson River at West Point to block British warships. The Sterling Ironworks also played a strategic role during the War of 1812 and the Civil War.

Subsequently owned by the Harriman family, the land was offered to the state as parkland in the 1940s, but the offer was declined and the property sold to private interests. In the late 1980s, the corporate owners proposed a massive development: homes for 35,000 people, along with abundant office and commercial space. Hikers had a strong interest in preserving this rugged forest. Spearheaded by NY–NJTC Executive Director JoAnn Dolan and her husband, Paul, a public-private partnership to save Sterling Forest was formed. Thanks to generous appropriations by the states of New Jersey and New York and the United States Congress, as well as substantial donations by the Open Space Institute,

Scenic Hudson, the Doris Duke Charitable Foundation, and other groups and individuals, the PIPC acquired 14,500 acres of Sterling Forest in 1998. Subsequent acquisitions have increased the size of the park to nearly 22,000 acres.

A corridor of federal land surrounding the Appalachian Trail bisects the park at its northern end. Passaic County, New Jersey, owns a 2,000-acre tract in the south, acquired by eminent domain. Some hiking trails in Sterling Forest State Park follow footpaths (two of the Sterling Forest hikes in this book, Hikes #36 and #38, primarily use hiking trails routed along these footpaths), but many other trails follow woods roads, some of which are eroded. Some of the trails are multi-use. The park allows seasonal turkey and deer hunting (permit required).

A generous donation of $1.75 million from the family of the late US Senator Frank Lautenberg (D–NJ) has endowed a visitor center at the south end of Sterling Lake, which also serves as the park's administrative headquarters. For more information, call 845-351-5907.

35

Sterling Lake Loop

TOTAL DISTANCE: 4.2 miles
WALKING TIME: 2.5 hours
ELEVATION GAIN: 640 feet
MAPS: USGS 7.5′ Greenwood Lake; NY–NJTC Sterling Forest Map #100
TRAILHEAD GPS COORDINATES: N 41°11′ 56.0″ W 74°15′ 24.6″

This relatively easy hike circles the scenic Sterling Lake and offers many panoramic views over the lake. It passes the remains of the historic Sterling Furnace as well as other remnants of former mining activity in the area. Unfortunately, to avoid private residences, the last part of the hike follows a roundabout route some distance from the lake, but this section includes an interesting crossing of a wetland on the embankment of a mining railroad.

The historic Sterling Furnace, passed near the start of the hike, is where the iron chain used during the Revolutionary War to fortify the Hudson River was forged. Built in the 1770s and abandoned in 1802, the furnace thereafter fell into ruin and remained in a ruined condition until it was rebuilt in the late 1950s by the City Investing Company, which then owned the property. To protect the rebuilt furnace, a dome was placed atop neo-Classical wooden columns. The dome has since disappeared, but the rather incongruous-looking wooden columns remain.

GETTING THERE

Take the New York State Thruway to Exit 15A. Turn left at the bottom of the ramp onto NY 17 and head north for 1.4 miles to the exit for Sterling Forest. Follow Sterling Mine Road (County Route 72) west for 3 miles, then turn right onto Long Meadow Road (County Route 84). Proceed north on Long Meadow Road for 3.6 miles, then turn left onto Old Forge Road and continue for half a mile until you reach the Sterling Forest State Park Visitor Center. Turn right at the sign for VISITOR PARKING and park your car, then cross the road and head downhill to the visitor center to obtain a map and view the exhibits.

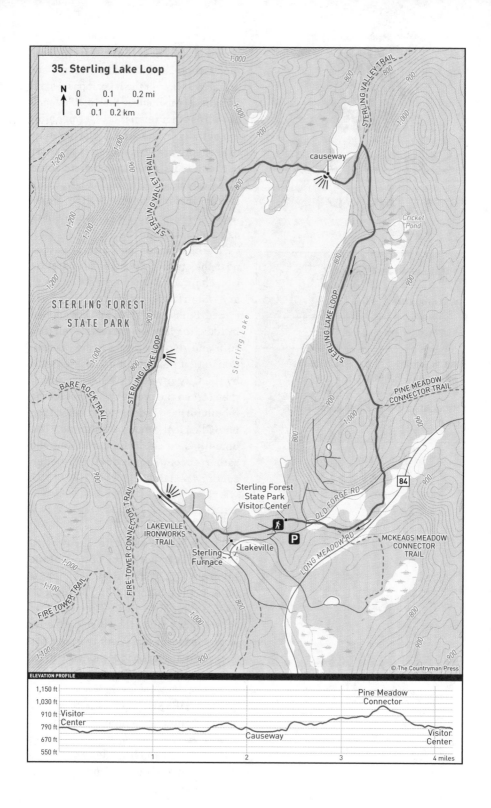

35. Sterling Lake Loop

N
0   0.1   0.2 mi
0   0.1   0.2 km

1,000

800

STERLING VALLEY TRAIL

900

1,000

1,200

causeway

Cricket Pond

900

STERLING VALLEY TRAIL

1,200

1,100

800

900

1,200

900

STERLING FOREST

STATE PARK

1,000

STERLING LAKE LOOP

Sterling Lake

800

STERLING LAKE LOOP

900

PINE MEADOW CONNECTOR TRAIL

BARE ROCK TRAIL

800

1,000

900

900

Sterling Forest
State Park
Visitor Center

84

FIRE TOWER CONNECTOR TRAIL

LAKEVILLE
IRONWORKS
TRAIL

OLD FORGE RD

P

Lakeville

MCKEAGS MEADOW
CONNECTOR
TRAIL

Sterling
Furnace

LONG MEADOW RD

900

1,000

1,000

1,100

FIRE TOWER TRAIL

1,000

900

800

900

1,100

© The Countryman Press

ELEVATION PROFILE

1,150 ft			Pine Meadow	
1,030 ft			Connector	
910 ft	Visitor			
790 ft	Center			
670 ft		Causeway		Visitor
550 ft				Center
	1	2	3	4 miles

STERLING LAKE

THE HIKE

Leave the park visitor center, using the front entrance, and turn right (west) on a dirt path, following the blue blazes of the Sterling Lake Loop. The trail briefly joins the paved entrance road, then bears right and crosses a grassy field, passing the stone foundations of a former church on the right. It enters the woods on a footpath and soon reaches a junction with the yellow-blazed Lakeville Ironworks Trail, which begins on the left. Here, the ruins of the Sterling Furnace are visible below.

Continue ahead, following the blue blazes of the Sterling Lake Loop, which crosses the outlet of Sterling Lake on a wooden bridge. Just beyond, the trail turns left and descends to a paved road. It turns right and follows the road, soon passing ruins of concrete-and-brick structures on the left. These are remnants of the former mining operations in the area. Sterling Forest was once a center of mining activity, with the first mines opened in the 1700s. The last active mine in the area closed down nearly 100 years ago.

Just beyond these ruins, you'll pass the western end of the Lakeville Ironworks Trail. Continue ahead along the road, which soon begins to run alongside Sterling Lake, with views across the lake. About three-quarters of a mile from the start, a sign marks the start of the Bare Rock and Fire Tower Connector Trails, and the paving ends just beyond. Continue ahead on a woods road, blocked by a wooden gate. The road runs inland for some distance, then again parallels the lakeshore.

Near the northern end of the lake, the yellow-blazed Sterling Valley Trail

EMBANKMENT OF FORMER MINING RAILROAD

joins from the left, and you now follow both yellow and blue blazes. Soon, you'll pass a former boat-launching ramp on the right. Just beyond, the trail crosses an earthen causeway, with broad views over the lake. A quiet, picturesque pond is on the left.

The trail now goes slightly inland and climbs over two rises. After descending through a mountain laurel thicket, it again emerges on the lakeshore at a small sandy beach, with a dead pine tree overhanging the water. The trail crosses another earthen causeway over an arm of the lake, with a beaver lodge on its east side. At the end of the lake, the trail

along the road, which climbs gradually, then descends a little. It crosses the outlet of Cricket Pond, visible on the left, and continues to run above the lake, climbing gently. You can catch some glimpses of the lake through the trees on the right.

After a mile of pleasant walking, the woods road turns away from the lake and reaches a fork. Bear left to continue along the blue-blazed trail, which narrows to a footpath. The trail crosses a wet area and soon widens to a rocky woods road, which climbs rather steeply.

Just beyond the crest of the rise, the blue-blazed trail turns right and descends on a footpath. (The orange-triangle-blazed Pine Meadow Connector begins here and continues along the road.) Soon, the trail turns right on a gravel road and follows it for about 75 feet, then turns left, leaving the road, and continues to descend more gradually to the paved Old Forge Road, which it crosses. Just before reaching a second paved road (County Route 84), the trail turns right and crosses a wetland on an earth-and-rock embankment of a former mining railroad. The trail bears left at the end of the embankment, then soon turns right and joins a gravel road.

When the road curves to the right to end in a paved parking area, continue straight ahead on a footpath. Just ahead, the orange-triangle-blazed McKeags Meadow Connector begins on the left. Proceed ahead on the Sterling Lake Loop, which soon emerges onto a grassy area. Continue to the paved Old Forge Road, then turn left and follow the road a short distance. Bear right at a sign for OVERFLOW PARKING, cross the parking area, then reenter the woods and follow the blue-blazed trail on a footpath back to the visitor center, completing the loop.

bears left and heads north, running parallel to the narrow arm of the lake.

When you reach the end of this arm, follow the blue-blazed Sterling Lake Loop as it turns sharply right onto another woods road (the yellow-blazed Sterling Valley Trail continues straight ahead). The blue trail proceeds south

Sterling Ridge to the Fire Tower

TOTAL DISTANCE: 7.4 miles, one-car hike (5.5 miles, two-car hike)

WALKING TIME: 4.5 hours, one-car hike (3 hours, two-car hike)

ELEVATION GAIN: 807 feet

MAPS: USGS 7.5' Greenwood Lake; NY–NJTC Sterling Forest Trails #100; Sterling Forest State Park

TRAILHEAD GPS COORDINATES: N 41° 11' 56" W 74° 15' 23.5"

This hike follows the Sterling Ridge Trail, with some moderate ups and downs, to a fire tower with panoramic views. It then descends to Sterling Lake and passes historical remnants of the iron mining operations that took place in the area for over 150 years. The hike ends at the Sterling Forest State Park Visitor Center, which has informative exhibits on the history of the area and its mining operations.

Today, Sterling Forest is a favorite destination for hikers, but it was not always this way. When the first edition of the *New York Walk Book* was published in 1923, most landowners did not object to hikers (then often referred to as "trampers") traversing their properties in rural areas; indeed, the 1923 *Walk Book* described many hiking routes that traversed private property. The book referred to the Sterling Forest area, however, as "forbidden territory," stating that it "is posted against trespassers; and this prohibition is being enforced against trampers." The 1934 edition of the *Walk Book* reiterated that the area "is forbidden to trampers," who are "at the risk of arrest by the employees of the Sterling Iron and Railway Company," but added the hope "that some time it will come into public ownership, possibly by a western extension of the Palisades Interstate Park."

By the time the fourth edition of the *New York Walk Book* appeared in 1971, the Sterling Ridge Trail had already been established. Even then, "NO TRESPASSING signs were at both ends of the trail," although it was also stated that the trail was "open to bona fide hikers, particularly those of the member clubs of the New York–New Jersey Trail Conference."

With the acquisition of Sterling Forest by New York State in 1998 and the

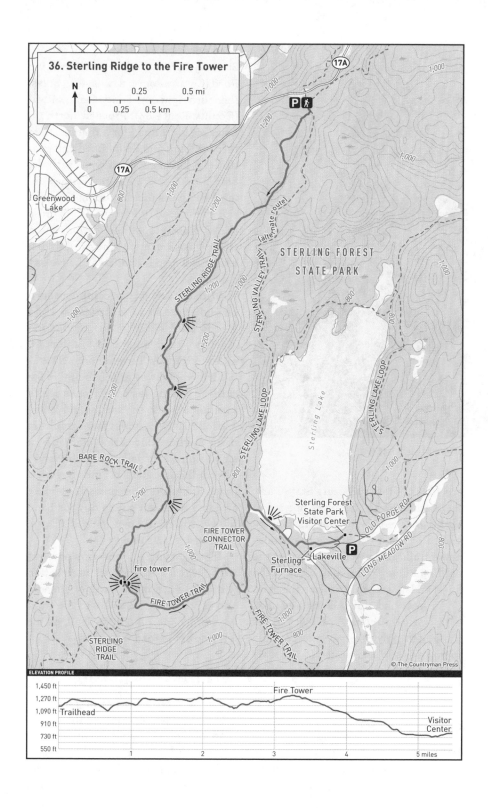

36. Sterling Ridge to the Fire Tower

STERLING FOREST STATE PARK

Greenwood Lake

STERLING RIDGE TRAIL

STERLING VALLEY TRAIL (alternate route)

STERLING LAKE LOOP

Sterling Lake

BARE ROCK TRAIL

FIRE TOWER CONNECTOR TRAIL

fire tower

Sterling Forest State Park Visitor Center

OLD FORGE RD

Sterling Furnace

Lakeville

LONG MEADOW RD

FIRE TOWER TRAIL

STERLING RIDGE TRAIL

© The Countryman Press

ELEVATION PROFILE

Trailhead

Fire Tower

Visitor Center

1,450 ft
1,270 ft
1,090 ft
910 ft
730 ft
550 ft

1   2   3   4   5 miles

STERLING FOREST FIRE TOWER

creation of Sterling Forest State Park, the Sterling Ridge Trail was opened to all hikers, and additional trails were blazed in the area. But most of these newer trails follow woods roads, and the Sterling Ridge Trail remains one of the finest and most scenic trails in the park.

As described, this is a one-way hike, with two cars required. However, for those with only one car, it is possible to make a loop and return to the start via the Sterling Lake Loop and Sterling Valley Trail.

GETTING THERE

If you have two cars available, take the New York Thruway to Exit 15A. Turn left at the bottom of the ramp onto NY 17 and head north for 1.4 miles to the exit for Sterling Forest. Follow Sterling Mine Road (County Route 72) west for 3 miles, then turn right onto Long Meadow Road (County Route 84). Proceed north on Long Meadow Road for 3.6 miles, then turn left onto Old Forge Road and continue for half a mile until you reach the Sterling Forest State Park Visitor Center. Park in the parking lot on the right side of the road (you may wish to cross the road and stop at the visitor center, where there are interesting exhibits and a free trail map is available). Leave one car here.

With the second car, continue ahead on Old Forge Road to its end at Long Meadow Road. Turn left onto Long Meadow Road and follow it for 3.6 miles to NY 17A. Turn left onto NY 17A (a divided highway at this point; make sure to cross the eastbound lanes before turning left onto the westbound lanes) and follow it for 4.1 miles to the trailhead of the Sterling Ridge Trail (marked by a small sign on the left side of the road). The trailhead is about 0.1 mile beyond a green-and-white sign indicating a hiker crossing. Turn left onto a dirt road and follow it past an open gate to a large parking area in a grassy field.

If you have only one car, proceed west on NY 17A from its intersection with NY 17 (2.5 miles north of Tuxedo) and continue for 5.5 miles to the trailhead of the Sterling Ridge Trail, on the left side of the road.

THE HIKE

From the rear of the parking area, go around the gate and follow the woods road which leads south. This road is marked with the blue-on-white blazes of the Sterling Ridge Trail, the teal diamond blazes of the Highlands Trail, and the yellow blazes of the Sterling Valley Trail. In 100 feet, turn right, leaving the road, and follow the blue-and-white and teal diamond blazes, which climb on a footpath (the yellow blazes continue ahead on the road). After reaching the top of a small rise, the trail levels off. Soon, the trail begins to run along the edge of a ravine, gradually descending, with limited views to the left through the trees. A short distance beyond, the trail crosses a seasonal stream and then begins to ascend. About a mile from the trailhead, it goes under a power line, with good views to the east and west.

After a short but steady ascent, the trail crosses a large rock outcrop. The trail continues along the ridge, now following a relatively level route. In about half a mile, you'll come out on another large rock outcrop, with a limited east-facing view. After another level stretch, the trail continues on undulating terrain and then emerges onto a third rock outcrop, with a stunted red cedar tree growing out of a crack in the rock. There are only very limited views from the outcrop (which features a number of cairns), but after a brief descent, you'll reach a panoramic viewpoint over Sterling Lake to the east, with a log supported by stones serving as a bench.

The trail continues along the ridge. After descending a little, it crosses a woods road—the route of the orange-blazed Bare Rock Trail. The trail then climbs to another, more limited viewpoint over Sterling Lake from open

STERLING LAKE FROM THE FIRE TOWER

rocks. It continues over undulating terrain, and after traversing an area dominated by hemlock and mountain laurel, reaches a ranger cabin and the Sterling Forest Fire Tower, about 3.5 miles from the start of the hike.

The expansive view from the top of the fire tower, built in 1922, is well worth the climb. Sterling Lake is visible to the northeast, and a portion of the much larger Greenwood Lake can be seen to the west. On a clear day, North and South Beacon Mountains of the East Hudson Highlands may be viewed in the distance to the northeast, and Schunemunk Mountain is visible to the north, with the Catskills on the horizon. A picnic table at the base of the tower makes this spot a good place to stop for lunch.

When you're ready to continue, find the white-stripe-on-red-blazed Fire Tower Trail and follow it as it descends from the ridge on a pleasant gravel road, with many grassy sections (do not follow the joint Fire Tower/Sterling Ridge Trail, which heads south on a footpath). After about half a mile, as the road levels off, you'll come to a junction. The Fire Tower Trail turns off to the right on a branch road, but you should bear left and continue ahead on the main road, now marked with red-triangle-on-white blazes as the Fire Tower Connector Trail. The trail continues to descend, and after passing a private residence and going around a locked gate, it ends at a paved road near the shore of Sterling Lake.

If you have only one car and need to return to the trailhead on NY 17A, turn left onto the road, marked with the blue blazes of the Sterling Lake Loop. Just ahead, the paving ends and the road is blocked by a wooden gate. Soon, the road begins to follow the scenic shoreline of Sterling Lake. In about three-quarters of a mile, you'll come to a Y-junction. Bear left here and follow the yellow-blazed Sterling Valley Trail, another woods road that leads slightly uphill, away from the lake. After a level stretch, the road begins to climb. It passes under the same power line that you crossed earlier in the hike, and then continues to ascend steadily. In about 1.5 miles, the trail ends at the parking area where you began the hike.

If you have spotted a second car at the Sterling Forest State Park Visitor Center, turn right onto the paved road, following the blue blazes of the Sterling Loop Trail (the trail is very sparsely blazed along the road). Soon, the road begins to run along the shore of Sterling Lake, with panoramic views across the lake. A short distance beyond, you'll pass ruins of concrete and brick structures on the right. These are remnants of former mining operations.

Just beyond, follow the blue-blazed Sterling Lake Trail as it turns left, leaving the road, and enters the woods on a footpath. The trail soon crosses the outlet of Sterling Lake on a wooden bridge, and just beyond, the yellow-blazed Lakeville Ironworks Trail begins on the right. Here, the ruins of the Sterling Furnace are visible below. After passing through an area with low, dense vegetation, the trail emerges onto a grassy field, passing the stone foundations of a former church. Continue to follow the blue blazes, which lead you to the Sterling Forest State Park Visitor Center, with its informative exhibits. From the visitor center, head uphill and cross the road to reach the parking area where you left your first car.

Mount Peter to Arden on the Appalachian Trail

This arduous hike should not be attempted by anyone in poor physical condition or without motivation. It crosses several mountains with many false summits, includes some short sections of rock scrambling, and ends with a very steep descent down a precipitous hill—Agony Grind—that can be hard on tired knees. Fitzgerald Falls and Little Dam Lake are highlights of the trip, but the hike covers other interesting terrain and passes a number of panoramic viewpoints. For its entire length, the hike follows the route of the Appalachian Trail (AT). Two cars are needed for a shuttle, and an option to shorten the hike is included.

TOTAL DISTANCE: 12.3 miles (8.7-mile alternate)

WALKING TIME: 9 hours (6.5-hour alternate)

ELEVATION GAIN: 2,956 feet

MAPS: USGS 7.5' Sloatsburg; Appalachian Trail Guide to New York–New Jersey, Map #2; NY–NJTC Sterling Forest Trails #100

TRAILHEAD GPS COORDINATES: N 41° 14' 38" W 74° 17' 15.5"

GETTING THERE

Drive two cars north on NY 17 through Sloatsburg and Tuxedo. Turn right onto Arden Valley Road 5.5 miles north of the Tuxedo railroad station, and continue for 0.3 mile to the ample parking at the Elk Pen on the right. Leave one car here. (During the early 1920s a herd of elk was indeed penned here. Transported from Yellowstone National Park in December 1919, the animals didn't flourish, and the survivors were sold in 1942.)

Now return to NY 17 and drive south for 2.8 miles to the junction of NY 17A. Bear right at the light and turn right again at the stop sign at the end of the commuter lot. Proceed west along NY 17A. The hiker sign you may notice about 5.5 miles down NY 17A indicates the trailhead of the Sterling Ridge Trail (Hike #36) and the Allis Trail. After 7.4 miles on NY 17A you'll reach a junction with NY 210. Bear right at the fork. Almost immediately, at another fork, you must decide whether to take the 12.3-mile hike or the 8.7-miler. For the longer hike, bear left, staying on NY 17A

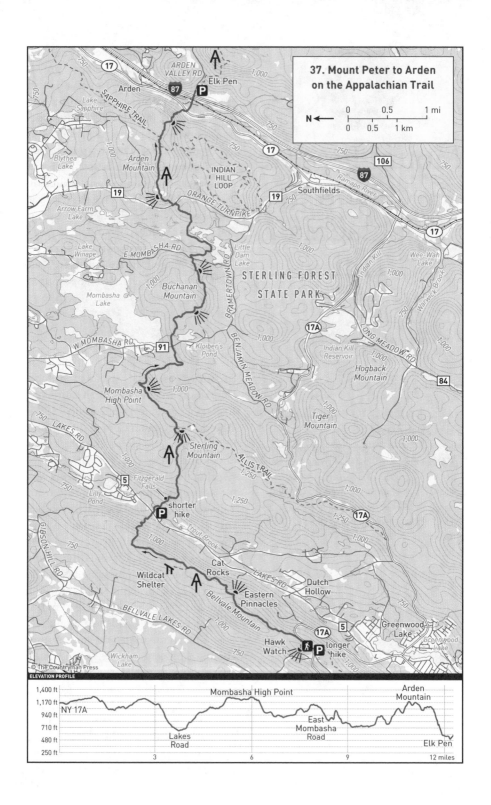

37. Mount Peter to Arden on the Appalachian Trail

ELEVATION PROFILE

toward Warwick. Continue for about 2 miles to the crest of Mount Peter, and park in the large dirt parking area for the AT on the left side of NY 17A.

For the shorter hike, take the right fork toward Monroe on Lakes Road. Continue straight ahead for 0.3 mile, paralleling Greenwood Lake on the right, to a stop sign. Drive straight ahead, now on County Route 5, and proceed 3.7 miles to a small parking area on the east side of the road near a large power-line stanchion.

THE HIKE

For the longer hike, proceed north on the AT from the parking area. Almost immediately, you'll notice a blue-blazed side trail on the left. Turn left and follow this trail, which leads in 0.2 mile to the Hawk Watch platform (used for monitoring spring and fall raptor migration), with views to the west and north. After taking in the scenery, retrace your steps to the AT and continue ahead. At first, the trail parallels the noisy NY 17A, but the road soon bends to the right, away from the trail.

The AT proceeds gently uphill, crosses a gas pipeline, and continues through an area with dense hemlock and mountain laurel. It then begins a gradual descent. About 1.3 miles from the start, you'll reach an outcrop of puddingstone rock known as the Eastern Pinnacles. You'll have to scramble up rocks to reach the top of this outcrop, which offers views to the north and east over the hills of Sterling Forest. Neither this scramble nor the next is particularly difficult, though both call for concentration and require the use of your hands as well as your feet.

There are alternatives to following the AT route up Eastern Pinnacles. A blue-blazed side trail avoids the climb by completely bypassing Eastern Pinnacles, and another blue-blazed trail, partway up the rocks, indicates an easier route. Unless the trail is wet or the weather is icy, by all means follow the white blazes, which offer the most scenic route.

The AT now heads gently downhill. It goes through dense mountain laurel thickets and traverses a wet area, then climbs to Cat Rocks—a dramatic rock outcrop with a steep drop. The east-facing view from Cat Rocks has largely grown in, but you'll want to take a break here to appreciate the fascinating puddingstone rock formations. Note particularly the deep crevice to the left of the trail. Again, an easier route that bypasses the steep climb is indicated by blue blazes. From Cat Rocks, the trail begins to descend.

Just over 2 miles from the start, a blue-blazed side trail on the left leads to the Wildcat Shelter. It is worthwhile to take the short side trip to the shelter—a favorite stop for many through-hikers on the AT. Return to the trail and turn left. The AT now climbs over a rise. After descending about 100 vertical feet, it turns sharply right and soon begins a steeper descent to Lakes Road, using rock steps for part of the way. When you reach Lakes Road, you've hiked for 3.6 miles. (The 8.7-mile hike begins here.) The teal-diamond-blazed Highlands Trail joins the AT here.

The AT crosses Lakes Road, descends through an area with dense vegetation, goes under a power line, and crosses a wooden bridge over Trout Brook. The trail proceeds across a flat expanse, climbs a rise, and continues through a hemlock grove. Soon, a blue-blazed high-water bypass trail, which avoids two crossings of the brook on rocks, begins on the left. A short distance beyond, the AT recrosses the brook on large boulders just below Fitzgerald Falls, a 25-foot waterfall in a rocky cleft. Water at the falls tumbles spectacularly through a split in the jagged rocks, and this is a good spot to take a break.

The AT now ascends steeply on rock steps to the right of the falls. The beautiful steps were constructed by volunteers of the New York–New Jersey Trail Conference in 2013. At the top, the trail briefly bears right, away from the stream, but soon bears left and crosses the stream on rocks (the blue-blazed bypass trail rejoins the AT just beyond). A short distance beyond, the trail crosses a gravel road, bears right, and begins a steady ascent, continuing to parallel the stream (below on the right). In another quarter mile, as the trail levels off, you'll notice several old stone walls on the left. These walls, and others encountered along the hike, are remnants of abandoned settlements in the area. After a level stretch, the trail continues to climb, crossing a boulder field along the way.

About 1.5 miles from Lakes Road, you'll reach a junction with the blue-blazed Allis Trail, which begins on the right. The Highlands Trail departs from the AT here and heads south on the Allis Trail. You'll notice a register box at the junction (please sign). The Allis Trail is named after a banker, J. Ashton Allis, who was an early treasurer of the Appalachian Trail Conference and a pioneer trail builder. There is an excellent west-facing viewpoint just 100 feet down the Allis Trail, and it's worth taking the short detour to this viewpoint, from which the High Point Monument in northwestern New Jersey can be seen on a clear day.

After another 0.8 mile of mostly level walking, you'll reach the summit of Mombasha High Point (elevation 1,280 feet), which offers limited south-facing views over the hills of Sterling Forest. On a clear day, you might be able to see the New York City skyline in the distance. You've now hiked 2.3 miles from Lakes Road and nearly 6 miles from NY 17A (if you've opted for the longer hike).

The AT now proceeds over rock slabs amid a forest of pitch pine—very different from the forest you've encountered so far on the hike. The trail curves sharply to the right and descends on a switchback, paralleling the escarpment that the trail followed above, then begins a steady descent. The trail next passes through a gap in a stone wall, levels off, then continues to descend. At the base of the descent, the path crosses several streams and wet areas on puncheons. After passing a small unnamed pond and crossing an overgrown field (a designated butterfly refuge), you'll reach West Mombasha Road.

Walk across the road, cross a ditch on planks, and proceed ahead on what seems to be the top of an old rock wall. After crossing a dirt road, the trail follows another woods road. It soon bears right, leaving the road, crosses the outlet of Kloiber's Pond, and climbs over a rise. It descends to cross a stream in a valley lined with moss-covered rocks and hemlocks, then climbs steadily. After a steep jaunt over jumbled rocks, the AT bears right and follows the edge of an escarpment, which leads to the first summit of Buchanan Mountain (1,142 feet). The views from the summit are obstructed by trees, but a rock ledge a short distance beyond offers panoramic south-facing views. This is another good spot for a break. You've now hiked 4.4 miles from Lakes Road and 8 miles from NY 17A.

FITZGERALD FALLS

The AT descends into a valley, where it crosses four streams. Just beyond the fourth stream crossing, the trail climbs very steeply over large boulders to reach a limited viewpoint to the east from a secondary summit of Buchanan Mountain. The AT now descends steeply to East Mombasha Road. Cross the road and continue on a winding woods road to the inlet of Little Dam Lake, which is crossed on large boulders (the crossing may be impassable in times of high water). The AT follows the northern shore of the lake and proceeds over a ridge to emerge onto Orange Turnpike.

Turn left onto Orange Turnpike for 250 feet, and reenter the woods on the right-hand side of the road at the end of the guardrail. The AT now undulates over several shoulders of Arden Mountain, with the best views coming after the first rock climb. On the way, you'll pass a register box (please sign).

About a mile beyond Orange Turnpike, you'll see a triple blue blaze on the right, which marks the start of a connector to the Indian Hill Loop Trail (Hike #38). A short distance beyond, the blue-blazed Sapphire Trail begins on the left.

CAT ROCKS

After climbing over a rise, you'll begin the steep downhill of Agony Grind. The trail is routed through two rock gullies but has no exposure due to tree cover. The sounds of the busy traffic on NY 17 begin to intrude on the quiet of the wilderness. At the base of the descent, bear right, and parallel NY 17 before emerging from the woods and crossing the road to walk the 0.3 mile on Arden Valley Road back to your car at the Elk Pen.

Indian Hill Loop

TOTAL DISTANCE: 4.3 miles	

WALKING TIME: 3 hours

ELEVATION GAIN: 1,010 feet

MAPS: USGS 7.5' Monroe; NY–NJTC Sterling Forest Trails #100; Sterling Forest State Park

TRAILHEAD GPS COORDINATES: N 41° 15' 11" W 74° 10' 59"

Although comprising part of Sterling Forest State Park, the Indian Hill tract traversed by this hike was not acquired by the State of New York directly from the Sterling Forest Corporation. Rather, the property was acquired by Scenic Hudson, which invited the New York–New Jersey Trail Conference to lay out and construct hiking trails on the land before it was transferred to the State of New York for inclusion in the park. The trails used by this hike, which, for the most part, follow footpaths, are among the most attractive in the park, as most other trails in Sterling Forest State Park are routed along woods roads, many of which are eroded.

The remains of the historic South-fields iron furnace, situated at the edge of the Indian Hill property, are along the trail near the start of the hike. The hike also passes by several viewpoints over other sections of the park, the Ramapo River Valley, and Harriman State Park.

Hunting is permitted in much of Sterling Forest State Park (845-351-5907), including Indian Hill. If you choose to hike here during deer season, usually mid-November to mid-December, you should make sure to wear some item of blaze orange.

GETTING THERE

From the south, take NY 17 north about 3.5 miles from Tuxedo. Just after passing the now-closed landmark Red Apple Rest, turn left onto Orange Turnpike (County Route 19). (If coming from the north, this junction is on the right, about 6 miles south of Exit 16 of the New York State Thruway, just past the Tuxedo Heights Condominiums.) In 0.6 mile, turn left onto Hall Drive and park in a parking area on the left side of the road at a curve.

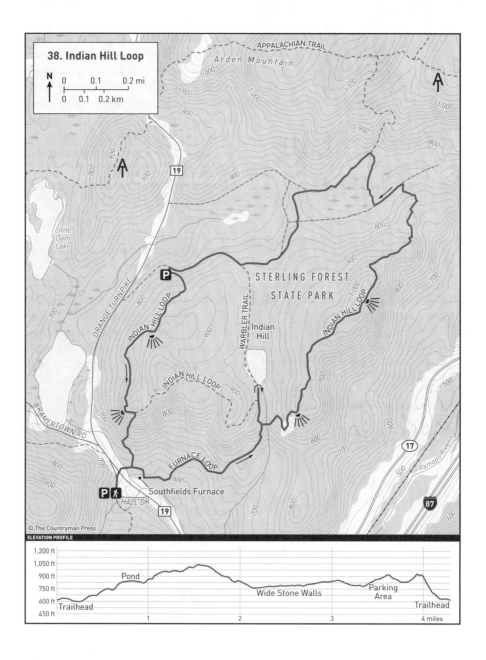

THE HIKE

From the parking area, proceed ahead (north) on Hall Drive, following the white blazes of the Wildcat Mountain Trail. When you reach Orange Turnpike, turn right and cross the road, climb over the guardrail, and descend to cross a footbridge over Mombasha Creek. The trail now turns right and heads east, parallel to the stream.

Just beyond, the white-blazed trail ends, and you should continue ahead on the red-blazed Furnace Loop Trail.

You now approach the historic Southfields Furnace, protected by a chain-link fence. Construction of the first furnace on this site began in 1804, and the furnace was "in blast" about a year later. By 1868, the Southfields Iron Works complex comprised not only a furnace but also a blacksmith shop, stamping mill, sawmill, gristmill, wheelwright, branch rail line, and manor house, among other facilities. Although the charging bridge (supported by arches) and some of the walls of the casting room remain intact, the furnace has suffered decay from neglect and weathering. Its "last blast" was in the fall of 1887. The complex was acquired by the Scenic Hudson Land Trust in 1997 and was transferred in 2002 to the State of New York for inclusion in Sterling Forest State Park.

Some 100 to 200 years ago, iron was produced in stone furnaces, like Southfields, by mixing iron ore, charcoal, and limestone. Once a furnace was lit, the blast would run continuously, producing as much as 25 tons of pig iron a week. In those days, a furnace might have required cutting an acre of hardwood forest a day to be used in making the charcoal. Today you would never know that almost the entire area of this hike had been clear-cut. Trees and

FOOTBRIDGE OVER MOMBASHA CREEK

WIDE STONE WALLS ALONG THE INDIAN HILL LOOP TRAIL

other ground cover are again abundant. Nature has renewed and restored.

The Furnace Loop Trail continues along an old railroad bed, then turns left and begins to climb on a woods road. After descending a little, the trail climbs rock steps below rock outcrops on the left to reach a junction (marked by a cairn) with the white-stripe-on-yellow-blazed Indian Hill Loop Trail. You will be continuing north on this trail, but for now take a side trip by turning left and following both red and white-stripe-on-yellow blazes. The trail soon bends to the right and, in about three minutes, turns sharply left at a cairn. Continue ahead (do not turn left), now following the yellow-bird-on-green blazes of the Warbler Trail, and you'll soon reach the dam of a pond—a tranquil location worth a short visit.

When you're ready to continue, retrace your steps back to the junction of the red-blazed Furnace Loop and white-stripe-on-yellow-blazed Indian Hill Loop Trails and continue ahead, now following only the white-stripe-on-yellow blazes of the Indian Hill Loop Trail. The trail crosses a stream on rocks and climbs to a panoramic south-facing viewpoint from a rock ledge. It then ascends to the ridgetop, which it follows north.

After a relatively level stretch, the trail climbs to the highest point on the ridge (1,047 feet). Turn right and walk a short distance to the edge of the ridge for a panoramic east-facing view over the Thruway and the Ramapo River Valley, with Harriman State Park beyond.

From the ridge, the trail descends gradually on switchbacks. Near the bottom, it briefly follows a stone wall, then turns right onto a woods road. At the base of the descent, it turns left onto a woods road between unusually wide stone walls. Now you've reached one of the area's mysteries.

The trail proceeds for some distance between two truly massive eight-foot-wide stone walls—much wider and larger than the stone walls encountered elsewhere. Why were they built so wide? Did farmers just have lots and lots of rocks to clear? Did these walls have something to do with mining activity? So far, no one has been able to offer more than conjecture.

Soon the trail turns right, passes through a gap in a massive stone wall, and continues on a footpath. To the right, you'll notice a row of massive white oaks, over 100 years old (one of the trees is adjacent to the trail). After crossing a stone wall, the Indian Hill Loop Trail reaches a junction with a blue-blazed trail that begins on the right and heads north to connect, in 0.4 mile, with the white-blazed Appalachian Trail (Hike #37). Here, the Indian Hill Loop Trail turns left and begins to parallel the stone wall. It soon crosses two more stone walls, as well as a woods road lined on both sides with wide stone walls.

After passing through a wide gap in yet another stone wall, the trail turns left onto a grassy woods road. At a T-junction, it turns right onto another woods road, which it follows for about a quarter mile to a barrier gate. Here, you'll see a triple blaze that marks the official end of the Indian Hill Loop Trail. Turn left and climb to the parking area, where you'll notice a kiosk on the left and a triple blaze that marks the start of the Indian Hill Loop Trail.

Turn left and reenter the woods on a footpath. The trail proceeds through a hemlock grove, bears right, and climbs to the crest of a rise. After descending a little, it climbs through mountain laurel to reach an open granite ledge, with west-facing views over the hills of Sterling Forest.

A short distance beyond, you'll reach a junction with the red-blazed Furnace Loop Trail (marked by a cairn). Turn right and descend steeply on this red-blazed trail, passing lichen-covered cliffs and interesting rock outcrops along the way. This is the steepest slope that you'll encounter along the hike, and you should use extreme care, especially if the trail is wet or covered with snow or ice. At the base of the descent, you'll reach a junction with the white-blazed Wildcat Mountain Trail. Turn right, now retracing your steps, and follow the white blazes across the stream and along Hall Drive back to the parking area where the hike began.

Schunemunk via High Knob

TOTAL DISTANCE: 8 miles

WALKING TIME: 6 hours

ELEVATION GAIN: 1,913 feet

MAPS: USGS 7.5' Cornwall; NY–NJTC West Hudson Trails #114

TRAILHEAD GPS COORDINATES: N 41° 21' 41" W 74° 06' 29"

This hike traverses the spectacular ridge of Schunemunk Mountain for 3 miles, following slabs of the distinctive Shawangunk conglomerate which tops the mountain. It climbs to the summit on the Long Path via High Knob, follows the Jessup Trail along the ridge, and descends to Otterkill Road via the Trestle Trail. Because this is a one-way hike, it requires two cars for a shuttle.

The hike begins with a rather demanding climb of about 1,200 feet elevation gain up to the ridge. It continues with an undulating ridge walk, passing many panoramic viewpoints. After dropping into the valley between the two ridges of Schunemunk Mountain, the route climbs rather steeply to the western ridge, then descends gradually to your second car. (If a second car is not available, a walk to the summit and back still makes for a splendid day's outing, and you can perhaps hike to the summit from the other direction at another time.)

GETTING THERE

Take the New York State Thruway (I-87) to Exit 16 (Harriman) and proceed north on NY 32 for 7.3 miles to the large black sign for the Black Rock Fish and Game Club. Turn left onto Pleasant Hill Road and left again onto Taylor Road. Taylor Road crosses Woodbury Creek and then I-87, and passes a hikers' parking area on the right. About 2 miles from NY 32, you'll reach a T-junction with Otterkill Road. Turn left and, in half a mile, you'll notice a massive railroad trestle ahead. There is space for a few cars immediately below the trestle, but the official parking area is another 0.2 mile farther down Otterkill Road, on the right-hand side of the road. Leave one car here.

Return in the second car to NY 32.

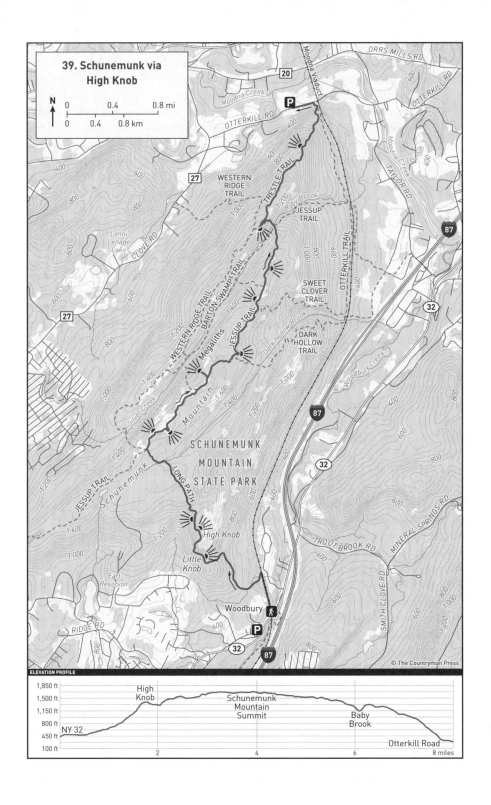

ELEVATION PROFILE

Turn right and continue south on NY 32 for 3.3 miles, passing under another railroad trestle (known as the Woodbury Viaduct). Continue for another 0.2 mile beyond the trestle and park in the grassy area on the west side of NY 32, just before its intersection with Evans Drive. (For those using one car and planning to walk to the summit and back, this parking area is 4 miles north of Exit 16 of I-87.)

THE HIKE

Walk north on NY 32 for 0.2 mile and cross under the trestle. Just north of the trestle, at the end of the guardrail, a driveway goes off to the left. Turn left here and, almost immediately, you'll see a sign for the Long Path on the left. Turn left again and climb rock steps, then turn left at the top of the first pitch and continue under the trestle. Immediately turn right, and again climb rock steps until you reach the level of the tracks. Turn left and head north, following along the railroad tracks. Remember that this is an active railroad line, and a bend in the tracks behind you makes it impossible for the engineer of a northbound train to see you. You may find it easier to cross the tracks and head north with the tracks on your left. The Long Path is marked with aqua blazes, but there are relatively few Long Path blazes in the section along the tracks.

Just past a dirt road that leads down to an active quarry on the right, and as a chain-link fence begins on the right, watch carefully for a double aqua blaze on the west side of the tracks. Follow the Long Path as it leaves the railroad and turns sharply left onto a woods road. The road briefly parallels the tracks, but just before the road crosses a stream, the Long Path turns right, leaving the road.

It crosses an old stone wall and soon bears right at a fork. A short distance beyond, at a T-intersection, the Long Path turns right onto an old woods road.

The trail now begins a steady climb, following the woods road for most of the way. After climbing about 500 vertical feet above the railroad, you'll notice a large rock outcrop on your right. This is Little Knob, which offers an east-facing view.

A little farther up, the trail bends right and begins a very steep climb up a rock outcrop. At the top of the outcrop, amid pitch pines, you'll be afforded a panoramic south-facing view, with a relatively new housing development visible directly below. To the west, you can see the ridge of Schunemunk Mountain, where you'll soon be headed. You've now climbed nearly 1,000 feet from the trailhead, and you'll want to rest here and take in the view. Keep in mind, though, that this is only the first of four viewpoints that you'll encounter on High Knob.

The Long Path continues along the relatively flat summit ridge and soon arrives at the summit of the knob, which offers a panoramic view to the north and east. North and South Beacon Mountains and Breakneck Ridge are visible across the Hudson River, and you can see as far north as the Newburgh-Beacon Bridge. To the east, Storm King Mountain and the hills of Black Rock Forest can be seen on the other side of I-87. Just below you is the quarry that you passed as you walked along the railroad at the start of the hike.

When you're ready to continue, proceed ahead across the summit ridge. After descending just a little, the trail emerges on the edge of an escarpment, with views of the ridge of Schunemunk Mountain (note the communications

HIGH KNOB

antennas along the ridge). It follows rock slabs along the escarpment, studded with pitch pines, then turns left and descends into a valley.

The trail now climbs a steep, rocky slope and turns right. It soon reaches yet another viewpoint—this one to the north. Beyond this viewpoint, the trail climbs gently to the crest of a ridge. Along the way, a faded red paint blaze and a cairn mark an intersection with an unmarked trail that heads north, roughly paralleling Dark Hollow Brook, but you should continue ahead on the Long Path. After descending a little, the trail turns left and briefly parallels the upper reaches of the brook. It then turns right and climbs steadily to reach an intersection with the Jessup/Highlands Trail on the ridge of Schunemunk Mountain.

The Long Path turns left at this intersection, but you should turn right, now following the yellow blazes of the Jessup Trail and the teal diamond blazes of the Highlands Trail, and head north along the crest of the mountain. You'll

immediately climb a large rock outcrop and emerge onto a large open area where the conglomerate bedrock has been smoothed by glacial action. The rock slabs here are so smooth that you can almost imagine that they were carefully evened out by heavy construction equipment! You'll also notice stunted pitch pines growing out of cracks in the bedrock.

The trail now reenters the woods. Soon, you'll emerge onto another open area of smooth conglomerate bedrock with a panoramic west-facing view. A short distance beyond, you'll reach the base of a steep rock outcrop. You'll need both your hands and your feet to climb this one! When you reach the top, you'll be rewarded with a broad east-facing view.

You'll be following the Jessup Trail along the eastern ridge of Schunemunk Mountain for the next 3 miles. Open slabs of smooth conglomerate rock studded with pitch pines alternate with wooded areas. Along the ridge, the trail is marked not only with paint blazes and

ALONG THE JESSUP TRAIL ON SCHUNEMUNK MOUNTAIN

metal markers, but also with cairns. In addition, in some places along the ridge, lines of small rocks have been placed to indicate the trail route. You'll encounter a number of viewpoints on both sides of the ridge, making this stretch of trail one of the most spectacular in the entire region.

In 0.8 mile from the Long Path/Jessup Trail junction, you'll reach a junction with the blue-dot-on-white-blazed Ridge-to-Ridge Trail, which begins on the left and heads over to the western ridge of the mountain. Continue ahead on the Jessup/Highlands Trail, which soon reaches the summit of the mountain (1,664 feet), marked with white paint on the bedrock. Although there once was a 360-degree view from the summit, it has largely been obscured by growth.

The Jessup/Highlands Trail now bears left and descends, almost immediately reaching a junction with a white-blazed side trail (also marked by cairns) that leads to the Megaliths—a group of huge blocks of conglomerate rock that have split off from the bedrock. The Megaliths also offer a fine west-facing view. This is a good place for a lunch break. If you have not spotted a second car, this should be your turnaround point.

If you have left a car at Otterkill Road, return to the Jessup/Highlands Trail and turn left. Almost immediately, the trail drops down into an attractive laurel grove that arches overhead. Soon, you'll reach a junction with the black-dot-on-white-blazed Dark Hollow Trail, which begins on the right and descends the east face of the mountain, but you should continue ahead on the Jessup/Highlands Trail. In a short distance, you'll come out onto another spectacular viewpoint over the Hudson River and the East Hudson Highlands.

About half a mile beyond, after passing yet another viewpoint, the white-blazed Sweet Clover Trail joins from the right. Continue ahead along the ridge, now following the white blazes of the Sweet Clover Trail, the yellow blazes of the Jessup Trail, and the teal diamond blazes of the Highlands Trail. The trail drops down to cross an intermittent stream and soon emerges onto a panoramic viewpoint. To the west, you can see the western ridge of Schunemunk Mountain in the foreground, with the Shawangunks and Catskills visible beyond on a clear day. You can also see the Hudson River to the northeast, with North and South Beacon Mountains and Breakneck Ridge across the river.

A short distance beyond, the Sweet Clover Trail departs to the left at a viewpoint over the western ridge. If you carefully scan the ridge to the left, you may be able to see the High Point Monument at the northwestern tip of New Jersey. Continue ahead on the Jessup/Highlands Trail, which soon begins a gradual descent, with more views along the way. After reaching another panoramic viewpoint to the west and north, the trail bears left and descends more steeply.

At the base of the descent, the Jessup/Highlands Trail reaches a woods road in the valley. Here, the Jessup/Highlands Trail turns right, but you should cross the road and continue ahead, now following the red-dot-on-white-blazed Barton Swamp Trail, which comes in from the left. Almost immediately, you'll cross Baby Brook on rocks and begin a rather steep climb. Soon, the trail turns left and follows along a rock ledge, with a sharp drop-off to the left. It then turns right, climbs through a cleft in the rock, and emerges onto a large expanse of conglomerate rock, with views to the northeast over the Hudson River. Continue ahead a

short distance to a junction with the white-blazed Trestle Trail.

Turn sharply right and follow the Trestle Trail downhill on a relatively smooth footpath. After about five minutes, you'll notice a side trail on the right that leads to a viewpoint. This is the first northeast-facing view you reach when you climb the mountain on the Trestle Trail, but you've already seen a number of broader vistas, so you might want to skip this viewpoint. Continue downhill on the Trestle Trail, and in another 0.6 mile you'll come to an overlook on the left with a bench. From here, you can see the trestle that gives the trail its name.

The official name for the trestle is the Moodna Viaduct. It was built between 1904 and 1908 by the Erie Railroad as part of a new freight bypass which became known as the Graham Line. Until the 1980s, the trestle was used only for freight service. Regularly scheduled passenger trains used this spectacularly scenic trestle for the first time in 1983, when the original Erie Railroad main line through Goshen and Middletown was abandoned. Today, Metro-North operates 13 passenger trains in each direction over the trestle every weekday (service is also provided on weekends). Most of these trains run between Port Jervis, New York, and Hoboken, New Jersey.

Continue heading downhill on the Trestle Trail, and in another half mile, you'll reach a junction where a triple-red blaze marks the start of the Otterkill Trail. Turn left to continue on the Trestle Trail, which soon approaches the trestle on the right. The trail bears left, away from the trestle, and descends to Otterkill Road. Turn left and follow the white-blazed trail along the road until you reach the parking area on the right where you left your car.

40

Schunemunk Mountain Loop

TOTAL DISTANCE: 7.8 miles

WALKING TIME: 5.5 hours

ELEVATION GAIN: 1,864 feet

MAPS: USGS 7.5' Cornwall; NY–NJTC West Hudson Trails #114

TRAILHEAD GPS COORDINATES: N 41° 24' 28" W 74° 04' 53"

Schunemunk Mountain, which sits in solitary splendor, is not nearly as popular as Harriman-Bear Mountain State Parks, a short distance to the south. This is partially due to the fact that any hike from the base of the mountain to its 1,664-foot summit involves an elevation gain of over 1,200 feet. But for those who are willing to make this rather strenuous ascent, the rewards are great. The light sandstones, shales, and conglomerates that crown its summit provide for a ridge walk replete with panoramic views, gnarled pitch pines, and unusual rock formations. This loop walk from the north highlights the deep cleft that creases Schunemunk Mountain, and it takes you to vantage points on both the eastern and western ridges.

GETTING THERE

To reach the trailhead, take the New York State Thruway (I-87) to Exit 16 (Harriman), and drive north on NY 32 for 7.3 miles to a sign for the Black Rock Fish and Game Club. Turn left here onto Pleasant Hill Road (County Route 79). At the bottom of the hill, turn left again onto Taylor Road, then bear right and cross the bridge over I-87. The trailhead parking area is on the right side of the road, just beyond the junction with Creekside Lane.

THE HIKE

From the western end of the parking area, cross the road and proceed south on the joint Jessup (yellow blaze), Sweet Clover (white blaze), and Highlands (teal diamond blaze) Trails, which climb gently to the crest of a field and then descend to a woods road. To the right, you can see Schunemunk Mountain, which you'll soon climb.

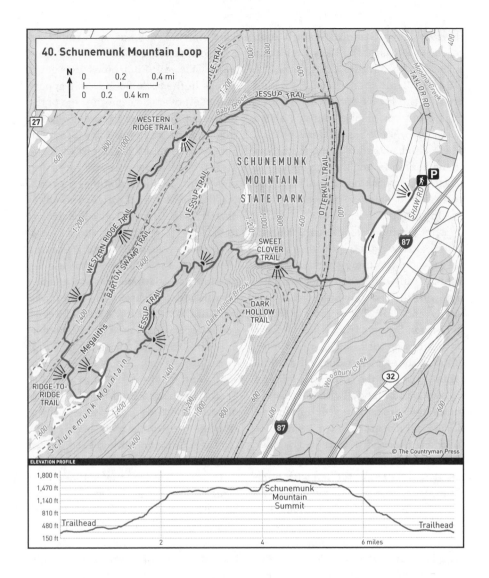

40. Schunemunk Mountain Loop

N
0   0.2   0.4 mi
0   0.2   0.4 km

WESTERN
RIDGE TRAIL

JESSUP TRAIL

SCHUNEMUNK
MOUNTAIN
STATE PARK

WESTERN RIDGE TRAIL

BARTON SWAMP TRAIL

JESSUP TRAIL

SWEET
CLOVER
TRAIL

OTTERKILL TRAIL

DARK
HOLLOW
TRAIL

Megaliths

RIDGE-TO-
RIDGE
TRAIL

Schunemunk Mountain

Dark Hollow Brook

Baby Brook

SHAW RD

TAYLOR RD

Woodbury Creek

87

32

87

27

P

© The Countryman Press

ELEVATION PROFILE

1,800 ft
1,470 ft
1,140 ft
810 ft
480 ft
150 ft

Trailhead

Schunemunk
Mountain
Summit

Trailhead

2   4   6 miles

Turn right on the woods road, going past a chain that blocks off the road. When the white-blazed Sweet Clover Trail leaves to the left, continue ahead, now following the yellow blazes of the Jessup Trail. (You're also following the Highlands Trail, but the teal-diamond Highlands Trail blazes appear mainly at intersections.) The Jessup Trail traverses a field diagonally to the right, crosses a footbridge over a stream, reenters the

woods, and soon climbs to a woods road, where it turns right.

Follow the yellow blazes along the woods road for about half a mile. Watch for a sharp left turn, where the trail leaves the road and climbs to cross the railroad tracks. This is an active rail line, so be sure to stop, look, and listen for approaching trains before crossing.

On the other side of the tracks, the Jessup Trail turns right, briefly joining the red-blazed Otterkill Trail. It soon reaches the cascading Baby Brook and turns left to parallel the brook. The Otterkill Trail then turns right and crosses the brook on a wooden footbridge, but you should continue ahead along the yellow-blazed Jessup Trail, which climbs steadily along the brook. In the next mile, you'll climb about 700 feet. If you're taking this hike in the spring, wild oats, spring beauty, and trailing arbutus line the way.

After joining a woods road, the trail detours to the right to pass by a beautiful cascade. Continue ahead along the Jessup Trail, which soon reaches a junction with the red-on-white-blazed Barton Swamp Trail. Turn right and follow the Barton Swamp Trail, which crosses Baby Brook on rocks and begins a steep climb up the western ridge of the mountain. At the top, the trail turns left and follows a rock ledge, with east-facing views over Storm King Mountain and Black Rock Forest. The trail continues to climb through a cleft in the rock and emerges onto a large expanse of conglomerate rock studded with pitch pines, with even broader views to the northeast over the Hudson River. The Newburgh–Beacon Bridge is visible in the distance. Near the top of the western ridge of Schunemunk Mountain, northwest-facing views to the Shawangunks and Catskills begin.

Continue to follow the red-dot-on-white blazes, passing a junction where the white-blazed Trestle Trail departs to the right, until the Barton Swamp Trail ends at a junction with the orange-blazed Western Ridge Trail. Bear left here and proceed south along the Western Ridge Trail, which follows the western ridge of Schunemunk Mountain over conglomerate rock outcrops studded with pebbles of white quartz and pink sandstone.

This unusual rock has been smoothed by glacial action, sometimes resembling a level sidewalk. Pitch pines grow out of cracks in the rock. Soon, views appear to the left over the eastern ridge of the mountain, separated from the western ridge by the valley of Baby Brook. In about ten minutes, the Western Ridge Trail reaches a panoramic west-facing viewpoint. A short distance beyond, you'll come to a junction with the white-blazed Sweet Clover Trail, which leaves to the left.

Continue ahead on the orange-blazed Western Ridge Trail for about a mile, passing more viewpoints as well as a fascinating deep fissure in the rock to the right of the trail. After a brief descent, you'll reach a junction with the blue-dot-on-white-blazed Ridge-to-Ridge Trail. Turn left, leaving the Western Ridge Trail, and follow the Ridge-to-Ridge Trail, which descends to the valley between the two ridges. Here, it turns right onto a woods road, briefly joining the red-dot-on-white-blazed Barton Swamp Trail.

In about 500 feet, turn left and continue to follow the blue-dot-on-white-blazed Ridge-to-Ridge Trail as it crosses a wet area and then steeply ascends the eastern ridge of the mountain. After a very steep pitch, the trail turns right along a ledge and reaches a panoramic west-facing viewpoint. The trail continues to climb more gradually. After traversing an open area of exposed conglomerate bedrock, the Ridge-to-Ridge Trail ends, on the crest of the eastern ridge, at a junction with the yellow-blazed Jessup Trail and the teal-diamond-blazed Highlands Trail.

Turn left and follow the joint Jessup/Highlands Trail, which reaches the 1,664-foot-high summit of Schunemunk Mountain—marked on the rock with

EAST-FACING VIEW FROM SCHUNEMUNK MOUNTAIN

white paint—in another 0.1 mile. The Jessup/Highlands Trail bears left and descends, almost immediately reaching a junction with a white-blazed side trail (also marked by cairns) that leads to the Megaliths—a group of huge blocks of conglomerate rock that have split off from the bedrock. This is a good place for a break, as the interesting geologic features are complemented by a fine vista to the west.

When you're ready to continue, return to the Jessup/Highlands Trail and turn left. In another 0.3 mile, the black-on-white-blazed Dark Hollow Trail departs to the right. This trail descends the mountain and could be used as an alternate return route. But for now, continue ahead on the Jessup/Highlands Trail, soon coming out onto another spectacular overlook over the Hudson River and the East Hudson Highlands.

About half a mile beyond, after going by yet another viewpoint, you'll reach a junction with the white-blazed Sweet Clover Trail. Turn right, leaving the Jessup/Highlands Trail, and follow the Sweet Clover Trail downhill. After passing an east-facing overlook, the trail descends on rock steps, crosses the northern branch of Dark Hollow Brook, then again approaches the brook just above a series of cascades. The trail descends some more, follows along the side of a hill, then resumes its descent, with portions of the trail having been relocated to avoid eroded sections.

Having descended over 1,200 feet from the summit, the Sweet Clover Trail arrives at a junction with the red-blazed Otterkill Trail just before reaching the Metro-North railroad tracks. Turn left onto the Otterkill Trail, then almost immediately turn right and cross the

THE MEGALITHS

railroad tracks (use extreme caution, as the crossing is on a curve in the tracks, and it is difficult to see or hear approaching trains). Continue to follow the Sweet Clover Trail as it descends through the woods, turns right onto a woods road, then bears left and follows a grassy road through fields. When you reach the junction with the yellow-blazed Jessup Trail (also the route of the teal-diamond-blazed Highlands Trail), turn right, then left, following the joint Sweet Clover/Jessup/Highlands Trails back to the parking area where the hike began.

Storm King Mountain

TOTAL DISTANCE: 2.5 miles

WALKING TIME: 2.5 hours

ELEVATION GAIN: 852 feet

MAPS: USGS 7.5' Cornwall; USGS 7.5' West Point; NY–NJTC West Hudson Trails #113

TRAILHEAD GPS COORDINATES: N 41° 25' 23" W 74° 00' 03"

"The Montaynes look as if some Metall or Minerall were in them. For the trees that grow on them were all blasted, and some of them barren with few or no trees on them." Thus did Robert Juet describe his view of the Hudson Highlands in September 1609 after his first trip up the Hudson in Henry Hudson's vessel *Half Moon*, anchored in what is now Newburgh Bay. The centuries have done little to alter the sight.

The noble ring of hills through which the Hudson flows south of Newburgh is as impressive as any range in the state. Storm King guards the west bank, and Beacon Mountain—giving way to Breakneck Ridge and Bull Hill on the south—guards the eastern shores. They are all mountains you will want to climb again and again.

Storm King and Butter Hill form a semicircular crest, which noted American historian Benson Lossing believed the Dutch skippers thought of as a huge lump of butter, hence the original name "Boterberg." Nathaniel Parker Willis, who settled at Idlewild at the foot of Storm King in present-day Cornwall, wrote weekly letters to the *Home Journal* in the 1850s, describing his bucolic surroundings. It was he who was able to change the name of part of the mountain to the more romantic Storm King.

Storm King Mountain is also linked to a major environmental court case. In the early 1960s, the Consolidated Edison Company (Con Ed) announced plans to build a hydroelectric plant at the base of the mountain, with a pumped storage reservoir in the adjacent Black Rock Forest. What is now known as Scenic Hudson was formed by the New York–New Jersey Trail Conference and others to fight this project. A 17-year legal fight ended with a

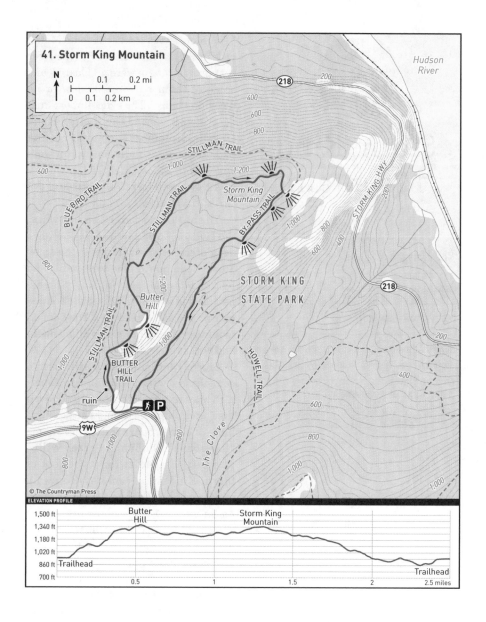

41. Storm King Mountain

N
0   0.1   0.2 mi
0   0.1   0.2 km

Hudson River

STILLMAN TRAIL

BLUE BIRD TRAIL

STILLMAN TRAIL

Storm King Mountain

BY-PASS TRAIL

STORM KING HWY

Butter Hill

STILLMAN TRAIL

STORM KING STATE PARK

BUTTER HILL TRAIL

HOWELL TRAIL

ruin

9W

The Clove

© The Countryman Press

ELEVATION PROFILE

1,500 ft — Butter Hill
1,340 ft
1,180 ft
1,020 ft
860 ft — Trailhead
700 ft

Storm King Mountain

Trailhead

0.5   1   1.5   2   2.5 miles

settlement in which Con Ed essentially gave up. This court case established the right of citizens' groups to take government agencies to court to protect scenic beauty and recreational interests. For more on this historic case, see library .marist.edu/archives/mehp/scenic decision.html.

GETTING THERE

From the circle at the west end of the Bear Mountain Bridge, proceed north on US 9W for 8.5 miles to a parking area on the right, at a sharp bend in the road. (This is the second parking area along US 9W in Storm King State Park, but the only one which is designated by a blue PARKING AREA sign; it has a yellow-on-blue historical marker entitled Freedom Road and an adjacent marker commemorating the completion of the Storm King Bypass Highway.) This parking area cannot be accessed from the southbound lanes of US 9W. If you are coming from the north, go to the junction of US 9W and NY 293/ NY 218, and use the underpass to turn around and head back north 3.1 miles to the parking area.

THE HIKE

From the parking area, walk north along the grassy shoulder of the road. Soon, you will see a triple-orange blaze, which marks the start of the Butter Hill Trail. Follow the orange blazes as they bear right, away from the road, and begin to ascend steeply. Soon, views over the

Hudson River begin to appear to the right. The mountain across the river is Bull Hill (Mount Taurus), and the point of land jutting into the river is Little Stony Point.

In 0.2 mile, you'll reach three stone pillars, with a stone foundation behind the pillars. These are the remains of Spy Rock House, the summer cottage of Dr. Edward L. Partridge, who served on the Palisades Interstate Park Commission from 1913 to 1930.

The trail now descends slightly into a rugged, stone-filled valley, then continues to climb Butter Hill, first gradually, then more steeply. At the top of the steep climb, you'll reach open rock ledges that afford a wide panorama to the east, south, and west. US 9W is visible straight ahead to the south, with the North Ridge of Crows Nest Mountain to its left. The Hudson River is to the east.

NORTH-FACING VIEW FROM STORM KING MOUNTAIN

SOUTH-FACING VIEW OVER COLD SPRING AND CONSTITUTION ISLAND

You'll want to pause here for a little while to enjoy this expansive view, but the best is yet to come.

After a short level stretch, the Butter Hill Trail ends at a junction with the yellow-blazed Stillman Trail (also the route of the teal-diamond-blazed Highlands Trail). Turn right and follow the Stillman Trail up to the summit of Butter Hill. A rock outcrop to the left of the trail offers a 360-degree view. The East Hudson Highlands are visible across the river, with towers marking the summits of North and South Beacon Mountains to the north. Bull Hill is directly to the east. On the west side of the river, the

high, the viaduct was constructed from 1904 to 1908 by the Erie Railroad and is the highest and longest railroad trestle east of the Mississippi River. In the distance to the northwest are the Shawangunks and, behind them, the Catskills. To the north, the Newburgh–Beacon Bridge spans the Hudson River.

After enjoying this spectacular view, continue ahead on the yellow-blazed Stillman Trail, which descends slightly. Soon, you'll reach a junction with the blue-and-red-blazed Bluebird Trail, marked by a large cairn. Turn right, uphill, and continue on the Stillman Trail. A short distance ahead, you'll reach the northern end of the blue-blazed Howell Trail, which departs to the right. Bear left here, continuing along the yellow-blazed trail, which follows a relatively level route for the next 0.7 mile. After a short, steep climb, you'll reach a limited view to the north. About five minutes ahead, though, you'll come to a much better viewpoint looking north over the Hudson River. Pollopel Island is directly below, with the ruins of Bannerman's Castle on its high point.

This mysterious island, now a state park, has been named Pollepel (or some variant thereof) since the 1600s, when the Dutch governed the area. The name appears on a Dutch map of the Hudson River valley dating back to the mid-1600s. Jasper Dankers, a minister, recorded in 1680 that it was called Potlepels Eylant, Dutch for Potladle Island. Another version of the name's origin relates that a young girl named Polly Pell was rescued from the breaking river ice near the island by her sweetheart, to whom she was promptly married. In 1777, General Henry Clinton fortified Pollepel Island, along with Constitution Island to the south. In the 1850s, Benson Lossing reported that it contained a solitary

north ridge of Crows Nest Mountain is directly to the south, with Black Rock Forest visible to the southeast. Schunemunk Mountain may be seen to the west, with the Moodna Viaduct (on the Metro-North rail line to Port Jervis) towering over the valley just north of the mountain. Some 3,200 feet long and 193 feet

house that looked like a wren's nest, inhabited by a fisherman with an insane wife who thought herself to be the queen of England. Francis Bannerman bought the island in 1900 to house his arsenal of secondhand military supplies—arms captured in the Spanish-American War. To store his surplus military supplies, he constructed a Scottish-style "castle," which became a landmark along the river. The castle was damaged by an explosion in 1920 and was essentially abandoned after 1950. New York State acquired the property in 1967, but two years later a fire destroyed much of its interior. The shell remained largely intact until December 2009, when a large portion of the castle collapsed during a storm. For more history and a tour schedule, visit www.bannerman castle.org.

Continue ahead, past the summit of Storm King Mountain, with some more views from rock ledges to the left. After a short descent, you'll reach a panoramic north-facing outlook with superb views. To the east, Breakneck Ridge (marked by the rail tunnel) is visible across the river. The stone building at the foot of Breakneck Ridge (partially obscured by the vegetation) caps a shaft of the Catskill Aqueduct, which tunnels 1,100 feet below the river. North Beacon Mountain (with communications towers) and South Beacon Mountain (with a fire tower) are to the northeast. To the northwest, the village of Cornwall can be seen along the west bank of the river.

The Stillman Trail now continues to descend, soon reaching a junction with the white-blazed By-Pass Trail. Turn left at this junction and walk about 25 feet to a rock ledge that affords a broad south-facing view down the Hudson River. The village of Cold Spring is visible across the river to the southeast, and Constitution Island juts into the river just beyond.

Now return to the junction and continue along the white-blazed By-Pass Trail, which descends along the side of the mountain—first gradually and then more steeply. There are several views of the river from rock ledges on the left, but they are not as broad as those from the junction with the Stillman Trail. After crossing a seasonal stream, the By-Pass Trail climbs briefly to end at a junction with the blue-blazed Howell Trail, which joins from the right.

Bear left and continue ahead on the Howell Trail, which soon begins to follow an old road. In about 500 feet, the blue-blazed trail turns sharply left, leaving the old road, but you should continue ahead on the road, which is now blazed white. The road climbs briefly, then descends steadily. As it approaches US 9W, the road again climbs rather steeply to end just beyond the parking area where the hike began.

Black Rock Forest— Southern Ledges

TOTAL DISTANCE: 9 miles
WALKING TIME: 6.5 hours
ELEVATION GAIN: 2,277 feet
MAPS: USGS 7.5' Cornwall; NY–NJTC West Hudson Trails #113; Black Rock Forest
TRAILHEAD GPS COORDINATES: N 41° 25' 07" W 74° 00' 39"

The hiking trails in Black Rock Forest are among the region's least frequented. They wind around and over a number of peaks, several with elevations of more than 1,400 feet. But generally these peaks rise less than 400 feet from the high plateau that is a westward continuation of the Storm King intrusion of the Hudson Highlands. That plateau drops precipitously to the north and east, with the summit of Black Rock Mountain, namesake of the forest, standing out above the valley near Cornwall.

This hike starts at the forest's main parking area, climbs to three peaks in the eastern end of the forest, and winds along the southern ledges that border on the lands of the United States Military Academy at West Point. It passes four of the best viewpoints in the forest: Mount Misery, Hill of Pines, Rattlesnake Hill, and Eagle Cliff (two more outstanding viewpoints, Black Rock Mountain and Split Rock Trail, are included in Hike #43).

Please note that the forest is closed to hikers during deer hunting season, usually mid-November to mid-December.

GETTING THERE

From the traffic circle at the western side of the Bear Mountain Bridge, proceed north on US 9W for 8.8 miles and turn right onto Mountain Road at a sign for the Storm King School. Immediately turn right again and proceed through a very narrow underpass beneath US 9W (large vehicles may not fit through this underpass). Continue ahead for 0.2 mile to a parking area on the right side of the road, just before a gate.

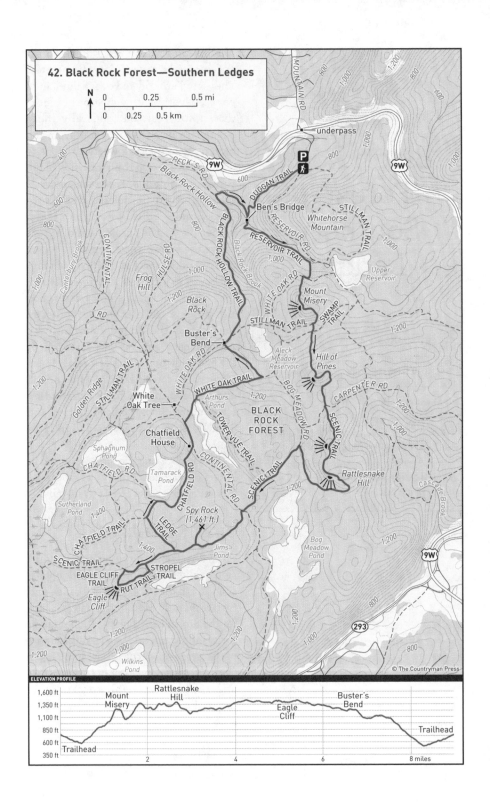

42. Black Rock Forest—Southern Ledges

N

| 0 | 0.25 | 0.5 mi |
| 0 | 0.25 | 0.5 km |

underpass

9W

P

MOUNTAIN RD

PECK'S RD

9W

Black Rock Hollow

DUGGAN TRAIL

Ben's Bridge

RESERVOIR RD

Whitehorse Mountain

STILLMAN TRAIL

RESERVOIR TRAIL

BLACK ROCK HOLLOW TRAIL

Black Rock Brook

WHITE OAK RD

Upper Reservoir

Mount Misery

Frog Hill

CONTINENTAL

HULSE RD

Black Rock

Buster's Bend

STILLMAN TRAIL

SWAMP TRAIL

Aleck Meadow Reservoir

Hill of Pines

RD

Golden Ridge

STILLMAN TRAIL

WHITE OAK RD

WHITE OAK TRAIL

Arthurs Pond

BLACK ROCK FOREST

BOG MEADOW RD

CARPENTER RD

SCENIC TRAIL

White Oak Tree

Chatfield House

Sphagnum Pond

CHATFIELD RD

Tamarack Pond

TOWER-VUE TRAIL

CONTINENTAL RD

SCENIC TRAIL

Rattlesnake Hill

Sutherland Pond

CHATFIELD TRAIL

CHATFIELD RD

LEDGE TRAIL

Spy Rock [1,461 ft.]

Jims Pond

Bog Meadow Pond

9W

SCENIC TRAIL

EAGLE CLIFF TRAIL

STROPEL TRAIL

RUT TRAIL

Eagle Cliff

Wilkins Pond

293

© The Countryman Press

ELEVATION PROFILE

1,600 ft		Rattlesnake				
1,350 ft	Mount Misery	Hill			Buster's Bend	
1,100 ft				Eagle		
850 ft				Cliff		
600 ft	Trailhead					Trailhead
350 ft		2	4	6		8 miles

BOG MEADOW POND FROM RATTLESNAKE HILL

THE HIKE

From the kiosk at the end of the parking area, bear right and proceed ahead on the red-blazed Duggan Trail, which heads downhill. In about half a mile, you'll reach a gravel road. Here, the red trail ends at a junction with the blue-blazed Reservoir Trail. Continue ahead on the blue trail, which immediately crosses Ben's Bridge (a wooden footbridge) and climbs along a picturesque stream, with cascades and waterfalls, following an old woods road.

In half a mile, you'll notice a shiny pipeline crossing the stream. On the other side of the stream, you can see the Black Rock Forest's Science Center. A short distance beyond, you'll reach a junction where the white-blazed Honey Hill Trail departs to the right. Proceed ahead on the blue trail, which soon curves to the right and continues to parallel the stream. When the blue trail ends, bear right and continue ahead on the yellow-blazed Stillman Trail, which joins from the left.

Soon, the Stillman Trail reaches the dirt White Oak Road. Turn right onto the road, joining the teal-diamond-blazed Highlands Trail, but in 100 feet, turn left, leaving the road, and begin a steep climb of Mount Misery on a footpath. At the top (elevation 1,268 feet), you'll reach a limited viewpoint to the west and northwest. Continue ahead for a short distance, and you'll come to a much better outlook, with Black Rock Mountain visible directly ahead and Aleck Meadow Reservoir below to the left. This is a good place to take a break (you've climbed nearly 700 vertical feet from Ben's Bridge).

Continue ahead on the yellow/teal-diamond trail, which begins its descent of Mount Misery, first gradually and then more steeply. In a rugged, boulder-strewn area at the base of the descent, you'll notice a triple-white blaze, which marks the start of the

VIEW FROM HILL OF PINES

Scenic Trail. Turn left and follow the white-blazed Scenic Trail, which crosses the blue-blazed Swamp Trail at the end of the rocky area and begins a steady climb of the Hill of Pines, passing through attractive mountain laurel and hemlock.

At the top of the climb, the trail emerges onto open rock, with a spectacular west-facing view. Black Rock Mountain may be seen on the right, and the Black Rock Forest fire tower is to its left. (Despite the name "Hill of Pines," there are only two pine trees near the summit, which is mostly covered with oaks.)

The trail climbs a little to the true summit (elevation 1,400 feet), descends the hill, and soon crosses the dirt Carpenter Road diagonally to the right. You'll now begin a gradual climb of Rattlesnake Hill. After reaching a high point and descending a little, you'll arrive at a spot with a viewpoint about 100 feet to the right of the trail (from a rock ledge adjacent to a large pine tree). If you can't find the path to this overlook, don't be

concerned, as you'll soon reach two more viewpoints that are directly on the trail. You'll now make a short but steep descent. After a relatively level stretch, you'll reach a second overlook—this one marked by a cairn and a gnarled, nearly horizontal pine tree. The fire tower may be seen on the right, and Bog Meadow Pond lies directly below.

Continue ahead through a dense mountain laurel thicket to the third viewpoint on Rattlesnake Hill, which offers a panoramic view from open rocks. Bog Meadow Pond is directly ahead, with the rolling hills of Orange County beyond. Continue ahead on the white trail, which begins to descend—first steeply, then more gradually. The trail briefly runs along the southern boundary of Black Rock Forest, with Bog Meadow Pond visible through the trees to the left.

After crossing the inlet stream of the pond, the trail climbs to the dirt Bog Meadow Road. Turn left onto the road, continuing to follow the white-blazed

Scenic Trail. In a quarter mile, the yellow-blazed Tower Vue Trail begins on the right, but continue ahead on the road, following the white blazes. Soon you'll reach a T-junction with Continental Road. Continue to follow the white-blazed Scenic Trail, which crosses the road diagonally to the right, reenters the woods, and begins to climb gradually.

When the trail levels off, watch carefully for a small cairn. Here, the blue-blazed Spy Rock Trail departs to the right. Turn right and follow this short trail, which leads in about 750 feet to Spy Rock, marked by a single pitch pine. This is the highest point in Black Rock Forest (1,461 feet). During the Revolutionary War, this rock outcrop was used as a lookout by Continental soldiers to monitor the area, but today, vegetation obscures most of the views, and only a limited north-facing view remains.

Retrace your steps to the white-blazed Scenic Trail and turn right. Soon you'll pass the yellow-blazed Ledge Trail, which begins on the right, and then the Stropel Trail (also yellow blazed), which goes off to the left. Proceed ahead on the white-blazed Scenic Trail, but a short distance beyond, turn left onto the blue-blazed Eagle Cliff Trail, which soon reaches Eagle Cliff—a huge rock outcrop with glacial striations. You'll have to use both your hands and your feet to climb to the top of the outcrop, but when you reach it, you'll be rewarded with a panoramic south-facing view. Wilkins Pond (on the grounds of the United States Military Academy at West Point) is straight ahead, and Jim's Pond is on the left. On a clear day, you may be able to see the New York City skyline in the distance. This is a good place to take a break.

When you're ready to continue, bear right onto the orange-blazed Rut Trail, which runs near the edge of the escarpment, with views through the trees on the right. Be alert for a sharp left turn, where the trail turns slightly away from

VIEW FROM EAGLE CLIFF

the cliff edge and goes down through a narrow passage between boulders. Soon you'll reach a trail junction, where the Rut Trail ends. Turn left onto the yellow-blazed Stropel Trail, which leads in a very short distance to the white-blazed Scenic Trail. Turn right and rejoin the Scenic Trail.

In another 0.2 mile, the yellow-blazed Ledge Trail begins on the left. Turn left onto this trail, which climbs over a rise, descends gently, then climbs a little more to end at a T-junction with the blue-blazed Chatfield Trail. Turn right onto the Chatfield Trail and descend to Chatfield Road, then turn right onto the road and follow it past Tamarack Pond, visible on the left through the trees. At the end of the pond, as the road curves to the right, a path straight ahead leads to the Moretti Outpost (a covered open pavilion). A short distance ahead, you'll reach the intersection of Chatfield and Continental Roads.

At this intersection, you'll notice an old stone building with a distinctive bulging chimney, indicative of a beehive oven inside. This is the Chatfield House, built in 1834—the oldest building in Black Rock Forest. The house was gutted by fire in 1913 and restored in 1932 by Dr. Stillman. The lands nearby were once pastures and orchards, and Tamarack Pond, originally called Orchard Pond, was used as a cranberry bog. Today, the Chatfield House is used for educational programs.

Turn left onto Continental Road, but follow it for only 500 feet and turn right onto the white-blazed White Oak Trail (here on a wide gravel road). After passing the northern end of Arthurs Pond and crossing the outlet stream of the pond just below the dam, you'll reach a junction with the yellow-blazed Tower Vue Trail, which begins on the right.

Continue ahead on the white-blazed White Oak Trail, which descends to White Oak Road near the Aleck Meadow Reservoir. Turn left onto the road and head toward Black Rock Mountain (visible in the distance). (NOTE: If the water is high and you are unable to cross the outlet stream of Arthurs Pond below the dam, retrace your steps to Continental Road and turn right. Continue to the next intersection, marked by a huge oak tree, and turn right onto White Oak Road. In half a mile, you'll reach Buster's Bend, marked by a sign. Turn left here onto a short unmarked trail and continue with the route of the hike as described in the next paragraph.)

Just beyond a stream crossing (the stream is the outlet of Arthurs Pond), the road curves to the left. This spot is marked by a sign identifying it as BUSTER'S BEND. Here, on the right, you'll notice a short unmarked trail which leads up to the yellow-blazed Stillman Trail (also the route of the teal-diamond-blazed Highlands Trail). Turn right onto this short connector trail, then turn right onto the Stillman/Highlands Trail, which follows a woods road. A short distance beyond, the yellow and teal-diamond blazes turn right, but you should continue ahead, now following the white-blazed Black Rock Hollow Trail along a section of the road which has narrowed to a footpath. The trail descends along the road, with portions rerouted to bypass very eroded sections of the road.

At the base of the descent, the white-blazed trail ends at a filtration plant. Turn right onto the blue-blazed Reservoir Trail and follow it around the plant and along the brook to a junction with the red-blazed Duggan Trail just before Ben's Bridge. Turn sharply left onto the red-blazed trail and follow it uphill to the parking area where the hike began.

Black Rock Forest— Northern Loop

TOTAL DISTANCE: 5.5 miles	
WALKING TIME: 3.5 hours	
ELEVATION GAIN: 1,182 feet	
MAPS: USGS 7.5' Cornwall; NY–NJTC West Hudson Trails #113; Black Rock Forest	
TRAILHEAD GPS COORDINATES: N 41° 24' 7.5" W 74° 02' 51.5"	

This hike, which explores the little-used northern section of Black Rock Forest, begins from the trailhead on Mine Hill Road. The route of the hike includes a climb of the 1,410-foot Black Rock Mountain, which offers panoramic views to the north. It also includes a south-facing viewpoint over Sutherland Pond, from which the New York City skyline can be seen on a clear day.

Please note that the small parking area at the Mine Hill Road trailhead accommodates only five cars (and roadside parking is strictly prohibited). The parking area fills up early on weekends, so you might want to plan this hike for a weekday. Please make sure that you do not block the road or hamper access by emergency vehicles.

GETTING THERE

To reach the trailhead, drive north on US 9W to Angola Road near Cornwall. Head southwest onto Angola Road for 1.6 miles, turn left onto Mine Hill Road, and continue for 0.9 mile to the parking turnout on the right side of the road, just beyond a very sharp, steep hairpin turn.

From the New York State Thruway (I-87), take Exit 16 and follow NY 32 north for 7 miles to Mountainville, where you turn right onto Angola Road. After 0.8 mile, you will come to a stop sign. Turn left to continue on Angola Road. In another 0.8 mile, turn sharply right onto Mine Hill Road. Follow Mine Hill Road uphill for 0.9 mile to the parking turnout described above.

THE HIKE

The hike begins by following the yellow-diamond-blazed Mine Hill Trail, which starts on the opposite side of the road, just beyond the parking turnout. The

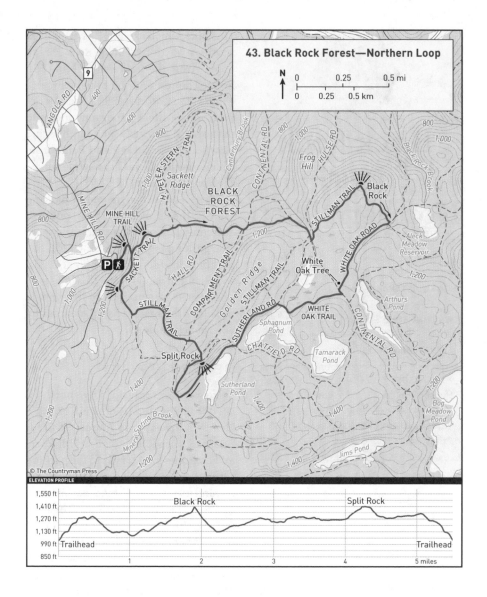

43. Black Rock Forest—Northern Loop

N

| 0 | | 0.25 | | 0.5 mi |
| 0 | 0.25 | | 0.5 km | |

ELEVATION PROFILE

1,550 ft
1,410 ft — Black Rock — Split Rock
1,270 ft
1,130 ft
990 ft — Trailhead — Trailhead
850 ft

1   2   3   4   5 miles

© The Countryman Press

trailhead is marked by a triple blaze. Follow the trail uphill, steeply in places. Just before a switchback turn, there are views over Schunemunk Mountain, the Moodna Viaduct, and the Shawangunks from open rocks to the left of the trail. The Mine Hill Trail now heads south and soon ends at a junction with the yellow-circle-blazed Sackett Trail. (You'll encounter four different yellow-blazed trails on this hike, so it's important to

note the shape of the blazes, in addition to their color.)

Turn left and follow the Sackett Trail, which soon climbs rather steeply over rock ledges, with views to the northwest. After descending a little, the trail climbs some more. Just beyond the crest of the rise, the red-blazed H. Peter Stern Trail, which leads down to the Hudson Highlands Nature Museum, departs to the left, but you should continue ahead on

SUTHERLAND POND FROM THE SPLIT ROCK TRAIL

the yellow-blazed Sackett Trail, which begins a steady descent. At the base of the descent, the trail crosses a stream and continues through a wet area. After climbing a little, the trail crosses a second stream. Just beyond, you'll notice a stone chimney to the left of the trail—the remnant of an old cabin, built many years ago as a family camping retreat.

A short distance beyond, the yellow blazes turn left and follow the grassy Hall Road for about 300 feet. Where the road bears left, continue along the yellow-blazed trail as it bears right, leaving the road. The path descends to a low point, with many fallen trees, then ascends gradually, traversing a rocky area along the way. About 1.6 miles from the start of the hike, the Sackett Trail turns right onto Continental Road, another woods road, which it follows for a short distance to its junction with Hulse Road. Here, the Sackett Trail ends.

Turn left onto Hulse Road, now following the route of the Stillman Trail, blazed with yellow rectangles, which is coaligned with the Highlands Trail (teal-diamond blazes). The trail follows the road for only 150 feet. Just past a stream crossing, watch carefully as the yellow and teal blazes bear right, leaving the road, and continue ahead on a footpath. Follow the Stillman and Highlands Trails through a thick stand of mountain laurel and hemlock and then steadily but gradually uphill. About 0.4 mile from the last intersection, the trail climbs steeply over a rock outcrop and reaches the 1,410-foot summit of Black Rock Mountain (after which the forest is named), with panoramic views. The best are from a rock ledge just north of the trail. Schunemunk Mountain is on the left, with the Moodna Viaduct to its right. You can also see the Hudson River on the right, with the Newburgh-Beacon

VIEW FROM THE SUMMIT OF BLACK ROCK MOUNTAIN

Bridge visible in the distance. On the horizon, you can see the Shawangunks, with the Catskills beyond. You'll want to take a break here to rest from the climb and enjoy the spectacular vistas.

When you're ready to continue, return to the trail and turn left, following the teal and yellow blazes as they descend rather steeply on a wide footpath. At the base of the descent, the trail makes a sharp left turn. Here, you should leave the yellow-and-teal-blazed trail and turn right onto a grassy path that leads 50 feet down to White Oak Road, a wide gravel road (a sign along the road identifies this location as BUSTER'S BEND). Turn right on White Oak Road and follow it as it climbs gently, paralleling the outlet stream from Arthurs Pond on the left. In half a mile, you'll reach a Y-junction, with a giant white oak tree (after which the road is named) in the middle of the intersection.

Bear left at the road intersection onto the gravel Continental Road, passing a pine plantation on the left. In 200 feet, you'll reach a junction with the white-blazed White Oak Trail. Turn sharply right and follow the white blazes, which run along a grassy woods road for a short distance, then continue ahead where the main woods road turns left. The White Oak Trail soon narrows to a footpath and goes through dense mountain laurel thickets, with an understory of blueberry bushes. In about 0.3 mile, after passing on the right an unmarked side trail that leads to the Phil Faurot Birding Platform at the edge of a wetland, you'll cross a stream and reach the stone impoundment of Sphagnum Pond. The trail skirts the dam, crosses a wet area on puncheons, bears left and climbs to the pond, then bears right and reaches Sutherland Road.

Turn left onto the road, which parallels Sphagnum Pond, visible below on the left. At the next intersection, Chatfield Road begins on the left, and a triple-blaze on the right marks the trailhead of the white-blazed Split Rock Trail (with a boulder inscribed in memory of William Golden above on the hillside). You should take the right fork of the road to continue on Sutherland Road. Just beyond, you'll pass a large cut into the hillside—the site of an abandoned mine.

The road now begins to parallel the shore of Sutherland Pond, the only natural pond in Black Rock Forest (the other ponds were created by the construction of dams). As the road moves away from the pond, keep your eyes open for an unmarked trail on the left that leads to a rock ledge overlooking the pond. Swimming (at your own risk) is permitted in Sutherland Pond, but not in the other ponds in Black Rock Forest, which are reservoirs for nearby towns.

When you're ready to resume the hike, return to Sutherland Road and turn left. In another 0.2 mile, you'll reach an intersection with Hall Road—the route of the blue-blazed Compartment Trail and the teal-diamond-blazed Highlands Trail. Turn right and, almost immediately, you'll reach the Hall Road Gate (marked by a sign). Just beyond, the Compartment/Highlands Trail turns right, leaving the road. Follow the blue and teal-diamond blazes, which climb steadily on a footpath through mountain laurel thickets.

Near the crest of the rise, you'll reach an intersection where the white-blazed Split Rock Trail begins on the right. Bear right and follow the Split Rock Trail, which climbs to the top of a rock outcrop, with a panoramic view to the southeast. Sutherland Pond is directly below, and the New York City skyline may be visible in the distance on a clear day. The Black Rock Fire Tower (closed to the public) can be seen on the left. This is a good spot to take a break.

When you're ready to continue, look for a yellow diamond blaze on a tree. Here, you should turn left and proceed for 100 feet to the intersection of the blue-blazed Compartment Trail (which enters from the left) with the yellow-rectangle-blazed Stillman Trail (which enters from the right). Continue straight ahead and proceed downhill (northwest), following both blue and yellow blazes. At the base of the descent, the Compartment Trail departs to the right. Bear left and follow the yellow rectangle blazes, which in 100 feet turn right and continue along Hall Road. (Note that the yellow-triangle-blazed Short Cut Trail begins on the left at this intersection; make sure that you follow the yellow rectangles, not the yellow triangles.)

Near the crest of a slight rise, at a sign for MINE HILL ROAD, follow the yellow-rectangle-blazed Stillman Trail as it turns left, leaving the road, and proceeds through dense mountain laurel thickets. The Stillman Trail soon reaches a T-junction, where the yellow-circle-blazed Sackett Trail begins. Turn right and follow the Sackett Trail past a limited west-facing viewpoint. When you reach the next intersection, turn left and follow the yellow-diamond-blazed Mine Hill Trail down to Mine Hill Road, where you began the hike.

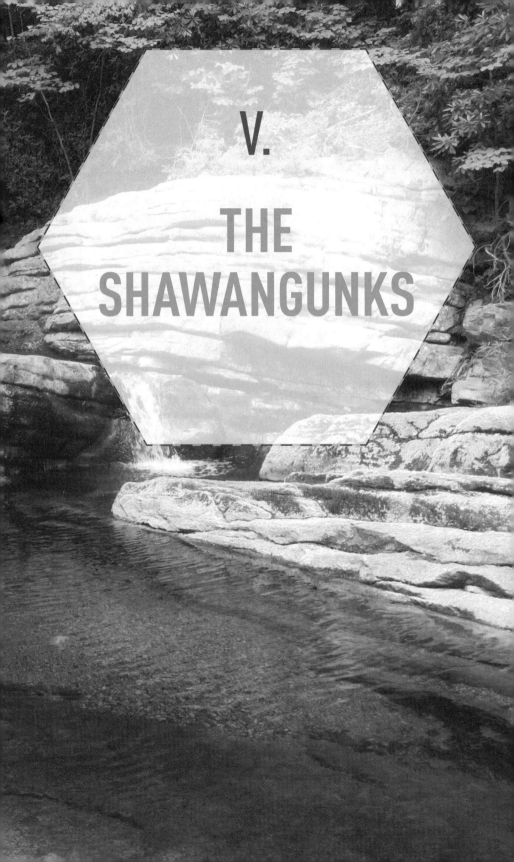

V.

THE
SHAWANGUNKS

Introduction to the Shawangunks

The Shawangunks (pronounced "shon-gum" and commonly called "the Gunks" by local folks and visiting climbers) is a continuation of the northern end of the ridge called the Kittatinnies in New Jersey and the Blue Mountains in Pennsylvania. The long ridge of the Northern Shawangunks, edged with sparkling white cliffs, is visible to the west of I-87 and has been designated a "Last Great Place" by The Nature Conservancy. Mohonk Mountain House's Sky Top Tower atop the ridge can be seen from many miles away.

The Shawangunks—meaning "white rock"—are world famous for rock climbing. An often-told legend has it that Fritz Wiessner, a celebrated and accomplished climber who had emigrated from Germany, became aware of these dazzling cliffs one afternoon in 1935 from across the Hudson while on Breakneck Ridge after a thunderstorm. Climbing first at Sky Top, he and his friend Hans Kraus were responsible for many of the first climbs of the Shawangunk cliffs.

Recreation opportunities abound in the Gunks. Cross-country skiing and snowshoeing are popular in winter, when the high elevation of the ridge attracts snow that remains longer than in lower-lying areas. Mountain bikes are allowed on many of the carriage roads.

This picturesque 30,000-acre preserved area can be divided into four jurisdictions: Mohonk Preserve, Mohonk Mountain House, Minnewaska State Park Preserve, and the Sam's Point Preserve—each with its own trails, access points, and fee structures. The area is a delight throughout the year, with its combination of white rock slabs and cliffs, green pitch pines, blueberry bushes that turn bright red in the fall, sheep laurel, mountain laurel, and rhododendron blooming in June—and, with luck, a clear, blue sky as a backdrop. The ridge contains five "sky lakes" and several waterfalls.

There has long been a human presence on the Shawangunk Ridge. Arrowheads have been found throughout the area, indicating use of caves and rock shelters by Native Americans. Trees on the ridge were consumed for the production of charcoal and barrel hoops, hemlock trees were cut for their bark and used to tan hides, and millstones were hammered out of the bedrock. Among the best-known residents were the berry pickers, whose shacks can still be seen along the Smiley Road, which runs 7 miles from Ellenville to Lake Awosting. Berry pickers invaded the area each summer as early as 1862. Their practice of setting fires to handicap the growth of competing vegetation resulted in improved berry crops for them and the development of a pygmy pine forest probably unique in the world.

The Shawangunks owe their development to the vision of Alfred Smiley, who first saw the Shawangunk escarpment in 1869. Alfred was so impressed by the spectacular beauty of the area that he persuaded his twin brother Albert, the principal of a Quaker boarding school, to purchase the 300-acre property at Mohonk Lake for $28,000. To finance the cost of running the property, they opened a hotel the following year. In 1876, Alfred purchased 2,500 acres at Lake Minnewaska, where he opened a hotel three years later. By Albert's death in 1912, the property had grown through more than 100 purchases to encompass 5,000 acres. The brothers transformed a boulder-strewn land into a premier resort by the systematic construction of carriage roads and walking paths.

MOHONK PRESERVE

Organized in 1963 as the Mohonk Trust, the Mohonk Preserve is New York State's largest privately owned nonprofit nature sanctuary. Its lands are open to the public for recreational activities compatible with preservation. Hikers on Mohonk Preserve lands need to be either Mohonk Preserve members or to have purchased a day pass, which they may be required to show to a ranger. The per-person day fee is currently $12. Day passes, memberships, and trail maps are available for purchase at the visitor center. To reach the visitor center, drive west about 6 miles on NY 299 from the village of New Paltz to its end at a T-junction with US 44/NY 55. Turn right, continue for half a mile, then turn right again onto the entrance road to the Mohonk Preserve Visitor Center. Inside the center is a small gift shop and much information on the natural history of the area. Outside there are nature trails to be explored.

MOHONK MOUNTAIN HOUSE

This elegant building is a private hotel that reflects the leisure and elegance of Victorian vacations. The trails that surround the hotel were laid out with the same nineteenth-century attitude that

fostered the resort. Today, these paths are a marvel of rock climbs, deep-woods walks, and vantage points that reflect their builders' humor. A Mohonk Preserve annual or day pass is honored on Mountain House lands, but day visitors are requested not to enter the hotel.

You may easily become infatuated with the area and wish to return to the Mountain House. Delicious meals are provided for overnight guests as well as for those reserving in advance by purchasing "A Day at Mohonk." This voucher allows you to drive to the hotel, hike its surrounding lands, and enjoy a meal and entry to the hotel.

MINNEWASKA STATE PARK PRESERVE

This spectacular state park preserve owes its existence to a chain of events beginning in 1879, when Alfred Smiley opened the first of two hotels overlooking Lake Minnewaska. The Smileys constructed many carriage roads and walking trails for the guests at their hotels. In the 1950s, Kevin Phillips, the general manager of the hotels at Lake Minnewaska, bought the property and endeavored to update the facilities by adding a golf course and a downhill-ski slope. However, financial difficulties forced the sale of part of the acreage, including Lake Awosting, to New York State in 1971, creating Minnewaska State Park Preserve. Continuing financial problems and a proposal by the Marriott Corporation to build condominiums, a 450-room hotel, an 18-hole golf course, and other amenities resulted in a long legal battle. In 1987, a 1,200-acre parcel that includes Lake Minnewaska was added to Minnewaska State Park Preserve. Today Minnewaska, administered by the Palisades

Interstate Park Commission, is one of New York State's most beautiful parks. Thanks to the work of the Open Space Institute, additional lands have been added to the park, which now includes over 22,000 acres.

Lakes Awosting and Minnewaska are renowned for their aquamarine color and exceptionally clear water. Swimming is allowed in designated areas in both lakes, and bicycles are allowed on many of the carriage roads. In winter, when snow conditions permit, the carriage roads are groomed for cross-country skiing. There is a $10 parking fee, with a $6 per-person entrance fee charged when cross-country skiing is available.

SAM'S POINT PRESERVE

The Sam's Point area was formerly owned by the village of Ellenville, with Lake Maratanza—the highest of the "sky lakes"—serving as the village's water supply. For three decades, some 4,800 mountaintop acres were leased to Ice Caves Mountain, Inc., a private corporation, and public access was limited to the ice caves on the escarpment, southeast of the Sam's Point promontory. In 1997, with the assistance of the New York–New Jersey Trail Conference, the land was acquired by the Open Space Institute. It has subsequently been transferred to the State of New York and added to Minnewaska State Park Preserve. Although part of the Minnewaska park, it is administered separately. There are informative exhibits at the visitor center at the entrance to the area. A $10 parking fee is charged. Lake Maratanza, near Sam's Point, is still part of the water supply system of the village of Ellenville, and no recreational use of the lake is permitted.

Shawangunk Ridge

TOTAL DISTANCE: 6.2 miles

WALKING TIME: 4.5 hours

ELEVATION GAIN: 1,799 feet

MAPS: USGS 7.5' Wurtsboro; NY–NJTC Shawangunk Trails #106

TRAILHEAD GPS COORDINATES: N 41° 40' 09" W 74° 24' 20"

This one-way hike (which requires a car shuttle) traverses a spectacular section of the Shawangunk Ridge that was preserved through the efforts of the New York–New Jersey Trail Conference. This route for the Long Path/Shawangunk Ridge Trail was created as an alternative to avoid roadwalks on the lowland route through Orange County. It follows the Shawangunk Ridge, which in New Jersey is referred to as the Kittatinny Ridge. The hike offers many spectacular views and passes fascinating rock formations.

GETTING THERE

A car shuttle is needed. Leave the New York State Thruway (I-87) at Exit 16 (Harriman), and drive two cars west on NY 17 (I-86) for 22 miles to Exit 114 (Wurtsboro, Highview). Exit 114 is only available going westbound. Turn right at the end of the exit ramp onto Old NY 17 (County Route 171), and proceed for half a mile. Turn left onto Shawanga Lodge Road, and follow it for 3 miles to a stop sign at Pickles Road. Continue ahead, but almost immediately turn left onto Ferguson Road. Continue for 0.1 mile and turn left into a parking area at a sign for the Wurtsboro Ridge State Forest. Leave one car here.

Drive the second car back to the stop sign at the end of Ferguson Road and turn right, then immediately turn left onto Pickles Road. In 0.7 mile, turn left at a stop sign onto the unsigned Roosa Gap Road. (Pickles Road becomes Ski Run Road on the other side of Roosa Gap Road.) Continue on Roosa Gap Road for 2 miles. When you reach an intersection where Frey Road begins on the right, bear left to continue on Pleasant Valley Road, and cross a bridge. In 0.2 mile, bear left at another stop sign onto Cox

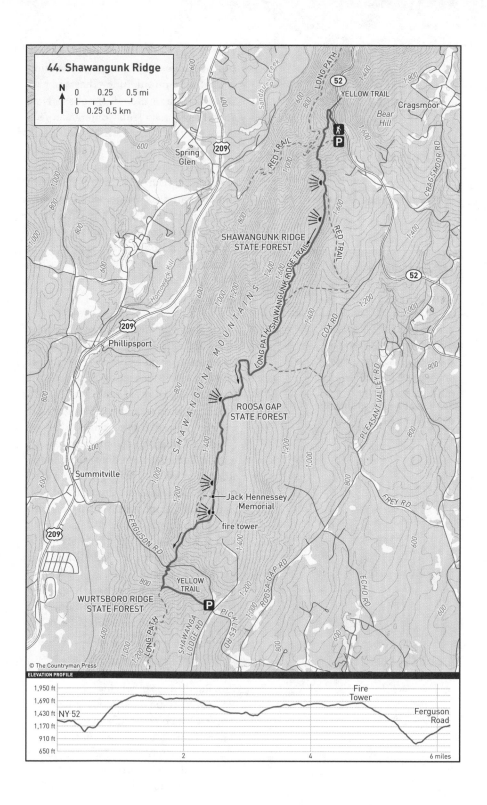

44. Shawangunk Ridge

N
0   0.25   0.5 mi
0 0.25 0.5 km

Sandburg Creek

LONG PATH

52

YELLOW TRAIL

Cragsmoor

Bear
Hill

Spring
Glen

209

CRAGSMOOR RD

RED TRAIL

SHAWANGUNK RIDGE
STATE FOREST

RED TRAIL

52

Homowack Kill

LONG PATH/SHAWANGUNK RIDGE TRAIL

COX RD

PLEASANT VALLEY RD

Phillipsport

209

ROOSA GAP
STATE FOREST

S H A W A N G U N K   M O U N T A I N S

Summitville

FREY RD

Jack Hennessey
Memorial

fire tower

FERGUSON RD

ECHO RD

ROOSA GAP RD

209

YELLOW
TRAIL

P

WURTSBORO RIDGE
STATE FOREST

LONG PATH

SHAWANGA LODGE RD

PICKLES RD

© The Countryman Press

ELEVATION PROFILE

			Fire Tower	
1,950 ft				
1,690 ft				
1,430 ft	NY 52			Ferguson Road
1,170 ft				
910 ft				
650 ft		2	4	6 miles

Road. Follow Cox Road for about 2 miles to NY 52. Turn left onto NY 52, and continue for 1.4 miles to a parking area on the left side of the road. Park the second car here.

THE HIKE

From the northern end of the parking area, follow the yellow trail into the woods. The yellow trail soon reaches a junction with a red-blazed trail, which begins on the left, but continue ahead on the yellow trail. After turning sharply left at the point of a switchback, the yellow trail continues downhill, with views through the trees over the valley below on the right. The trail descends steadily through a deciduous forest with a dense understory of blueberry and mountain laurel, then crosses an intermittent stream. The trail turns right onto a woods road, then immediately turns left and continues downhill to a magnificent cascading stream. Use care when crossing the rock slabs, as they are often slippery. Once on the other side, turn sharply left, paralleling the stream uphill. (If the water is high, the crossing may be impassable. If so, continue uphill along the stream; you should be able to cross it on rocks just above the top of the steep climb.)

The yellow trail now climbs steeply, then bears right, away from the stream. After a short level section, the yellow trail ends at a red-blazed woods road. Turn right and follow the road for only 20 feet, then turn sharply left and reenter the woods on a footpath—the route of the aqua-blazed Long Path (do not follow the Long Path straight ahead on the woods road). You will follow the Long Path for the next 5 miles. In addition to aqua

WEST-FACING VIEW FROM THE SHAWANGUNK RIDGE TRAIL

ALONG THE SHAWANGUNK RIDGE TRAIL

paint blazes, this section of the Long Path is marked with blue circular plastic discs of the New York State Department of Environmental Conservation (DEC), as you are now on state land.

For the next 0.6 mile, you'll be climbing, steeply in places, toward the crest of the Shawangunk Ridge. The trail proceeds through a dense understory of blueberry and mountain laurel—particularly beautiful in June, when the mountain laurel is in bloom. Soon you'll reach an open area with pitch pines, which offers a broad west-facing view. After taking in the view, continue climbing to the crest of the ridge. You'll be ascending over 500 vertical feet in only 0.6 mile.

Near the top of the climb, the grade moderates, and you'll soon reach a junction with a red-blazed trail that begins on the left. Continue ahead on the Long Path/Shawangunk Ridge Trail, which soon arrives at a spectacular west-facing viewpoint. This is a good place to enjoy a respite from the steep climb up the ridge. The trail continues to ascend over slabs of conglomerate rock dotted with pitch pines, with more west-facing views. Just before reaching the high point on the ridge (1,791 feet), there is a panoramic north-facing view over Bear Hill, with the microwave towers at Lake Maratanza visible beyond.

As you continue along the ridge, you'll notice the effects of a forest fire that burned the area in May 2015. Low vegetation and small tree branches were destroyed in the fire, but the trunks of larger trees remained unscathed. The vegetation has begun to regenerate, and the scarred pitch pines are producing new branches in rather unusual patterns. You'll also notice some fascinating rock formations on the east side of the ridge, with the trail in places running near the edge of steep 30-foot-high cliffs. The trail switches to the west side of the ridge, moves back to the east side, then comes out again on the west side.

After reaching another broad west-facing viewpoint from open slabs of Shawangunk conglomerate rock, you'll reach a junction with a red-blazed trail that departs to the left. Continue ahead on the Long Path/Shawangunk Ridge Trail, which begins a gradual descent through a deciduous forest. After crossing an old woods road, you'll notice a stone wall—evidence of former agricultural activity in the area.

The next section of the trail is relatively level and often wet. You'll cross a number of stone walls and pass a stand of barberry, an invasive species. This entire route of the Long Path from NY 52 to Ferguson Road is remarkably free of invasives, and this one large patch of barberry is the only exception you'll encounter along this entire segment of the Long Path/Shawangunk Ridge Trail.

After descending a little more and then climbing briefly, the Long Path/Shawangunk Ridge Trail bears right and follows the base of a rock escarpment on the left, descending gradually. It crosses an intermittent stream and soon bears left, climbing through a crack in the escarpment. The trail now continues to climb toward the crest of the ridge.

As the trail approaches the ridge, scrub oak becomes the predominant vegetation. Because the scrub oak tends to grow relatively high, the views are limited in this section. Soon the trail descends to a col (see Glossary on page 297), then climbs to a rise (with limited views) marked by two glacial erratics. A short distance beyond, you'll reach another large erratic, known as Jack's Rock, which offers a broader west-facing view.

For the next three-quarters of a mile, you'll walk high along the western escarpment, with occasional views through the dense scrub oak. The end of this section is marked by a plaque in memory of Jack Hennessey, a dedicated volunteer trail maintainer of this section. Here, the Long Path/Shawangunk Ridge Trail bears left to continue along the ridge, soon reaching a fire tower at the crest of the ridge. The tower offers panoramic views. The Wurtsboro Airport is visible in the valley below to the southwest; the huge building just beyond is a Kohl's distribution center. The large wetland in the distance is the Basha Kill and, on a clear day, the High Point Monument can be seen in the distance.

The Long Path/Shawangunk Ridge Trail now begins a steady descent. The first part is on a graded footpath, but as you approach Ferguson Road, the trail heads more steeply downward along rock slabs, which can be slippery when wet. The trail crosses Ferguson Road and continues to descend on switchbacks.

At the base of the descent—just before the Long Path/Shawangunk Ridge Trail crosses a stream—you'll reach a junction with a yellow-blazed trail. Turn left and follow the yellow trail, which ascends steadily—first paralleling the stream, then crossing several tributaries. Near the top of the climb, just beyond a stream crossing, the trail approaches a spectacular waterfall that cascades down into the valley below. The yellow trail ends at the parking area where you left the first car.

45

Verkeerder Kill Falls Loop

TOTAL DISTANCE: 9.6 miles

WALKING TIME: 6.5 hours

ELEVATION GAIN: 1,332 feet

MAPS: USGS 7.5' Ellenville; USGS 7.5' Napanoch; NY–NJTC Shawangunk Trails #104

TRAILHEAD GPS COORDINATES: N 41° 40' 13.5" W 74° 21' 40"

This hike loops around the Sam's Point Preserve, home to the world's largest area of ridgetop dwarf pitch pines. It has been designated by The Nature Conservancy as one of the "Last Great Places" in the world. The first part of the hike follows a gravel road still used by service vehicles to access radio towers, but for most of the way, you'll be following narrow footpaths that traverse dense pitch pine forests.

The Sam's Point area was first publicized as a tourist attraction by Thomas Bosford, who acquired land in the area in 1858. In 1871, he built an observatory at the top of the promontory, as well as a hotel that used the cliff as one of its walls. The hotel burned down after its first season. Then, in 1922, the tract was acquired by the village of Ellenville for watershed protection. Subsequently, the village leased a portion of the property to an entrepreneur who permitted visitors (for a fee) to enter the lighted ice caves. Several groups worked together for the protection of this site, and after many years of negotiations, it was acquired by the Open Space Institute in 1997, with management provided by The Nature Conservancy. In 2007, the Open Space Institute conveyed 3,800 acres of the Sam's Point Preserve to the State of New York, and the remaining 1,000 acres were transferred to the state in 2013. The area is now managed as part of the Minnewaska State Park Preserve. The Sam's Point Visitor Center, which opened in 2005, is a dramatic "green" building which contains exhibits that highlight the unique landscape and spectacular scenery.

In April 2016, a fire burned over 2,000 acres of parkland in the Sam's Point area. Containing the fire required nearly a week of effort by over 300 responders from local and state agencies. To prevent

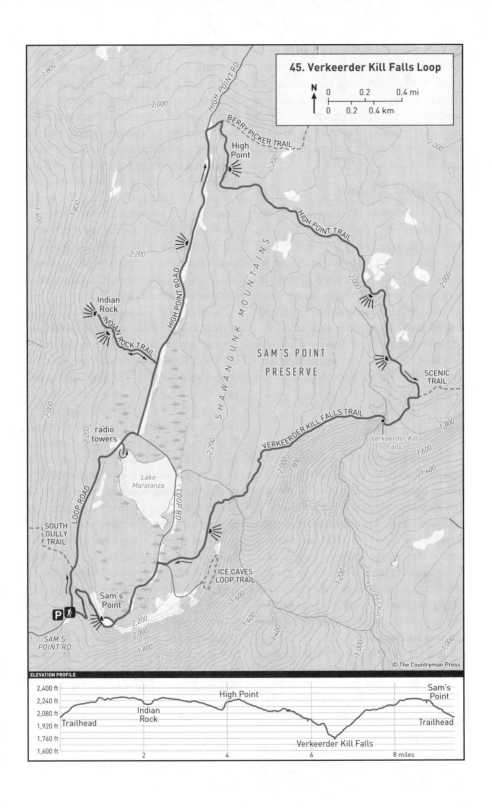

45. Verkeerder Kill Falls Loop

N

| 0 | | 0.2 | | 0.4 mi |
| 0 | 0.2 | | 0.4 km | |

HIGH POINT RD

BERRY PICKER TRAIL

High Point

HIGH POINT TRAIL

1,800

2,000

1,600

1,800

2,200

Indian Rock

INDIAN ROCK TRAIL

HIGH POINT ROAD

S H A W A N G U N K   M O U N T A I N S

SAM'S POINT PRESERVE

SCENIC TRAIL

2,000

2,000

1,800

VERKEERDER KILL FALLS TRAIL

Verkeerder Kill Falls

1,600

1,400

2,000

radio towers

2,000

Lake Maratanza

LOOP ROAD

LOOP RD

SOUTH GULLY TRAIL

ICE CAVES LOOP TRAIL

1,600

1,400

1,200

Verkeerder Kill

1,000

Sam's Point

P

SAM'S POINT RD

2,200

2,000

1,800

1,400

1,000

© The Countryman Press

ELEVATION PROFILE

	High Point		Sam's Point
2,400 ft			
2,240 ft			
2,080 ft	Indian Rock		
1,920 ft	Trailhead		Trailhead
1,760 ft			
1,600 ft		Verkeerder Kill Falls	

2   4   6   8 miles

the introduction of invasive species to the recovering landscape, many of the trails in the Sam's Point area remained closed for a number of months following the fire, but the trails described in this hike have since reopened. You will see many signs of this fire along the hike.

GETTING THERE

Take NY 17 (I-86) to Exit 119 and continue north on NY 302 for 9.6 miles to Pine Bush, where NY 302 ends. Turn left onto NY 52 and continue for 7.3 miles. Just before the crest of the hill, turn right onto Cragsmoor Road. In 1.3 miles, turn right in front of the Cragsmoor post office, then take the next right onto Sam's Point Road and follow it for about 1.2 miles to its end at the parking area for the preserve. A parking fee is charged.

THE HIKE

From the parking area, walk around the gate and take the left fork of the Loop Road (a gravel road, closed to private vehicles but open to service vehicles). Follow the road uphill, passing several dilapidated shacks on the left built to house the "berry pickers" who lived there seasonally while harvesting the area's abundant blueberries and huckleberries. The berry picking operations began here in the 1860s and continued for over 100 years.

In 0.3 mile, a sign on the left marks the start of the South Gully Trail, the route of the aqua-blazed Long Path. Continue ahead on the gravel Loop Road, which passes the site of a former quarry on the right and levels off.

About a mile from the start, you'll notice several radio towers on the left. These towers—an unwelcome intrusion

on the pristine beauty of the area— predate The Nature Conservancy's stewardship of the property. Service vehicles are allowed to use the Loop Road to access the towers, and you may be passed by one of these vehicles along the way. Soon an unmarked side trail begins on the right (opposite a road on the left that leads to one of the towers). Follow this side trail a short distance down to the scenic Lake Maratanza, which still serves as the water supply for the village of Ellenville (swimming is not permitted). The lake served as a tourist attraction around 1900, and a hotel was built along its shore.

Return to the Loop Road and turn right. When you reach a junction marked by a wooden sign, turn left onto the High Point Road, a wide gravel road constructed by the Civilian Conservation Corps (CCC) in the 1930s. In 0.4 mile, you'll notice a sign on the left. Turn left and follow the yellow-blazed Indian Rock Trail, which crosses a wet area on a long set of puncheons and continues on a level, narrow footpath through pitch pines with a dense understory of blueberries. This footpath is a welcome change of pace from the wide gravel road that you have been following up to now. (NOTE: As of September 2018, the Indian Rock Trail is closed for ecological reasons. It may reopen in spring 2019. If the trail remains closed, continue ahead on the High Point Road.)

In about 0.3 mile, as the trail curves to the right, an open rock ledge straight ahead offers panoramic views to the west and north, with the Catskill Mountains visible to the right. The Indian Rock Trail now begins to descend— emerging, in another quarter mile, onto an exposed rock ledge. The blazes lead down through a narrow crevice and out to Indian Rock—a large, fractured

INDIAN ROCK

boulder balanced on a smaller boulder, which offers views to the west and north.

After taking a break, retrace your steps back to the High Point Road and turn left. In about 0.7 mile, the improved gravel road ends and the road becomes grassier and somewhat narrower. Just beyond, you'll pass a west-facing viewpoint with a bench. A short distance ahead, you'll notice in the distance on the right a rock outcrop that marks High Point, which you'll soon climb.

In another half mile, you'll come to a junction marked by a sign. Ahead, High Point Road is somewhat overgrown, and you should turn right—now following the red-blazed High Point Trail, which will be your route for the next 2.5 miles. Most of the blazes are painted on the rocks on the footpath, but you will also notice some blazes on trees along the way. At times, the trail maintainer has placed rows of smaller rocks to keep the walker on track.

The trail begins by climbing rather steeply to a T-junction, where the blue-blazed Berry Picker Trail begins on the left. Turn right, continuing to follow the red-blazed High Point Trail, which is now joined by the Long Path (along the route of the High Point Trail, the Long Path is marked only by occasional logo blazes). In a short distance, you'll emerge onto a panoramic viewpoint from an open rock ledge, with views to the west and north. This was once the location of the High Point fire tower. Continue along the High Point Trail, which ascends very gently through dense stands of pitch pine. Some of these pitch pines

VERKEERDER KILL FALLS

are hundreds of years old. Their growth is stunted by the wind and the thin and unfertile soil.

In about a quarter mile, you'll reach High Point, the highest point in the area (2,240 feet), marked by a USGS benchmark. High Point offers a panoramic 360-degree view. To the north, you can see the Catskills, with Slide Mountain (the highest peak in the Catskills) and the Burroughs Range in the foreground, and the peaks of the Devil's Path (Plateau, Sugarloaf, Twin, and Indian Head Mountains) to the right in the distance. The radio towers you passed previously are visible to the southwest, and to the northeast you can see Gertrude's Nose in Minnewaska State Park Preserve. The Hudson Highlands can be seen to the east, and on a clear day, you might even get a glimpse of the Hudson River.

After taking a break to admire the spectacular view, continue along the High Point Trail, which steeply descends from the rock ledge and continues through a dense stand of pitch pines, with an understory of blueberries. There are several short but steep descents in the next section of the trail, and you'll need to use both your hands and your feet to negotiate them. After about a mile, you'll come out onto a rock outcrop, with panoramic views to the west and south. To the southwest, across the valley, you can see the radio towers you passed earlier in the hike, and the Wallkill Valley is visible to the south. For the next half a mile, you'll be following a dramatic escarpment, with many views along the way. Finally, the High Point Trail goes back into the woods and descends to reach a T-junction, marked by a sign.

The light-blue-blazed Scenic Trail begins on the left, but you should turn right onto the Verkeerder Kill Falls Trail (also the route of the Long Path), marked with aqua blazes. You will note that the pitch pines you've seen for most of the hike have been replaced by deciduous trees in this area. A short distance ahead, you'll come to a fork. The main trail bears left here, but you should take the right fork, which leads to an exposed rock ledge, with two glacial erratics, that offers views to the west and south.

Return to the main trail and follow it as it descends, steeply in places, toward the falls. As you approach the falls, the trail turns right, but you should continue ahead to a rock ledge overlooking the 180-foot-high Verkeerder Kill Falls—the highest waterfall in the Shawangunks. Use extreme care, as there is a sheer drop from here to the bottom of the falls! The falls are most dramatic after heavy rains, and might be reduced to a trickle in times of drought. They're particularly fascinating in winter when ice forms on the cliff.

When you're ready to continue, turn left on the Verkeerder Kill Falls Trail/Long Path, which almost immediately crosses the braided Verkeerder Kill above the falls (the crossing can be difficult if the water is high) and soon begins a gradual climb. At first, you'll pass through an area dominated by tall oak, birch, and maple trees, but after gaining some elevation, the pitch pine/blueberry forest returns.

Just beyond, the trail makes a sharp left turn (the overgrown path to the right, now abandoned, once led to the Loop Road near Lake Maratanza). The trail now levels off, and the vegetation soon changes to a birch forest with an understory of ferns. After the trail crosses an intermittent stream (the outlet of Lake Maratanza), the pitch pine/blueberry forest returns, and the trail resumes its ascent.

Soon, views appear to the northeast

over Minnewaska State Park Preserve. The three rock formations that you see are (left to right) Castle Point, Hamilton Point, and Gertrude's Nose. A short distance beyond, the Verkeerder Kill Falls Trail ends at a junction with the road that leads to the Ice Caves. Turn right, head uphill to the Loop Road, and turn left, following the sign that points to the visitor center.

Follow this deteriorated paved road for half a mile until a wide road departs to the right. Turn right and follow this road a short distance to Sam's Point, a large open rock slab with protective rock walls, which offers panoramic views to the southwest. Sam's Point was once called the Big Nose of Aioskawasting. The legend surrounding the current name of this magnificent promontory is that Samuel Gonsalus, a famous local hunter and scout constantly at odds with his Native American neighbors, was once alone at this promontory when he was surprised by a group who started in pursuit, as Sam ran away. Sam—a big man and always a good runner—outpaced his enemies and flung himself from the brink to land in a clump of bushes that broke his fall. His enemies retreated, mistakenly assuming that Sam had been killed by the fall.

Return to the Loop Road, turn right, and follow the road as it descends on switchbacks below the cliffs of Sam's Point and returns to the visitor center and the parking area where the hike began.

Minnewaska State Park Preserve Loop

TOTAL DISTANCE: 9.2 miles

WALKING TIME: 6 hours

ELEVATION GAIN: 1,654 feet

MAPS: USGS 7.5' Gardiner; USGS 7.5' Napanoch; NY–NJTC Shawangunk Trails #104

TRAILHEAD GPS COORDINATES: N 41° 44' 04" W 74° 14' 39"

Although this hike does not pass by either Lake Minnewaska or Lake Awosting, it traverses some of the most spectacular scenery in Minnewaska State Park Preserve. The route begins by following the cascading Peters Kill, continues to climb over conglomerate rock slabs with pitch pines, and reaches Castle Point, with panoramic views. The path follows along magnificent rock ledges, passes the fascinating Rainbow Falls, and climbs to a broad viewpoint over the Catskill Mountains. This hike can easily be completed by the average hiker in six hours, but the amazing sights you'll see along the way will tempt you to linger, and you might want to allow more time to savor all the special features of the backcountry of Minnewaska State Park Preserve.

GETTING THERE

Take the New York State Thruway (I-87) to Exit 18 (New Paltz). After paying the toll, turn left onto NY 299 and continue west through the village of New Paltz. When you cross the bridge over the Wallkill River at the west end of the village, continue ahead on NY 299 (do not turn right toward the Mohonk Mountain House). In another 5.6 miles (from the Wallkill River bridge), NY 299 ends at a T-junction with US 44/NY 55. Turn right and follow US 44/NY 55 as it negotiates a very sharp hairpin turn and climbs to pass under the Trapps Bridge (a steel truss overpass). Continue for 3 miles past the Trapps Bridge to the entrance to Minnewaska State Park Preserve, on the left side of the road (a parking fee is charged at the gatehouse). Immediately turn right and proceed for 0.2 mile to the Awosting parking area. Make a note of the park closing time, which is closely observed. On a fine weekend, it's

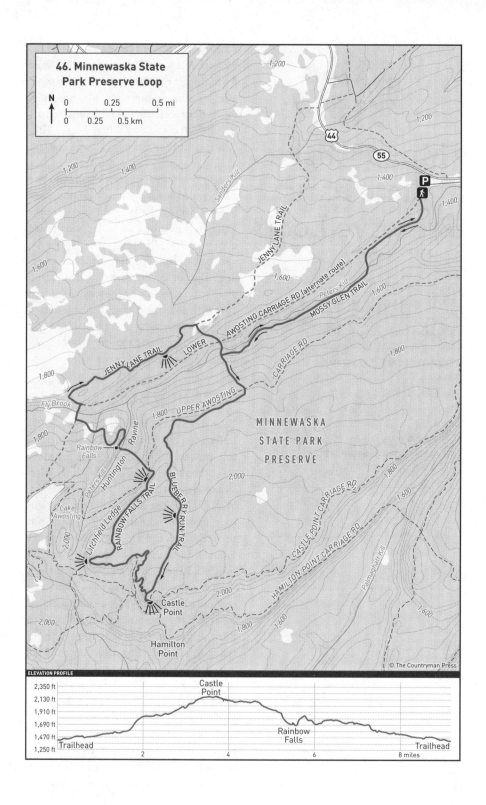

46. Minnewaska State Park Preserve Loop

N

0   0.25   0.5 mi

0   0.25   0.5 km

1,200

1,400

44

55

P

1,400

1,400

1,200

1,400

JENNY LANE TRAIL

Sanders Kill

1,600

AWOSTING CARRIAGE RD (alternate route)

Peters Kill

MOSSY GLEN TRAIL

1,600

1,600

JENNY LANE TRAIL

LOWER

CARRIAGE RD

1,800

1,800

Fly Brook

UPPER AWOSTING

1,800

MINNEWASKA
STATE PARK
PRESERVE

1,800

1,800

1,600

1,600

Rainbow
Falls

Ravine

Peters Kill

Huntington

Litchfield Ledge

RAINBOW FALLS TRAIL

BLUEBERRY RUN TRAIL

2,000

CASTLE POINT CARRIAGE RD

Lake
Awosting

2,000

HAMILTON POINT CARRIAGE RD

Palmaghatt Kill

Castle
Point

2,000

2,000

1,800

1,600

1,600

Hamilton
Point

© The Countryman Press

ELEVATION PROFILE

2,350 ft

2,130 ft

1,910 ft

1,690 ft

1,470 ft

1,250 ft

Castle
Point

Rainbow
Falls

Trailhead

Trailhead

2   4   6   8 miles

advisable to arrive early because the lot has been known to fill up and close by 10 a.m.

THE HIKE

From the kiosk at the rear of the parking area, continue past the gate onto the Lower Awosting Carriage Road. Almost immediately, turn left onto the yellow-blazed Mossy Glen Trail, built by volunteers of the New York–New Jersey Trail Conference in 1999 as a scenic alternative to the carriage road. In half a mile, after passing through an attractive forest of hemlock and mountain laurel, the trail approaches the carriage road, then turns sharply left and descends to the Peters Kill, which it crosses on a rustic wooden footbridge. The bridge, built in 1999, was washed away by Hurricane Irene in August 2011, but it was replaced by the park in 2013.

The Mossy Glen Trail now turns right and parallels the stream, which is tinged with brown from tannic acid in the trees. The Peters Kill rushes along through chutes, cascades, and falls, often slowing into deep pools. For part of the way, the trail follows polished rock slabs, smoothed by the glaciers, that slope toward the stream. These slabs can be very slippery, so care should be exercised, especially if they are wet or covered with pine needles. Rhododendron and white pine may be found along the trail, together with hemlock and mountain laurel. At one point, the trail tunnels under dense rhododendron.

In another mile, the Mossy Glen Trail ends in an open area, with stunted pitch pines and an understory of blueberries. Turn left here onto the blue-blazed Blueberry Run Trail, which climbs steadily through mountain laurel and blueberries. After a while, the grade moderates,

and the trail crosses the Upper Awosting Carriage Road.

A short distance after heading back into the woods, the Blueberry Run Trail turns right and begins to parallel the carriage road on a level footpath, passing through dense mountain laurel thickets (in full bloom in late June). Puncheons have been placed across several wet areas. In half a mile, the trail crosses under a power line, with the foothills of the Catskills and the Rondout Reservoir—one of the links in New York City's water supply chain—visible to the right.

After descending a little, the trail bears left and begins a gradual climb through mountain laurel, hemlock, blueberries, and pitch pines. During the next mile, the trail gains about 300 feet in elevation. Along the way, the trail traverses a number of rock slabs, with cairns indicating the route. After passing an interesting cliff on the right, the Blueberry Run Trail climbs more steeply and emerges onto an expansive conglomerate rock slab covered with stunted pitch pines and blueberries. To the north, you can see the Catskill Mountains in the distance. From the right, the peaks you see are Overlook Mountain and Indian Head, Twin, Sugarloaf, and Plateau Mountains of the Devil's Path. The trail continues to climb, soon emerging on another large conglomerate slab, with several large cairns.

After reaching an open rock ledge at the highest point on the trail, the Blueberry Run Trail descends slightly to end at the Castle Point Carriage Road. Turn left onto the carriage road, and almost immediately you'll reach Castle Point, a steep promontory with panoramic views. Lake Awosting is below to the west, and Sam's Point may be seen to the southwest (to the left of the communications

RUSTIC FOOTBRIDGE ON THE MOSSY GLEN TRAIL

towers visible in the distance). Directly ahead (south) you can see Hamilton Point, another rock promontory, with the Wallkill Valley beyond, and the cliffs of Gertrude's Nose may be seen across Palmaghatt Ravine to the east. Over to the left is the gorge of the Hudson River between Breakneck Ridge and Storm King. The hills of Harriman-Bear Mountain and Sterling Forest State Parks may also be visible on a clear day. You'll want to take a break here to savor the views from this spectacular point—the highest viewpoint in this area of the park.

When you're ready to continue, turn left onto the carriage road, marked with blue Shawangunk Ridge Trail logo blazes and blue diamonds. This carriage road is open to bicyclists, as well as hikers, and you should be alert for approaching bicycles. You'll immediately pass the trailhead of the Blueberry Run Trail on your right and soon begin to head downhill, passing more magnificent viewpoints over Sam's Point, Lake Awosting, and the Catskills. A short distance beyond the second hairpin turn on the Castle Point Carriage Road, watch carefully on the right for two rock steps that climb up into the woods just before another bend in the road. Turn right here onto the orange-blazed Rainbow Falls Trail (also the route of the Shawangunk Ridge Trail), which immediately bears left and follows along rock ledges, with the cliffs of Battlement Terrace visible on the other side of the Castle Point Carriage Road.

After steeply descending a rock ledge, the trail follows along low cliffs. Soon you'll come out on wide, open rock ledges that afford a panoramic view of Lake Awosting, with Sam's Point on the left and the Catskills on the right. This is another special place where you'll want to spend some time exploring the area and savoring the views.

When you're ready to continue, follow the orange-blazed Rainbow Falls Trail as it reenters the woods and makes several short but steep climbs over rock ledges. Soon the trail begins to descend over slabs of conglomerate rock studded with pitch pines. It continues downhill through mountain laurel thickets and dense hemlock groves. On the way down, you'll pass a rock ledge on the left that offers a panoramic north-facing view, with Huntington Ravine below and the Catskills in the distance.

The Rainbow Falls Trail continues to descend. As it approaches the Upper Awosting Carriage Road, it bends sharply to the left and descends along a cliff of fractured conglomerate blocks. The trail crosses the road, descends rock steps, and continues downhill through a stand of hardwoods and large hemlocks, crossing a stream on the way. Soon the sounds of the falling water at Rainbow Falls can be heard.

At the base of the descent, the trail crosses another stream and climbs over rocks to reach the base of the falls, where the water drops from overhanging rock ledges, forming a cool mist. Use caution as you approach the falls, as the wet rocks may be slippery.

Leaving the falls, the trail descends to the stream and parallels it for a few minutes, with cliffs above on the left. Pay careful attention to the trail blazes, as in a short distance the trail bears left, away from the stream, and steeply climbs through a gap in the cliffs. At the top, the trail turns left and comes out on open rocks, with south-facing views across Huntington Ravine. After climbing a little more, the trail emerges at the top of a sloping face of conglomerate rock dotted with pitch pines, with panoramic north-facing views of the Catskill Mountains. The Rainbow Falls Trail descends along the rock slabs, then bears left and crosses a stream just below a cascade (the stream crossing can be tricky if the water is high). It briefly bears left and climbs a little, then continues to descend. With Fly Brook in view to the right, the Rainbow Falls Trail bears left and climbs to its terminus at the Lower Awosting Carriage Road.

Turn right onto the carriage road and cross over Fly Brook on a concrete bridge. The road formerly crossed an earthen causeway over the stream, but the causeway was destroyed during Hurricane Irene and has been replaced by the bridge. Just beyond, turn left onto the blue-blazed Jenny Lane Trail (also the route of the Shawangunk Ridge Trail), which follows an old woods road. The road soon bears right and climbs rather steeply, then levels off. For part of the way, the road follows slabs of conglomerate rock.

In half a mile, the trail turns right under power lines. For a short distance, it runs parallel to them, but just beyond the next power line tower, the trail turns left and reenters the woods. Soon the trail begins to run close to the edge of the ridge, emerging occasionally onto open rocks, with views to the southeast across the valley of the Peters Kill.

After bearing left, away from the

VIEW OF THE CATSKILLS FROM THE RAINBOW FALLS TRAIL

edge of the ridge, you'll reach a junction with the Blueberry Run Trail (also blazed blue), marked by a sign on the right. Turn right onto the Blueberry Run Trail, which soon begins a rather steep descent. At the base of the descent, the trail turns left and passes through a hemlock grove, crossing a stream on rocks. A short distance beyond, the trail reaches the Lower Awosting Carriage Road.

Here you have two options. If you want to head directly back to your car, turn left and follow the carriage road for 1.5 miles to the parking area. The road is relatively uninteresting (although you will get a few glimpses of the Peters Kill, below on the right), but it is the shortest and fastest route back to your car.

If you have enough time and want to return by a more interesting route, you can continue along the Blueberry Run Trail, which descends to cross the Peters Kill on a log bridge and climbs to a junction with the Mossy Glen Trail. Turn left at the junction and retrace your steps back to the parking area on the Mossy Glen Trail. You've already hiked this trail on your way in, but it is certainly a nicer way to conclude your hike than walking on the rather boring carriage road.

Peters Kill Loop

TOTAL DISTANCE: 2 miles

WALKING TIME: 1.5 hours

ELEVATION GAIN: 545 feet

MAPS: USGS 7.5' Gardiner; NY–NJTC Shawangunk Trails #104

TRAILHEAD GPS COORDINATES: N 41°44' 18.8" W 74°13' 06.2"

Although this hike is relatively short, it samples some of the most attractive scenery in the "Gunks." Featuring a panoramic view of the Catskills from exposed ledges of Shawangunk conglomerate rock, the hike also parallels a magnificent section of the Peters Kill, with cascades, chutes, and pools. The hike also passes interesting historical remnants of the short-lived Ski Minne downhill ski facility, which was abandoned over 40 years ago. If you don't have the six hours needed to take the longer Minnewaska hike (Hike #46), this much shorter hike will allow you to experience the wonderful scenery of the area. The average hiker should be able to complete the hike in an hour and a half, but you might want to allow extra time to pause and take in the beautiful scenery.

GETTING THERE

Take the New York State Thruway to Exit 18 (New Paltz). After paying the toll, turn left onto NY 299 and continue west through the Village of New Paltz. When you cross the bridge over the Wallkill River at the west end of the village, continue ahead on NY 299 (do not turn right toward the Mohonk Mountain House). In another 5.6 miles (from the Wallkill River bridge), NY 299 ends at a T-intersection with US 44/NY 55. Turn right and follow US 44/NY 55 as it negotiates a very sharp hairpin turn and climbs to pass under the Trapps Bridge (a steel truss overpass). Continue for about 2 miles past the Trapps Bridge to the entrance to the Peters Kill area of Minnewaska State Park Preserve, on the right side of the road (a parking fee is charged at the gatehouse).

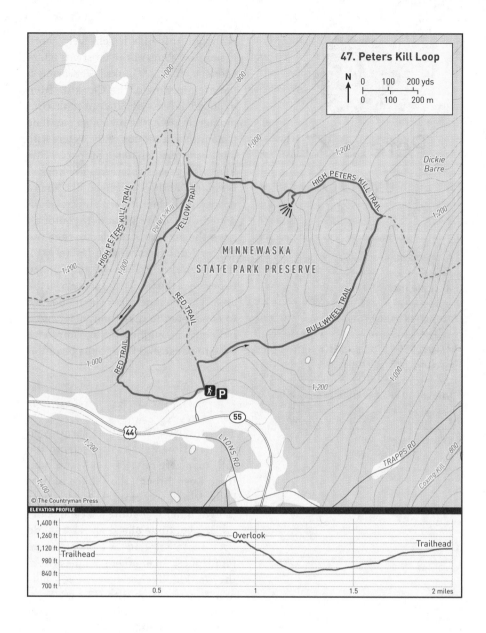

47. Peters Kill Loop

MINNEWASKA STATE PARK PRESERVE

Dickie Barre

© The Countryman Press

ELEVATION PROFILE

Overlook

Trailhead

Trailhead

THE HIKE

From a kiosk at the western end of the lower parking area, head north on a gravel road, following the Red Loop Trail. At the top of a rise, a sign and a triple-white blaze on a tree on the right mark the start of the Bullwheel Trail. Turn right onto this trail, which climbs

gradually on an old carriage road. After a short descent, the trail bears right at a fork and continues to climb on a rougher route.

After narrowing to a footpath, the trail reaches the crest of the rise, where it passes a concrete slab, with steel bolts protruding. A tower that was anchored to the slab via the bolts once supported a pulley for a ski lift—part of the Ski Minne downhill ski area, which operated from 1964 to 1978. The pulley is commonly referred to as a "bullwheel"—hence the name for the trail.

The trail now descends gradually, passing through mountain laurel thickets and blueberry bushes. Several side trails for rock climbers leave to the left. After passing the cliffs of Dickie Barre on the left, the Bullwheel Trail ends at a junction with the blue-blazed High Peters Kill Trail. Turn left onto this trail, which climbs briefly to cut through a notch in Dickie Barre (notice the tilted blocks of conglomerate rock on the left), then begins a long, gradual descent through mountain laurel thickets and blueberry bushes to the Peters Kill.

About halfway down, the trail emerges on exposed rock ledges, with pitch pines growing from the bedrock, and bears right. Before continuing ahead, you should bear left and cross the ledges to reach a dramatic viewpoint from the edge of the cliffs, with the Catskills visible in the distance to the right. Then return to the trail, which descends more steeply for a short distance. The grade soon moderates, and the trail runs close to the edge of the escarpment, with sheer drops on the left.

At the base of the descent, just before reaching the Peters Kill, turn left onto a yellow-blazed trail (at a sign PETERS KILL PARKING LOT). The trail parallels the picturesque stream amid hemlocks, rhododendron, and mountain laurel. After passing an interesting cascade, where the stream flows over slanted rock slabs,

SLANTED ROCK SLABS ALONG THE PETERS KILL

WATERFALL AND POOL ALONG THE PETERS KILL

the Yellow Trail bears left, away from the stream, and it soon ends at a sign for the Red Trail. You'll notice nearby another concrete slab with protruding bolts and steel cables along the ground—more remnants of the downhill Ski Minne operation.

Turn left onto the Red Trail, but in only 20 feet turn right and follow the red blazes parallel to the stream. This trail section is even more scenic than the previous one, as you pass numerous cascades and flumes in the stream.

After reaching a small waterfall and a pool on the right (a good place to stop and take a break), the Red Trail bears left, leaving the stream, and climbs back toward US 44/NY 55. At the top of the climb, the trail turns left and follows a gravel path through successional fields, soon returning to the parking area where the hike began.

The Trapps to Gertrude's Nose

TOTAL DISTANCE: 10.1 miles

WALKING TIME: 6 hours

ELEVATION GAIN: 1,836 feet

MAPS: USGS 7.5' Gardiner; USGS 7.5' Napanoch; NY–NJTC Shawangunk Trails #104 and #105; Mohonk Preserve-Northern

TRAILHEAD GPS COORDINATES: N 41° 44' 15" W 74° 11' 51"

For a special look at this geologically intriguing area known as the Gunks, try the hike along the Trapps to Gertrude's Nose. This hike follows trails on the escarpment edge but also features some easy walking on carriage roads, ending with a stroll through deeply forested areas. The route includes a visit to spectacular Millbrook Mountain and Gertrude's Nose. The beauty of the Shawangunks lies in the way the views continuously unfold, enlivening the walk.

It is the rock—and its history—that is so impressive about this hike. The Shawangunks were formed about 450 million years ago. The sediments that form the shining white conglomerates were once deposited along the shores of an inland sea, whose waters tumbled and smoothed the quartz pebbles later embedded in these gleaming white rocks. These sediments were shaped by heat and pressure, faulted and bent, and uplifted about 280 million years ago to form the magnificent cliffs of the Shawangunks' southwestern face, where the horizontal layers of deposits are worn away. The dip to the northwest produces the long slopes so characteristic of the area. The age of the uplift makes the Shawangunks one of the youngest formations in the East.

The trails followed in this hike often approach the edge of cliffs and cross deep crevices in the rock. These features make the hike a very special and dramatic one, but those who are fearful of heights might want to choose another hike.

GETTING THERE

Take the New York State Thruway (I-87) to Exit 18 (New Paltz). After paying the toll, turn left onto NY 299 and continue west through the village of New Paltz. When you cross the bridge over the

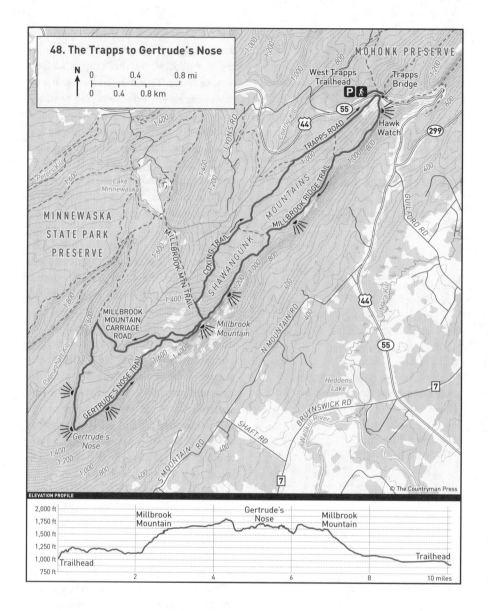

48. The Trapps to Gertrude's Nose

ELEVATION PROFILE

Wallkill River at the west end of the village, continue ahead on NY 299 (do not turn right toward the Mohonk Mountain House). In another 5.6 miles (from the Wallkill River bridge), NY 299 ends at a T-junction with US 44/NY 55. Turn right and follow US 44/NY 55 as it makes a very sharp hairpin turn and climbs to pass under the Trapps Bridge (a steel truss overpass). Continue for 0.3 mile past the Trapps Bridge and turn right into the West Trapps Trailhead parking area. A per-person daily use fee will be collected by the attendant (an annual membership is also available).

THE HIKE

The hike begins on lands of the Mohonk Preserve. The route heads southwesterly, following the Millbrook Ridge Trail, which runs close to the edge of dramatic cliffs. The thrills a hiker will experience by following this route are comparable to what a rock climber experiences while ascending the famous Shawangunk cliffs.

From the eastern end of the parking area, follow the yellow-blazed West Trapps Connector Trail, a gravel road which heads east parallel to US 44/NY 55. In about a quarter mile, you'll reach the Trapps Bridge. Climb the gravel road that leads up to this steel truss bridge, turn sharply right, cross the bridge, then turn right again onto the Trapps Road.

About 150 feet down Trapps Road from the bridge, watch for three light-blue blazes on the left that mark the start of the Millbrook Ridge Trail. Turn left and follow this trail—marked with paint blazes on the rocks—which steeply climbs over rock slabs dotted with pitch pines. Soon you'll reach a north-facing viewpoint (the first of many along the ridge).

A short distance beyond, after some more climbing, you'll reach the crest of the ridge (known as the Near Trapps). Here there is an even-broader vista from a point called the Hawk Watch. To the left, you can see Dickie Barre, with the Catskill Mountains in the distance beyond. To the right, there is a sweeping view over the Wallkill Valley, with New Paltz visible in the distance. This is a good spot to rest and take a break from the climb.

Follow the light-blue blazes of the Millbrook Ridge Trail as it undulates along the top of the ridge, alternating between rock slabs and soft pine-needle-covered paths. The trail now levels off and continues through a wooded area along the ridge, with scrub oak and pitch pine and an understory of blueberry bushes. Soon you'll reach another viewpoint on the left, with the Sky Top tower of the Mohonk Mountain House visible to the north, and the intersection of NY 299 and US 44/NY 55 directly below.

About a mile from the start, you'll descend slightly and reach a junction with the red-blazed Bayards Path, which begins on the right. Continue ahead on the light-blue-blazed Millbrook Ridge Trail, which bears left and climbs to the top of the next ridge, known as the Bayards. After passing several viewpoints over the Wallkill Valley, you'll traverse a long, relatively level section. Suddenly, the trail emerges onto a rounded outcrop with a view ahead (through the trees) of the dramatic cliff of Millbrook Mountain—the next destination of the hike.

After bearing right and descending through mountain laurel and hemlock, the Millbrook Ridge Trail arrives at a junction with the red-blazed Millbrook Cross Path, about 2 miles from the start. Continue ahead on the light-blue-blazed trail, which bends left and climbs to regain the crest of the ridge. Soon your path crosses a rock outcrop with several small glacial erratics. The trail continues on a relatively level footpath through laurel and hemlocks and emerges onto an open area, with many glacial erratics.

The trail now follows a rocky path through hemlocks, soon arriving at the base of a cliff. It climbs rather steeply over rocks to the right of the cliff and continues on a footpath below the crest of the ridge. Next, the trail bears left, climbs through a boulder field, and proceeds through an open area, with blueberries and pitch pines, to reach the crest of the ridge.

The trail turns right and continues to climb along exposed rock outcrops, with views to the south and east over

WALLKILL VALLEY FROM THE MILLBROOK RIDGE TRAIL

the Wallkill Valley as far as the Hudson Highlands. Sky Top may be seen to the northeast, and the Catskills in the distance to the north. Just beyond, the trail follows a narrow path to the right of a sloping rock slab. Next, the trail climbs to the very edge of the cliff, with a sheer 300-foot drop. Using extreme caution, you can peer over the sharp cliff edge and see the vast boulder field below—probably the moraine of a small glacier that remained after the main ice sheet had melted away.

Continue to follow the Millbrook Ridge Trail along the cliff edge. Soon, the trail heads slightly inland. Finally—a little over 3 miles from the start—you'll arrive at a junction with the red-blazed Millbrook Mountain Trail (marked by a sign for LAKE MINNEWASKA). Continue ahead on the trail (now blazed red) for a few hundred feet to a sign for MILLBROOK MOUNTAIN. Turn left here and climb the rock slab to the edge of the cliff. You're now at the summit of Millbrook Mountain, which offers an even broader view than those you've seen until now.

After taking in the scenery, walk down the slabs to the Millbrook Mountain Carriage Road and turn left. It's easy walking, even a bit dull, but it's the quickest way to make a loop walk around Gertrude's Nose. The carriage roads are the marvel of Mohonk and Minnewaska—miles and miles of well-graded paths. They were built over 100 years ago to enable guests at the hotels to experience the beauty of the area on horse-drawn carriages, but today they make for superb walking, bicycling, and cross-country skiing. The carriage roads are all paved with Martinsburg shale, a 2,000-foot layer of which underlies the Shawangunks. The shale weathers to a dense but surprisingly soft and smooth walking surface. Except on the trails, the shale is unnoticeable, for almost everywhere it is topped with the white conglomerate. You may encounter mountain bikers along this road.

After a gentle downhill section, the carriage road bends to the right before ascending slightly and then resuming its downhill trend. In about a mile, you'll reach a junction with the red-blazed Gertrude's Nose Trail, which begins on the left. The junction is marked by a sign.

Turn left and follow the Gertrude's Nose Trail, which climbs through a dense evergreen forest to reach a west-facing viewpoint over the Palmaghatt Ravine—the deep cleft between the trail you are following and the Hamilton Point Road. The trail now descends, first moderately, then more steeply through deep and shady hemlock woods, to cross a stream under a power line.

The next trail section is one of the most scenic in the entire Shawangunks. The trail climbs along bare rock ledges, with sheer drops of several hundred feet just to the right, and many views over the Palmaghatt Ravine to the west. Glacial erratics perched near the cliff edge, deep cracks and crevices in the rock (created as the soft shale foundations weathered and became displaced), and pitch pines growing out of these crevices make the hike even more interesting. The trail is sometimes a little difficult to follow (most of the blazes are painted on the rocks), and it detours away from the cliff edge and heads through the woods in a few places to protect the islands of fragile plants growing on the rock slabs. You'll want to take some time to savor the beauty of this magnificent area. Keep in mind, though, that the unprotected cliff edge can be dangerous (children should be kept well away from the edge).

In this area, there is evidence of another geological force: the glaciers that once covered the Shawangunks to a depth of 4,000 to 5,000 feet. As the ice mass moved along the northwestern slopes, the rocks it pushed along scraped the conglomerate, leaving striations—long, thin scratch marks—that can be seen occasionally. The smooth polish of many surfaces is also the work of the glaciers.

You'll eventually come out at the promontory of Gertrude's Nose, the southern tip of the ridge, which features broad views to the east and south. After taking in the spectacular views, begin the return trip by continuing around the point and heading northeast, following the red blazes along the ridge. This part of the ridge is not as dramatic as the western section that you just traversed, as it lacks the many open rock slabs. However, there are a number of good viewpoints over the Wallkill Valley to the east from rock ledges to the right of the trail.

After a relatively flat section, the trail descends to once again cross beneath the power line. A short distance ahead, you'll notice an unmarked trail on the right. Follow this trail a short distance to a deep crevice in the rock. You can feel the cool air escaping from this crevice—quite refreshing on a hot day! Stand here for a few moments to experience the cool air, then return to the main trail and turn right.

The Gertrude's Nose Trail now begins a steep climb. At the top, you can look back to the southeast at the ridge you just traversed. After a relatively level stretch, you'll emerge onto an area where pitch pines grow out of long expanses of bedrock. There are several panoramic east-facing viewpoints along this trail section.

About three-quarters of a mile from the second power line crossing, you'll notice that the Millbrook Mountain Carriage Road begins to parallel the trail just to the left. Soon, you'll reach the turnaround at the end of the carriage road, just below the summit of Millbrook Mountain. Continue ahead, following the red blazes, until you reach a sign

ALONG THE GERTRUDE'S NOSE TRAIL

pointing to Lake Minnewaska. This sign marks the start of the Millbrook Mountain Trail (also blazed red). Turn left here and follow this red-blazed trail as it begins to descend into the valley of the Coxing Kill.

In about a quarter mile, the blue-blazed Coxing Trail begins on the right. Turn right and head downhill on the Coxing Trail, first over rock slabs dotted with pitch pines and then through hemlocks and laurel, with an understory of blueberry bushes. The walking here is very different from the trek along the ridge and offers a peaceful end to an exhilarating outing. After traversing a wet area, watch for an attractive spring to the west (left) of the trail.

The spring, bordered and protected by a rock wall, is called the James Van Leuven Spring, after one of the early settlers in the area. Old maps that date to 1865 indicate that part of the Coxing Trail was once a public road and that the James Van Leuven cabin was probably located on the hump above the spring.

Cross the outlet of the spring on stepping stones and the subsequent swampy area on puncheons. The Coxing Trail becomes wider, and rock walls indicate where the land was once cleared and farmed. The area is quiet and serene, and the trail route is easily followed. The old road you are following runs parallel to the Millbrook Ridge Trail and passes by the two red-blazed connectors you encountered earlier, the Millbrook Cross Path and the Bayards Path.

After following the Coxing Trail for about an hour, you'll come to a junction with the Trapps Road. Turn right, and be aware that mountain bikers use the Trapps Road. After a while, you may notice traffic on US 44/NY 55 down to the left. Just past the trailhead of the Millbrook Ridge Trail, you'll reach the Trapps Bridge. Cross the bridge, turn sharply left, and follow the yellow-blazed West Trapps Connector Trail back to the parking area where you began the hike.

49

Old Minnewaska Trail Loop

TOTAL DISTANCE: 7.5 miles

WALKING TIME: 5 hours

ELEVATION GAIN: 1,552 feet

MAPS: USGS 7.5' Gardiner, Mohonk Lake; NY–NJTC Shawangunk Trails #104

TRAILHEAD GPS COORDINATES: N 41°44' 40.7" W 74°11' 50.2"

This hike follows little-used trails along the northwestern side of the Shawangunk escarpment, with many spectacular views. It returns on carriage roads, where you may observe climbers scaling the heights of the Trapps.

GETTING THERE

Take the New York State Thruway to Exit 18 (New Paltz). After paying the toll, turn left onto NY 299 and continue west through the Village of New Paltz. When you cross the bridge over the Wallkill River at the west end of the village, continue ahead on NY 299 (do not turn right toward the Mohonk Mountain House). In another 5.6 miles (from the Wallkill River bridge), NY 299 ends at a T-intersection with US 44/NY 55. Turn right and follow US 44/NY 55 as it negotiates a very sharp hairpin turn and climbs to pass under the Trapps Bridge (a steel truss overpass). Continue for half a mile past Trapps Bridge and turn right onto Clove Road. Follow Clove Road for 1 mile to Mohonk Preserve's Coxing parking area, on the left. A per-person fee is charged.

THE HIKE

From the parking area, cross the road and walk past a gate. Continue ahead along a gravel road, passing ruins of the Enderly barn on the right and their home on the left, then cross a wide wooden bridge over the Coxing Kill.

Just beyond the stream crossing, a yellow-blazed trail leads to the left, and then the red-blazed Shongum Path departs to the right. Continue ahead on the gravel road, known as the Old Minnewaska Trail. Built in 1879 to link Mohonk with Minnewaska, this carriage road was abandoned in 1907. It is

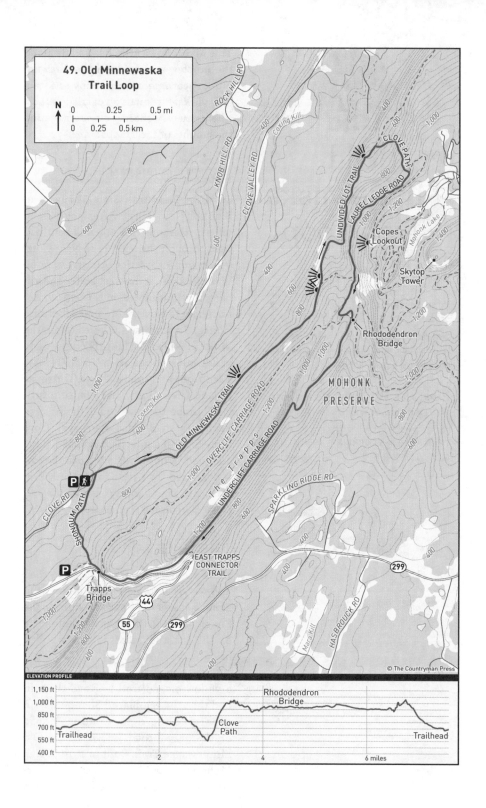

49. Old Minnewaska Trail Loop

N
| 0 | 0.25 | 0.5 mi |
| 0 | 0.25 | 0.5 km |

ROCK HILL RD
KNOB HILL RD
CLOVE VALLEY RD
Coxing Kill
CLOVE PATH
UNDIVIDED LOT TRAIL
LAUREL LEDGE ROAD
Copes Lookout
Mohonk Lake
Skytop Tower
Rhododendron Bridge
MOHONK PRESERVE
OLD MINNEWASKA TRAIL
OVERCLIFF CARRIAGE ROAD
UNDERCLIFF CARRIAGE ROAD
The Trapps
Coxing Kill
SPARKLING RIDGE RD
P
SHONGUM PATH
CLOVE RD
P
EAST TRAPPS CONNECTOR TRAIL
Trapps Bridge
44
55
299
299
HAS BROUCK RD
Mara Kill

© The Countryman Press

ELEVATION PROFILE

1,150 ft
1,000 ft
850 ft
700 ft
550 ft
400 ft

Trailhead
Clove Path
Rhododendron Bridge
Trailhead

2   4   6 miles

marked with light blue blazes (and also with the dark blue plastic discs of the Shawangunk Ridge Trail).

After climbing gradually through hemlocks, the road descends slightly to cross a stream. The stone abutments of a former bridge may be seen ahead, but the footpath dips down to the stream, which it crosses on rocks.

The route now narrows to a footpath and begins a gradual climb. As the trail levels off, the remains of an old quarry down to the left can be seen when the trees are leafless. The hand-cut drill holes at the edges of the large conglomerate stone blocks are still visible. The trail now continues along a relatively level route, with some minor ups and downs. Huge slanted rock slabs begin to appear on the right. After a while, you'll come to a broad viewpoint to the left, with pitch pines lining the slope below, and the Catskills visible in the distance.

The trail now begins a steady but gentle climb through mountain laurel thickets. In half a mile, the trail begins to descend. Soon, you'll reach a spot where the old road has been eroded down to the bedrock. Here, a slanted rock slab on the left affords a superb vista across the Rondout Valley to the Catskills. This is a good spot to take a break.

Just beyond this viewpoint, watch carefully for a trail junction (marked by a signpost). Here, a triple light-blue blaze on the left marks the start of the Undivided Lot Trail. Leave the Old Minnewaska Trail and turn left onto the Undivided Lot Trail. Immediately, you'll reach a rock ledge studded with

VIEW OF THE WALLKILL VALLEY FROM UNDERCLIFF ROAD

VIEW OF THE CATSKILLS FROM THE UNDIVIDED LOT TRAIL

gnarled pitch pines, with views to the north and west.

Carefully follow the light blue blazes as the trail descends rather steeply over rock slabs, then levels off. There are more views over the Catskills to the left, and up to the right, you may be able to see two gazebos at the Copes Lookout. Soon, the trail bears right, crosses an intermittent stream, and climbs steeply to the top of a cliff, passing an overhanging rock ledge on the left. At the top, the trail bears left and soon reaches an area with deep fissures in the rock. Use caution here, as the crevices crossed by the trail are quite deep!

After passing a stone fireplace on the right, the trail begins a steady descent, soon emerging onto open rocks, with views through the trees of the Rondout Valley below. As the trail continues to descend, you'll reach a particularly fine view from a lichen-encrusted rock outcrop to the left of the trail over the Devil's Path mountains in the eastern Catskills.

After passing a second viewpoint from a rock outcrop on the left, the trail levels off, crosses a stream, and reaches a junction with the red-blazed Clove Path. Turn right and follow this trail steeply uphill. You'll be climbing about 450 feet in less than half a mile; this is steepest sustained climb of the hike. After crossing a streambed, you'll reach a junction with the Plateau Path (also blazed red), marked by a sign. Turn right and follow the Plateau Path—a relatively level trail, which soon widens to a woods road—until it comes out onto Laurel Ledge Road.

Turn right onto Laurel Ledge Road, a wide, maintained carriage road, which is open to bicyclists as well as hikers. Soon, the road begins to follow a narrow shelf, with steep cliffs above to the left and below to the right. It then crosses a talus slope, with gigantic boulders on both sides of the trail.

After the Old Minnewaska Trail begins on the right, you'll pass the fascinating Rhododendron Swamp, where many rare plants are found, on the left. Imposing cliffs soon appear on the right, after which the road curves sharply left.

Continue ahead to the end of Laurel Ledge Road at Rhododendron Bridge. Do not cross the bridge; rather, continue straight ahead on Undercliff Road (marked by a sign). After the road makes a sharp S-curve, you'll reach the famous Trapps Cliffs, considered the best rock climbing area in the East. From here to the Trapps Bridge, you'll probably encounter many rock climbers along the road. You might want to stop and watch them scale the cliffs. There are views to the left over the Wallkill Valley.

After about 2 miles along Undercliff Road, you'll reach a junction with the yellow-blazed East Trapps Connector Trail, which begins on the left. US 44/ NY 55 now comes into view below to the left. Continue ahead along Undercliff Road. The Trapps Cliffs begin to approach the road, and you're likely to encounter more climbers at a closer range.

In another half mile, you'll reach the Trapps Bridge, where Undercliff Road ends at a junction with Overcliff Road. Bear left and descend on a gravel road (do not cross the bridge). Soon after the road levels off, you'll reach a junction with the red-blazed Shongum Path (marked by a sign). Turn right and follow the Shongum Path downhill.

The trail crosses rock outcrops, descends through a dense hemlock forest, and follows a stream, which it crosses twice on wooden bridges. It follows a long stretch of narrow boardwalk across a wet area and continues along a gravel path bordered by rocks. After approaching the Coxing Kill and briefly paralleling an old stone wall, the Shongum Path descends steps to end at the Old Minnewaska Trail. Turn left onto the Old Minnewaska Trail and follow it back to the Coxing parking area where the hike began.

Bonticou Crag

TOTAL DISTANCE: 4 miles

WALKING TIME: 3 hours

ELEVATION GAIN: 992 feet

MAPS: USGS 7.5' Mohonk Lake; NY–NJTC Shawangunk Trails #105; Mohonk Preserve-Northeastern Section

TRAILHEAD GPS COORDINATES: N 41° 47' 43" W 74° 07' 41"

This hike includes some easy walking through a deciduous forest, with sweeping views of the Catskills. It also features a challenging rock scramble up Bonticou Crag. This outcrop of white, shining Shawangunk conglomerate rises unexpectedly like a mirage from the valley floor and can be seen in the distance from many directions.

The rock scramble is an adventure in itself. Although not a technical rock climb, it comes as close to it as any "hike" does. Thus, it should not be tackled by young children, folks with inflexible bodies, or those who fear heights—and it certainly should not be attempted by anyone in wet or icy conditions. Both hands and feet will be needed to make the ascent, though the rock, by its nature, offers great handholds and grips. (If you'd like to reach the top of Bonticou Crag but don't want to attempt the rock scramble, you can follow an alternative route, described in the fourth paragraph below, under "The Trail".)

GETTING THERE

Take the New York State Thruway (I-87) to Exit 18 (New Paltz). After paying the toll, turn left onto NY 299 and continue west through the village of New Paltz. After crossing the bridge over the Wallkill River at the west end of the village, turn right onto Springtown Road, following signs for the Mohonk Mountain House. At the next intersection, turn left onto Mountain Rest Road and follow it for 3.3 miles to the entrance to the Mohonk Mountain House at the top of the hill. Continue ahead downhill for 1 mile and turn right onto Upper 27 Knolls Road. The Spring Farm parking area of the Mohonk Preserve is just ahead. A ranger is usually stationed at

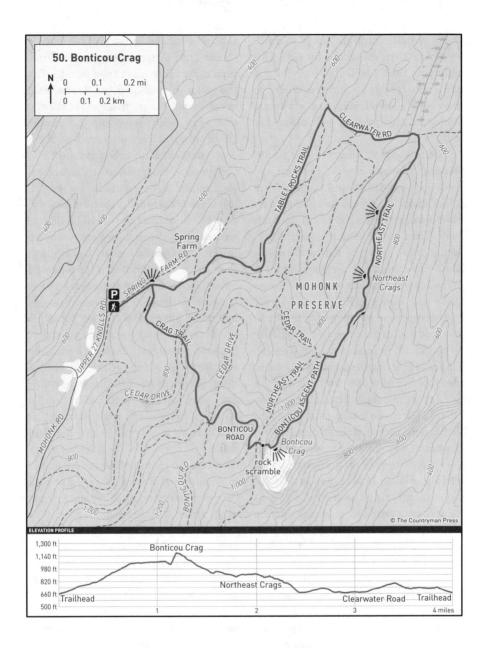

ELEVATION PROFILE

a kiosk to collect day-use fees and distribute maps.

THE HIKE

From the exit at the northern end of the parking area, follow a short unmarked trail uphill and turn left onto the blue-blazed Table Rocks Trail, which parallels Spring Farm Road. As the trail reaches the top of a rise, a broad panoramic view of the Catskill Mountains appears to the left. Just beyond, you'll reach a junction with the Crag Trail. The Table Rocks

Trail continues straight ahead and will be your return route, but for now turn right onto the Crag Trail, which follows a row of cedar trees, continues on a wide path across a field, and parallels an old stone wall along the left side of another field.

After about 15 minutes of uphill walking, the trail crosses two carriage roads—Cedar Drive and Spring Farm Road—in quick succession. You'll now notice some red blazes along the trail route. The Crag Trail continues to climb, rather steeply in places, reaching its terminus—about a mile from the start of the hike—at the intersection of Cedar Drive with Bonticou Road.

Make a broad left turn onto Bonticou Road (do not turn sharply left onto Cedar Drive, which descends rather steeply). This level carriage road soon curves to the right, with trees growing out of the thin layers of deeply tilted shale on the hillside. After the road bends to the left, then again to the right, the imposing Bonticou Crag comes into view through the trees on the left. Watch carefully for a triple-yellow blaze on the left side of the road, marking the start of the Bonticou Ascent Path. When you reach this yellow-blazed trail, turn left and follow it downhill to a junction with the blue-blazed Northeast Trail.

Now begins the fun. The ascent itself is only about 0.3 mile long and gains only 150 feet of elevation, but it involves a climb over large boulders and jagged ledges, and should not be undertaken lightly. It is generally considered the most difficult rock scramble in the Mohonk area. (For those who are intimidated by the sight of the steep and rocky route ahead and would prefer an easier route to the top of the cliff, turn left on the Northeast Trail and follow it for about half a mile, bearing right when the blue blazes meet the red-blazed Cedar Trail. After a rather steep climb, turn right again when the junction with the yellow-blazed Bonticou Ascent Path is reached. This route accesses the top of the crag without having to climb the challenging rock scramble, and the hike's continuation can then be followed.)

If you choose to climb the challenging rock scramble, be sure to follow the yellow blazes carefully, as they indicate the easiest route. After the initial boulder is surmounted, the route winds its way up the face of the crag, first to the right and then to the left. Stunted pitch pine and paper birch survive in occasional spaces between the huge rocks. There are excellent views almost from the beginning of the scramble, and they get better and better as you ascend. On a sunny day, the startling white of the rocks, the blue of the sky, and the green of the trees below are a wonderful contrast. The last hurdle of the climb is a cleft where it might be useful to remove your packs, handing them up to your fellow hikers, before tackling the chimney itself. Once having overcome this last obstacle, the trail becomes easy and, turning right, leads to the summit of the crag.

Walk out to the end of the ridge and admire the expansive views. The Catskill Mountains are prominent on a clear day, and the valleys of the Rondout, the Wallkill, and the Hudson can be seen. The village of New Paltz may be seen below to the southeast. The crag's summit is only 1,194 feet in elevation, but it's a fabulous place for lunch, relaxation, and contemplation of your achievement in reaching this place the difficult way.

The hard work is now over, and the remainder of the trip uses more traditional trails. Turn back toward the way you came, and, bearing right, pick up the northern branch of the yellow-blazed

BONTICOU CRAG

Bonticou Ascent Path. The trail heads north, descending through pines and laurels to end at a junction with the blue-blazed Northeast Trail.

Turn right onto the Northeast Trail, which climbs through mountain laurel and heads north along a ridge. In about 0.3 mile, the trail shifts to the north side of the ridge and emerges on an outcrop of fractured conglomerate rock, known as the Northeast Crags, which offers a spectacular unobstructed view over the Catskill Mountains. Continuing along the ridge, the trail descends—first gradually, with many views to the left, then more steeply—to its end at Clearwater Road.

Turn left, cross a bridge over a stream, and continue through a low-lying area. As you walk, look up to the right, where, on a slight rise, you'll see the stone ruins of an old homestead, the home of the Peter Stokes family in the late 1700s. The site was subsequently bequeathed to the Mohonk Preserve by his descendants.

Continue walking on the wide Clearwater Road, climbing gradually. Bear right at a fork near the crest of the rise and begin to descend, with a stone wall on the left, then turn left at a cairn and a sign indicating a junction with the Table Rocks Trail and the Farm Road. These two trails run concurrently for a very short distance, and either route would take you back to your car. However, the Table Rocks Trail is the more interesting route.

Within a few minutes, bear right onto the Table Rocks Trail, leaving the Farm Road, which continues ahead. Soon the trail emerges into the open, with a row

ALONG THE NORTHEAST TRAIL

of cedars on the right and open fields on the left. Near the end of the fields, Farm Road briefly rejoins, but be alert for another fork and continue to follow the Table Rocks Trail, which reenters the woods, crosses a bridge, and begins a slight ascent on a footpath to a junction with the red-blazed Cedar Trail. Turn sharply right here to continue on the Table Rocks Trail. The trail now descends, passing the Slingerland Pavilion, below on the right, then levels off and crosses Spring Farm Road.

Continuing ahead, the Table Rocks Trail now traverses two lovely fields. At the end of the first field, it passes through a gap in a tree hedge, then crosses the second field diagonally to the right. Milkweed is abundant here, and the mountains that comprise the Devil's Path in the Catskills can be seen to the right of the trail, just prior to accessing the gravel path leading back to the parking lot. You should recognize this final section of the hike because you walked this way on your outgoing journey.

Glossary

benchmark: A permanent metal disk at a known elevation used for surveying.

blaze: A trail marking that can be either a painted symbol on a tree or a metal or plastic marker.

bog bridges: A low boardwalk over fragile terrain that is often wet.

bushwhack: Walking off trail to reach a goal.

cairn: A pile of stones to indicate a trail junction or the route of a trail.

carriage roads: Also known as carriageways. Long-established horse and carriage routes. Most often found on old estates.

col: A pass between two peaks or a gap in a ridgeline.

erratic: A large boulder assumed to have been left by a retreating glacier and usually of a different rock type from that in its vicinity.

herd path: An unmarked footway.

lean-to: A three-sided shelter used for overnight stays.

"lollipop-loop" hike: Out and back on the same trails, with a loop in the middle.

marker: A metal or plastic disk nailed to a tree to indicate the route of a trail.

puncheons: See "bog bridges."

ravine: A deep narrow cleft in the earth's surface usually caused by runoff.

saddle: A ridge between two peaks.

scree slope: A slope covered with small rocks and gravel that have broken away from the cliffs above.

stile: A structure built over a fence or wall that allows hikers to cross without passing through a gate.

switchback: A trail that zigzags on the side of a steep ridge, hill, or mountain, which allows for a more gradual and less strenuous ascent or descent, thus preventing erosion.

talus slope: Talus slopes are more angled than scree slopes. Talus is also larger than scree, and the rocks have sharper edges, all of which makes a talus slope far more dangerous to cross and more difficult to scramble up or down.

through-hiker: A hiker attempting to hike an entire long-distance trail from end to end in one continuous journey.

trailhead: The beginning/end of a trail.

vernal pools: Small ponds that form in the spring from winter snowmelt and that usually dry up later in the year. Breeding grounds for frogs and salamanders.

woods road: Old dirt road formerly used for farming, logging, or mining activities.

Bibliography

Adler, Cy A. *Walking the Hudson: From the Battery to Bear Mountain.* Woodstock, VT: Countryman Press, 2012.

Anderson, Scott Edward. *Walks in Nature's Empire: Exploring The Nature Conservancy's Preserves in New York State.* Woodstock, VT: Countryman Press, 1995.

Appalachian Trail Guide to New York–New Jersey, 17th edition. Harpers Ferry, WV: Appalachian Trail Conservancy, 2011.

Binnewies, Robert O. *Palisades: 100,000 Acres in 100 Years.* New York: Fordham University Press & Palisades Interstate Park Commission, 2001.

Buff, Sheila. *Nature Walks In and Around New York City.* Boston: Appalachian Mountain Club Books, 1996.

Burgess, Larry E. *Mohonk, Its People and Spirit: A History of One Hundred Years of Growth and Service,* revised edition. Fleischmanns, NY: Purple Mountain Press, 1993.

———. *Daniel Smiley of Mohonk: A Naturalist's Life.* Fleischmanns, NY: Purple Mountain Press, 1997.

Card, Skip. *Take a Hike: New York City,* 2nd edition. Berkeley, CA: Avalon Travel Publishing, 2012.

Case, Daniel. *AMC's Best Day Hikes Near New York City: Four-Season Guide to 50 of the Best Trails in New York, Connecticut, and New Jersey.* Guilford, CT: Globe Pequot Press, 2010.

Chazin, Daniel. *Hike of the Week: A Year of Hikes in the New York Metro Area.* Mahwah, NJ: New York–New Jersey Trail Conference, 2013.

Clyne, Patricia Edwards. *Hudson Valley Tales and Trails.* New York: Overlook Press, reprinted 1997.

Copeland, Cynthia C., and Thomas J. Lewis. *Best Hikes with Children in the Catskills and Hudson River Valley,* 2nd edition. Seattle: Mountaineers Books, 2002.

Daniels, Jane and Walter. *Walkable Westchester: A Walking Guide to Westchester County, NY,* 2nd edition. Mahwah, NJ: New York–New Jersey Trail Conference, 2014.

Dunwell, Frances. F. *Hudson River Highlands.* New York: Columbia University Press, 1992.

Fagan, Jack. *Scenes and Walks in the Northern Shawangunks,* 3rd edition. Mahwah, NJ: New York–New Jersey Trail Conference, 2006.

Fried, Marc. *Tales from the Shawangunk Mountains. A Naturalist's Musings: A Bushwhacker's Guide,* revised edition. Geneva, NY: W. F. Humphrey Press, 1981.

———. *The Huckleberry Pickers. A Raucous History of the Shawangunk Mountains.* Hensonville, NY: Black Dome Press, 1995.

———. *Shawangunk: Adventure, Exploration, History, and Epiphany from a Mountain Wilderness.* Gardiner, NY: M. B. Fried, 1998.

Harrison, Marina, with Lucy D. Rosenfeld. *A Walker's Guidebook: Serendipitous Outings Near New York City, Including a Section for Birders.* New York: Michael Kesend Publishing, 1996.

Kiviat, Erik. *The Northern Shawangunks:*

An Ecological Survey. New Paltz, NY: Mohonk Preserve, 1988.

Lenik, Edward J. Iron Mine Trails: A History and Hikers Guide to the Historic Iron Mines of the New Jersey and New York Highlands. New York: New York–New Jersey Trail Conference, 1996.

Myles, William J. and Daniel Chazin. Harriman Trails: A Guide and History, 4th edition. New York: New York–New Jersey Trail Conference, 2018.

New York Walk Book: A Companion to the New Jersey Walk Book, 7th edition, revised. Mahwah, NJ: New York–New Jersey Trail Conference, 2005.

O'Brien, Raymond J. American Sublime: Landscape and Scenery of the Lower Hudson Valley. New York: Columbia University Press, 1981.

Perls, Jeffrey. Paths along the Hudson: A Guide to Walking and Biking. Piscataway, NJ: Rutgers University Press, 1999.

———. Shawangunk Trails Companion: A Complete Guide to Hiking, Mountain Biking, Cross-Country Skiing, and More Only 90 Miles from New York City. Woodstock, VT: Countryman Press, 2003.

Ransom, James M. Vanishing Ironworks of the Ramapos: The Story of the Forges, Furnaces, and Mines of the New Jersey–New York Border Area. Piscataway, NJ: Rutgers University Press, 1966.

Stalter, Elizabeth "Perk." Doodletown: Hiking through History in a Vanished Hamlet on the Hudson, updated edition. Bear Mountain, N.Y.: Palisades Interstate Park Commission Press, 2017.

Turco, Peggy. Walks and Rambles in Dutchess and Putnam Counties: A Guide to Ecology and History in Eastern Hudson Valley Parks. Woodstock, VT: Countryman Press, 1990.

———. Walks and Rambles in Westchester and Fairfield Counties: A Nature Lover's Guide to 36 Parks and Sanctuaries just North of New York City. Woodstock, VT: Countryman Press, 1993.

———. Walks and Rambles in the Western Hudson Valley: Landscape, Ecology, and Folklore in Orange and Ulster Counties. Woodstock, VT: Countryman Press, 1996.

Waterman, Laura and Guy. Forest and Crag: A History of Hiking, Trail Blazing, and Adventure in the Northeast Mountains. Boston: Appalachian Mountain Club, 1989.

———. Backwoods Ethics. Environmental Issues for Hikers and Campers, 2nd edition. Woodstock, VT: Countryman Press, 1993.

———. Wilderness Ethics: Preserving the Spirit of Wildness, 2nd edition. Woodstock, VT: Countryman Press, 1993.

———. A Fine Kind of Madness: Mountain Adventures Tall and True. Seattle: Mountaineers Books, 2000.

Weinman, Steve. A Rock with a View: Trails of the Shawangunk Mountains. New Paltz, NY: One Black Shoe Productions, 1997.

Weise, Don. Circuit Hikes in Harriman: 37 Loop Hikes and Trail Runs in Harriman and Bear Mountain State Parks, 2nd edition. Mahwah, NJ: New York–New Jersey Trail Conference, 2017.

Yorktown Walk Book, 4th edition. Yorktown Heights, NY: Yorktown Land Trust, 2016.

Zuger, Sascha. Moon New York State Handbook, 5th edition. Emeryville, CA: Avalon Travel Publishing, 2010.

Zungoli, Nick. *Bear Mountain & Harriman State Parks*. Sugar Loaf, NY: Exposures Gallery Press, 2018.

HIKING MAPS PUBLISHED BY THE NEW YORK–NEW JERSEY TRAIL CONFERENCE:

East Hudson Trails, three-map set, 2018

Harriman-Bear Mountain Trails, two-map set, 2018

Hudson Palisades Trails, five-map set, 2018

Shawangunk Trails, three-map set, 2016

Sterling Forest Trails, one map, 2016

West Hudson Trails, two-map set, 2015

Westchester Trails, three-map set (expected to be available in 2019)

For latest information, see www .nynjtc.org/catalog/maps